CW00521345

CHILDCARE MARKETS

Can they deliver an equitable service?

Edited by Eva Lloyd and Helen Penn

To Selena,

with many thanks
and all good wishes,

Eva

25 June 2012

First published in Great Britain in 2012 by

The Policy Press
University of Bristol
Fourth Floor
Beacon House
Queen's Road
Bristol BS8 1QU
UK
t: +44 (0)117 331 4054
f: +44 (0)117 331 4093
tpp-info@bristol.ac.uk
www.policypress.co.uk

North American office:
The Policy Press
c/o The University of Chicago Press
1427 East 60th Street
Chicago, IL 60637, USA
t: +1 773 702 7700
f: +1 773-702-9756
sales@press.uchicago.edu
www.press.uchicago.edu

© The Policy Press 2012

British Library Cataloguing in Publication Data
A catalogue record for this book is available from the British Library.

Library of Congress Cataloging-in-Publication Data
A catalog record for this book has been requested.

ISBN 978 1 84742 933 9 hardcover

The right of Eva Lloyd and Helen Penn to be identified as editors of this work has been asserted by them in accordance with the Copyright, Designs and Patents Act 1988.

Cover design by The Policy Press.
Front cover: image kindly supplied by Paul Preacher
(www.paulpreacher.com/)
Printed and bound in Great Britain by MPG Book Group.
The Policy Press uses environmentally responsible print partners.

FSC
www.fsc.org
MIX
From responsible
sources
FSC® C018575

Contents

List of tables and figures

Tables

Figures

About the contributors

Philip Blackburn is a consultant business economist who since 1998 works predominantly with Laing & Buisson, a major UK social care market research organisation. He is author of Laing & Buisson's annual *Children's Nurseries UK Market Report*, and *Out of School Childcare UK Market Report*. Philip has wide access to business information within the childcare industry; his childcare consultancy projects include a 2006 report on *Future Childcare Services in the EU* for the European Monitoring Centre for Change. Before this he was an economist at the Office for National Statistics.

Jerome Davis started working for the Centre for Spatial Economics (C_4SE) in 2008. C_4SE is based in Ontario, Canada. Jerome provided assistance on several projects including an examination of the machinery and equipment sector at national and provincial level, occupational modelling and forecasting, and quantifying the economic implications of socioeconomic developments. He has an MSc in economics from University College London and a BA Honours in economics from Queen's University, Belfast.

Robert Fairholm is a partner with the Centre for Spatial Economics (C_4SE) based in Ontario, Canada and President of Robert Fairholm Economic Consulting Inc. He produces custom research for clients on a range of topics, including productivity, fiscal forecasting, labour supply, demand and occupational models and forecasts, and impact analyses. He has over 25 years of experience in economic analysis, modelling and forecasting. Before joining the C_4SE, he was the managing editor of the *International Bank Credit Analyst* and chief Canadian economist of Standard Poor's DRI where he won awards for forecast accuracy.

Kari Jacobsen practised as a preschool teacher and principal in Oslo before joining the Norwegian ministries responsible for early childhood education and care (ECEC) in 1976. Between 2006 and 2011 she was a senior adviser on ECEC in the Norwegian Ministry of Education and Research. Kari chaired a Council of Europe Programme for Children and Families working group drafting a 2002 Recommendation on Early Childhood Education and Care. She was Norwegian national coordinator for the OECD's *Thematic Review of Early Childhood Education and Care*, a member of the OECD ECEC network since 2006 and its chair in 2009 and 2010.

Eva Lloyd is reader in early childhood at the University of East London and co-director of the International Centre for the Study of the Mixed Economy of Childcare (ICMEC). She has held honorary positions at Cambridge University, London University's Institute of Education and Queen's University, Belfast. Currently she holds an honorary research fellowship at the School for Policy Studies, University of Bristol, where she previously was a senior lecturer in Early Childhood Studies. Her research interests include UK and international early childhood, family support and child poverty policies and strategies.

Linda Mitchell is associate professor in the Faculty of Education, University of Waikato. Her research interests in early childhood education and care policy, teacher and parent relationships in early childhood education and multimodal literacies, are reflected in a wide range of publications, including some dealing with the New Zealand childcare market. She has recently completed a longitudinal evaluation commissioned by the Ministry of Education of *Pathways to the Future: Ngā Huarahi Arataki,* New Zealand's early childhood education strategic plan and is now leading a four year national evaluation of the government's ECE Participation Programme.

Peter Moss is emeritus professor of early childhood provision at the Thomas Coram Research Unit, Institute of Education, University of London. His interests include early childhood education and care and other services for children, their workforces, critical approaches to research and practice in these areas, the relationship between care, gender and employment, and democracy in children's services. His work over the past 20 years has been mostly cross-national, in particular in Europe. Between 1986 and 1996 he was the coordinator of the European Commission Childcare Network; currently he coordinates the International Network on Leave Policies and Research together with Fred Deven of the Belgian Ministry of Well-Being, Public Health and Family.

Gillian Paull is an associate of Frontier Economics. Prior to joining Frontier Economics in 2010, she studied and taught at Princeton University and has held research positions at the International Monetary Fund, the World Bank, the London School of Economics and the Institute for Fiscal Studies. Her main research interests include labour market behaviour and family-related policy, focusing on gender comparisons, mothers' employment, childcare, child maintenance and family poverty. She has published in academic journals and in government publications, most recently quite extensively in the UK Department for Work and Pensions research report series.

Helen Penn is professor of early childhood at the University of East London and co-director of ICMEC. Her focus is on policy within early childhood, in particular the impact of the market on the supply of early education and care, the way families use private provision, and the impact on children of such provision. She takes a global overview of these issues. She has published in education and economic journals on the marketisation of childcare. Her latest book *Quality in Services to Young Children: an International Perspective* was published in 2010 by the Open University Press.

Janneke Plantenga is professor of economics at the University of Utrecht, the Netherlands. Her research interests focus on labour market flexibilisation, the reconciliation of work and family and (European) social policy. She is the Dutch member and coordinator of the EU Expert Group on Gender and Employment. She has written widely on redistribution of unpaid work, changing working time patterns, childcare issues and modernising social security.

Laura Stout Sosinsky is assistant professor in the Department of Psychology at Fordham University, Bronx, New York. She is also a faculty affiliate in the Edward Zigler Center in Child Development and Social Policy at Yale University in New Haven, Connecticut. Her major research interests centre on early childhood development in the context of parenting, childcare, early education, family, industry and policy contributors to early care and education quality and parental childcare decision making. She has written widely on these issues, including on the impact of sector auspice on quality in early childhood provision.

Jennifer Sumsion is foundation professor of early childhood education at Charles Sturt University, Bathurst, New South Wales, Australia. She is co-leader of the Early Years Education Collaborative Research Network, a major Australian government initiative to build capacity in early childhood education research. Her current research interests focus on multi-perspectival conceptions of quality and professional practice and policy in early childhood education and care, integrated service provision, early childhood curriculum, and workforce development. In 2008–09, Jennifer was co-leader of a national consortium to develop and trial Australia's first national curriculum framework for early childhood education and care.

Gerd Vollset holds a master's degree in sociology from the University of Oslo (1972). She has worked as a civil servant in the ministries responsible for questions concerning family policy, gender equality and early childhood education. Her current position is deputy director general in the Ministry of Children, Equality and Inclusion. Through her work she has contributed to many of the official committee reports on these subjects and prepared both law proposals and White Papers for the Norwegian Parliament. An important concern has been to promote the use of social science as part of the knowledge used to inform sound political decision making.

Gail Yuen is assistant professor in the Department of Education Policy and Leadership at the Hong Kong Institute of Education. Her work focuses on policy, advocacy and teacher development. Gail has been studying the early education voucher scheme since it was first introduced by the Hong Kong Government in 2007. Having already completed three related research projects, she is currently conducting another territory-wide study funded by the Central Policy Unit of the Hong Kong Government. Gail is also active in working with advocates and colleagues to influence the policy agenda and public discourse on local early childhood education development.

Acknowledgements

This is a global book that incorporates work from five continents. To work in this way has required a special effort from our contributors in order to collate and compare their work (and submit to our editing) and we are very grateful to them. The contributors in turn have drawn on work from their colleagues, and used those colleagues as a sounding board for their contributions, so we also wish to acknowledge our gratitude to the wider circle of people who have been indirectly involved in the preparation of this book. This book emerged from the work undertaken by the editors as co-directors of the International Centre for the Study of the Mixed Economy of Childcare (ICMEC), which they established at the University of East London's Cass School of Education and Communities in 2007. We want to acknowledge the support the Centre has attracted from our colleagues, particularly from the university's Royal Docks Business School, from a wide range of academics nationally and internationally, and from childcare business leaders, policy makers and others who have contributed to ICMEC seminars.

Part One

Introduction

Childcare markets: an introduction

Eva Lloyd

Introduction

The state's role in the provision of early childhood education and care (ECEC) services is of particular interest, since such services are closely linked to other social, educational, demographic and economic policy developments. Robust education systems, labour market policies which acknowledge the key contributions of women, family stability and ideas of inclusive citizenship all to an extent hinge on the provision of comprehensive and high quality early childhood education and care. This role requires states to strike a balance between serving the interests of parents and the wider family, of children and of the state itself. But negotiating the intersections between these policy interests is often conflictual (Archard, 2003; Kamerman and Moss, 2010). Agreeing and enabling a coherent mix of leave policies, financial support and childcare services, while also allowing for parental choice and achieving a satisfactory resolution to the macro-division of costs, may pose serious challenges for governments (Plantenga and Remery, 2009). One particular option for addressing these policy conundrums is the promotion of a market-based approach to the provision of early childhood education and care, the subject of this book.

Modern welfare states traditionally have varied in the amount of public support provided for early childhood education and care systems and in their response to economic challenges, such as the transition to post-industrialist economies and the rise of female labour market participation (Mahon, 2002). Viewed as a continuum, publicly supported universal systems in the Nordic countries (Rauhala, 2009) would be located at one end and at the opposite end would be provision in non-welfare states such as those in Sub-Saharan Africa (Prochner and Kabiru, 2008), almost entirely reliant on funding from private or supra-national agencies or NGOs.

Everywhere early childhood policies and systems appear in a state of flux, but in the present global economic climate childcare markets are a distinctive and rapidly growing phenomenon (Penn, 2009a). Compared to commodity markets, childcare markets tend to form part of a mixed economy, like other human services markets. In this mixed economy the state, private-for-profit and private-not-for-profit providers all play a role in the provision, funding and regulation of ECEC. Among the private-for-profit childcare providers that operate in such markets may be corporate businesses, whose primary commercial interest may lie elsewhere (Penn, 2011).

Fully state-funded early childhood education and care provision may be directly provided in parallel with privately provided services in some markets. Early education is often treated differently in public policy and may or may not be part of such a market. Or there may not be a consistent national approach to childcare markets. Privatisation of social welfare and education services may mean the participation of private sector interests in a predominantly publicly funded and delivered service system; it need not necessarily coincide with marketisation, that is the opening up of services to competitive delivery by private providers (Whitfield, 2006). These issues will be explored further in the next section of this chapter, while other contributions to this volume illustrate the operation of both processes.

In a childcare market parents are proxy customers on behalf of their children, the actual consumers of the service. Parental choice may be supported with the help of public subsidies such as tax credits or vouchers, as long as their income remains below any caps set by governments (Warner and Gradus, 2011). In some countries, including Britain (Kazimirski et al, 2006), employers may be encouraged to provide childcare support to employees in the form of childcare vouchers, in return for corporation tax rebates.

Childcare markets have become the dominant delivery model for early years provision in European countries such as the UK (Penn, 2007; Lloyd, 2012) and the Netherlands (Lloyd and Penn, 2010). In other European countries they are also increasingly substituting for the role of the public sector in respect of ECEC and other human services that may traditionally have been delivered directly by public bodies or have received substantial public funding. Childcare markets predominate in English speaking nations, including the US (Meyers and Gornick, 2003; Kamerman and Gatenio-Gable, 2007), Canada (Mahon and Phillips, 2002) and Australia (Brennan, 2002), as well as on the African continent (Penn, 2008) and in the Asia Pacific region (Yuen, 2010).

The alternative position is reflected in the policy rationale employed by a European country such as France (Martin and Le Bihan, 2009), where a state-funded and state-provided ECEC system has existed for some sixty years. In such cases the government considers that there are strong economic grounds for treating ECEC services as a 'public good', which justifies substantial public investment in the services themselves and in their infrastructure. Both this direct investment in ECEC services and in their infrastructures are seen as key to ensuring equitable and universal access for all children irrespective of their parents' socioeconomic position, ethnic background, rural or urban location, or health status (Cleveland and Krashinski, 2004; Leseman, 2009).

These contrasting policy positions produce different outcomes for the relevant early childhood education and care systems, particularly as the economic environment changes. Childcare markets also generate different consequences for the system's quality and sustainability, depending on the political and socioeconomic conditions in the localities, regions and nations where they operate. The chapters in this book illustrate the range of impacts and outcomes of childcare markets in different countries.

Background

Mixed economies of welfare and education services go back a long way (Stewart, 2007). Social welfare and education provision, delivered by religious or secular private, community or informal institutions, not only long predate state social welfare interventions and regimes, but continue to play a role within them (Hill, 2007). Sometimes such systems became embedded within early welfare legislation, such as the British Old and New Poor Laws and liberal welfare reforms. This trend predated the emergence of capitalist welfare states after the Second World War (Thane, 1996).

Non-parental childcare and early (nursery) education privately purchased within some kind of childcare market also have a long history. To explain the evolution of current childcare systems in Europe, Scheiwe and Willekens (2009) take a historical and institutional perspective. They illustrate how European ECEC systems are underpinned by much older national traditions rooted in earlier economic and social developments. These can both enable and inhibit innovations intended to address emerging social policy issues, e.g. the rise of female labour market participation. The UK is one of many nations where parents have for a long time used private for-profit

or not-for-profit centre-based provision for their children, alongside
family daycare or informal care by family and friends. The British and
other governments have had a long-standing interest in extra-familial
childcare and early education as a social welfare intervention (Lawrence
and Starkey, 2001; Hendrick, 2003).

But a policy interest in childcare as a service to enable parental, or
more pragmatically, maternal, labour market participation is a more
recent phenomenon in the UK and other industrialised nations
(OECD, 2006). According to Duncan and Williams (2002, p5), this
shift away from the male breadwinner family model has been a major
development in welfare states.

This edited volume focuses largely on childcare market developments
within capitalist mixed economies of welfare during the past thirty
years approximately. The Second World War forms a step change in
terms of the growing prominence of the state's direct role in supplying
welfare, health and educational provision (Stewart, 2007). The evolving
formats of ECEC systems in countries such as France (Martin and Le
Bihan, 2009), the Netherlands (Noailly and Visser, 2009) and the UK
(Penn, 2009b) bear witness to the impact of emerging 'welfare states'
around this period.

According to Hill (2007, p178) the emphasis within comparative
social policy analyses veered away from the welfare role of the state after
the publication of Esping-Andersen's regime theory (Esping-Andersen,
1990, 1999). Esping-Andersen used the concept of 'decommodification'
to describe the extent to which any state system of benefits and welfare
services is separate from market dynamics. He classified welfare-state
regimes in post-industrial economies from most to least decommodified.
This classification included: a) social-democratic regimes, as in the
Nordic countries; b) intermediate, including conservative, regimes
where extensive welfare provision is closely linked to employment
status, as in European countries; c) liberal regimes, where welfare is
largely conceived as a safety net for the poorest people, as in the US, the
UK and other English speaking countries. This theory has subsequently
been modified by others to include family and gender dimensions; a
comparison of European care regimes by Bettio and Plantenga (2004)
also included an analysis of childcare systems and arrived at a broadly
similar typology to Esping-Andersen's.

Taking the example of parental leave policies, Kamerman and Moss
(2010) illustrate how Esping-Andersen's typology can be related to
national policies, embedded within specific political systems. Leave
policies appear to be most developed under social democratic regimes,
such as the Nordic countries, and least developed in liberal regimes,

e.g. English speaking countries; conservative countries' leave policies are located halfway between the two (Kamerman and Moss, 2010, p 7). The authors then draw attention to alternative approaches, such as one employed within OECD, which relate the role of existing political and economic institutions to the emergence or inhibitions of particular welfare policies.

Since the late 1970s, capitalist welfare states have been entering a new transitional phase (Williams, 1999), where privatisation of social welfare services has gathered pace (Friedman et al, 1987; Swank, 2005). Such privatisation may take the form of a liberalisation of statutory regulations restricting market operations and introducing greater competition with publicly supported provision, rather than a full denationalisation of public services (Heald, 1988). Applying Esping-Anderson's classification, it can be argued that category b) and c) countries have either seen erstwhile publicly provided services, including childcare, increasingly commissioned out to private-for-profit and not-for-profit providers, or that existing mixed markets have been further consolidated.

Where social care and education service systems have traditionally operated through a mixed market of private and publicly funded provision, or where public provision used to be the norm, such services may also become increasingly marketised (Ball, 2007). This can lead to the emergence of 'quasi-markets' (Le Grand, 2002). For instance, in the first decade of the 21st century, both England and the Netherlands passed legislation explicitly encouraging the mixed market economy of childcare and assigning a 'market management' duty to local government (Lloyd and Penn, 2010).

Behind the transition of public to private provision lies the expectation that the market will create better incentives for providers to offer consumers more choice and competitive pricing, leading to a better balance between service supply and demand. If demand in such markets is supported by public funding in the form of vouchers, tax credits or other types of consumer subsidy, this is expected to boost the growth and sustainability of the private sector (Plantenga and Remery, 2009).

Arguably, the increasing privatisation and marketisation of childcare and parallel developments in other areas of education and social welfare signify a retrenchment in welfare states. Several authors recognise in these developments a distinct risk to the present and future wellbeing and development of young children within their families (Kamerman and Kahn, 2001; Penn, 2009b). Indeed, this trend may put the equitable delivery of such services in jeopardy. Evidence is presented in this volume that marketisation and privatisation risk deepening, consolidating or widening inequalities of access to ECEC provision and driving qualitative differences between types of provider. Research findings increasingly suggest that there is an uncomfortable relationship between childcare market provider aegis and quality (Mathers et al, 2007; Sosinsky et al, 2007; Cleveland and Krashinski, 2009). In particular there is an interaction between the politics of childcare and issues of class, ethnicity and gender equality (Michel and Mahon, 2002; Bettio and Plantenga, 2004). This book also explores how childcare markets reflect such issues.

The purpose of this book

This book emerged as a response to the editors' concern that the availability, quality and sustainability of publicly supported early childhood education and care may be at an important juncture within modern welfare states. Within childcare markets the equitable provision of ECEC is highly problematic, especially as parental income inequalities persist or widen. This is happening despite the acknowledgement of young children's rights in principle, as reflected in the almost universal acceptance of the Education for All Millennium Goals (UNESCO, 2006).

In view of these developments the editors in 2007 established the International Centre for the Study of the Mixed Economy of Childcare (ICMEC) in the Cass School of Education and Communities at the University of East London. This is a multidisciplinary research centre with close links to the university's business school. ICMEC has been developing an international and interdisciplinary approach to exploring mixed economies of childcare. It aims to generate greater knowledge about ECEC in countries which employ mixed economies of welfare and education. The Centre's work programme focuses on the critical analysis and documentation of the rapid trend toward privatisation and marketisation of early childhood provision in the UK and the rest of the world, setting this in the wider context of ECEC policies and their relationship with other social welfare and education policy developments.

This edited volume reflects recent work by the editors and an international group of experts in social policy, education, economics, psychology, early childhood studies and business and management studies who are committed to exploring the consequences of childcare markets for young children and their families in terms of equity. It brings together recent relevant policy research from eight nations operating childcare markets. Alongside this it offers material about 'raw' and 'emerging' childcare markets operating with a minimum of government intervention, mostly in low income countries or post-transition economies in the process of adopting a market model. In this way the book allows comparisons between privatisation and marketisation processes of ECEC services within their national policy and political contexts.

The subject is viewed through a multidisciplinary lens by the authors represented in this book. Rather than working to a template requiring descriptions of particular childcare markets, contributors have been encouraged to share key findings of their current and recent childcare market research, supported by brief descriptive and policy background sections concerning the markets in question. Those authors writing from an education or childcare background emphasise the position of children, especially vulnerable children, and consider the detail of the care and education they are likely to receive in a market climate. The economists' contributions to this book take a different perspective. They consider the childcare market from the perspective of wider economic analysis and prediction, and they view childcare as a more or less well-functioning sector of the market. Economists deal mainly with macro statistics and aggregates of data, and model their predictions on this basis, in line with standard economic precepts and assumptions, and using economic vocabularies. The non-economists contributing to this book are more interested in individual variations and qualitative differences, and consider the values which might be said to underpin provision. Both types of explanation are important, but at times they may appear to sit oddly together. We regard it as a strength, rather than as a weakness that these complementary approaches are juxtaposed in this book.

Given the potential impact of competitive markets on children's access to ECEC and the quality of their experience, the editors believe that current and robust research evidence should inform pertinent policy making, practice and academic discourse. So far this has been largely absent from academic, policy and political debate. The contributions in this volume aim to further the debate by offering evidence and analyses concerning many aspects of childcare market operations within the political and economic systems in which they are embedded. We hope this research on childcare markets allows us to begin to answer the question posed in the subtitle to this volume: can they deliver an equitable service?

This book particularly focuses on the impact which privatisation and marketisation have had on centre-based early childhood education and care. There are however other models of provision operating in the childcare market. In many countries there is a tradition of family daycare based in the home of the provider and run as a small business. Out-of-school provision is another model, usually forming part of school-based childcare services, targeted generally at older children and rarely delivered as free-standing private provision. These alternative models, together with informal care, deserve careful study. However, they have been less influenced by the dynamic of privatisation and marketisation and have not therefore been considered in any detail in this book.

Terminology

International and supranational bodies have over time come to play a substantial role in relation to social welfare systems, notably childcare policy systems and developments (UNESCO, 2006). Indeed, in majority world or poor countries, they often play the dominant role. This has influenced the choice of terminology adopted here to describe ECEC systems and their component parts. It is based on the terminology employed by OECD in its major comparative review of childcare and early education systems in 20 countries (OECD, 2001, 2006). The Education and Training Directorate of OECD in these two reports deliberately refers to early childhood education and care services (ECEC), since the system of early childhood provision in member states may encompass both types of provision.

Analyses emanating from within European Union Directorates employ the same terminology (Plantenga and Remery, 2009). Individually, member states may employ the term 'childcare' to refer to both education and care. In reports focusing primarily on early childhood education and care provision in the majority world, on the other hand, the term ECCE, an abbreviation of Early Childhood Care and Education, is more common (UNESCO, 2006). Other international organisations prefer to use Early Child Development (ECD) in order to stress the importance of healthcare interventions as part of the spectrum of early childhood programmes.

In this book, the term childcare is used to refer to provision catering for children while their parents are employed, unless the discussion requires making a distinction between early childhood care and early childhood education. For instance, in the Netherlands the term 'childcare' refers exclusively to non-parental care provision for young children whose parents are employed, whereas in England, the term has been employed in official documents, at least until recently, to refer to childcare for the children of working parents as well as to publicly funded and universal early education.

Most chapters also employ terminology that is particular to the early childhood and care system under discussion, such as the term 'kindergarten' used in chapter seven in relation to Norway. These terms are explained in the text where appropriate. Contributors were consulted on the implications of simplifying the terminology in this way, to ensure that their arguments and descriptions cohere.

The structure of this book

This book is arranged in three parts which complement each other by providing different perspectives on the same subject. Each part and each chapter can also be read independently from its wider context and should make sense on its own. This chapter and the subsequent two chapters in Part One aim to provide an overview of the subject of childcare markets, locating them within their current and recent policy context.

The chapters making up Part Two reflect divergent childcare market developments. They document the varied economic and policy backdrops against which different countries have developed their current childcare systems. The analyses explore the consequences for parents and children and in some cases for the pertinent workforce, of the strengthening of market operations or of their introduction.

The chapters in Part Three are concerned less with the immediate realities of particular childcare markets or early childhood service systems. Instead they examine the wider vision informing the policies encouraging childcare markets, explore alternative approaches and finally present a framework for drawing together the emerging themes. Questioning the status quo like this would appear to follow naturally from the body of evidence presented in the first two parts of this volume.

This introductory chapter explains the genesis of the book, puts the subject briefly in context, and discusses the nature of each contribution. In the second chapter, Helen Penn interrogates dominant market theories and their applicability to childcare markets. She explores the workability of the childcare market model from the perspective of providers seeking to make a profit out of childcare provision and contrasts the competing demands of profitability with those of equitable access, quality and sustainability of provision. Drawing on Harvey's (2010) notions of the geography of capitalism, she questions markets' supposed superiority compared to alternative approaches.

While acknowledging that she does not offer a direct comparison with publicly funded early childhood education and care systems, she concludes that the market model poses serious risks to equity.

Chapter three predicts future UK childcare market developments, on the basis of an analysis of market trends during the first decade of the 21st century. Here Philip Blackburn explores from an economic perspective the probable limits on further corporatisation in a now relatively mature childcare market.

Part Two examines divergent and occasionally contrasting developments within childcare markets in six advanced economies. The final chapter of the seven making up this part of the book focuses on 'raw' and 'emerging' markets in economies of a different kind. Part Two starts with Janneke Plantenga's economic investigation of consumer choice within the Dutch childcare market. First she documents the reorganisation of the Dutch childcare market following the passing of the 2005 Dutch Childcare Act. She then analyses in more detail ideas about consumer demand, in particular the notion of parental voice, and whether it is adequately understood in economic theorising about childcare markets. She concludes by asking whether childcare policy makers ought to pursue a reconfiguration of the division of responsibilities between childcare markets and the state.

In chapter five Gail Yuen discusses how the city of Hong Kong, a centrally operated economy, but nevertheless one with a strong market ethos, has recently introduced a market-based innovation, early education vouchers, with mixed results. Employing an ethic of care perspective grounded in Tronto's (1993) theory, she questions whether this market approach can alter existing power structures within Hong Kong society, which in her view negatively affect the status of women and young children.

New Zealand is often held up as a model example of an English speaking country which early on introduced a coherent national framework of public subsidies, regulatory control and a national early childhood curriculum. In chapter six Linda Mitchell demonstrates that market operations nevertheless prevail and that these have led to rapid growth among private for-profit, including corporate, childcare businesses, resulting in inequities of access.

In contrast, Norway, the subject of chapter seven, has managed to harness the talents of not-for-profit providers alongside public bodies to deliver an accessible ECEC service system. The system offers parents choice, but outside of a for-profit system. This was achieved by using a wide-reaching regulatory system and judiciously targeted – and generous – funding in line with this system. Kari Jacobsen and Gerd

Vollset describe how this came about as a result of a strong vision on the part of government and Norwegian society on how to ensure equity and quality for children and their parents.

The next two chapters, eight and nine, illustrate divergent childcare market dynamics in two politically liberal nations, the US and Canada. The huge US economy has very little in the way of a systematic ECEC system, because of its overriding views about the importance of family (woman's) responsibility and its belief in the viability of the market. Not only does the US lack a national childcare or indeed family policy, but it also deliberately minimises any federal centralised oversight of such provision. Laura Sosinsky carefully deconstructs the complexity of its childcare markets, exploring their effects in terms of their dual function of supporting child development and promoting maternal labour market participation. She draws attention to the one area where initiatives might have some limited success, namely in improving quality accreditation systems as an alternative to regulation. She concludes that parental childcare choice is thwarted by the complexity of US childcare markets.

Robert Fairholm and Jerome Davis, also writing from an economist's point of view, point to the difficulties of implementing national policies in federal states. They adopt the perspective of the – mostly small – providers in at present predominantly not-for-profit Canadian childcare markets (although in the oil rich state of Alberta the majority of provision is for-profit and increasingly corporate). These providers are faced with serious workforce shortages. The authors address the nature of these shortages, as well as employer support needs. They report on innovative solutions identified in their research. Their study derives in part from an economic survey carried out for the Child Care Human Resources Council. Canada is an interesting example since it is a federal state, where provinces have had considerable autonomy to set their own levels of investment in childcare and to determine their own regulatory frameworks. To this extent Canada represents a working laboratory, and a means of comparing shifts of policy in labour market interventions.

In chapter ten Helen Penn illustrates the gross inequalities likely to characterise 'raw' markets without public funding or regulatory support, using the case of Namibia. She contrasts these with 'emerging' markets such as in the former Soviet Bloc countries, which are faced with the privatisation or closure of the ECEC systems that once characterised centrally organised economies, and the difficulties of setting up regulatory systems. A welfarist safety-net model, promoted by international non-governmental organisations (INGOs) is replacing state systems in poorer post-transition states, with little acknowledgement of what went before. She points out the particular burdens experienced by women in both raw and emerging childcare markets.

Part Three concerns broad alternatives or checks to childcare markets. In chapter eleven Peter Moss questions whether there are alternatives to childcare markets. He argues that the choice of policy instrument to determine a particular childcare system's format, regulation and state support, represents a particular vision of society. This relates to the roles and responsibilities of men and women, of parents and the place of children within it. While acknowledging the challenges, he nevertheless believes that a demarketised system of early childhood services can be realised.

In chapter twelve Jennifer Sumsion applies the concept of an ethical audit framework to the development of for-profit childcare within an Australian context. She asks whether this approach can and should be generalised to the other human services and should in fact constitute a precondition for public subsidy. This chapter revisits the story of the recent virtual demise of Australian corporatised childcare, in doing so adding an eighth country 'case study' to this volume. It questions whether such developments could ever have been in the public interest.

In chapter thirteen, the final chapter, Gillian Paull, an economist, argues that drawing together the wide range of arguments presented in the preceding chapters from within different academic disciplines and informed by different concerns and social objectives, is not feasible within a single comparative framework. Instead she reviews the evidence for the role of the market in childcare and the case for government intervention from an economic perspective. She concludes that there is considerable scope for mutual learning between countries with experience of childcare policy development, implementation and their consequences in order to generate workable ECEC systems of market and non-market elements. In her view neither the market's role nor that of government needs to become more uniform to achieve those objectives.

References

Archard, D. W. (2003) *Children, family and the state*, Aldershot: Ashgate.

Ball, S. J. (2007) *Education PLC: Understanding private sector participation in public sector education*, London and New York: Routledge.

Bettio, F. and Plantenga, J. (2004) 'Comparing care regimes in Europe', *Feminist Economics*, vol 10, no 1, pp 195–214.

Brennan, D. (2002) 'Australia: Child care and state-centered feminism in a liberal welfare regime', in: S. Michel and R. Mahon (eds) *Child care policy at the crossroads – Gender and welfare state restructuring*, New York and London: Routledge, pp 95–112.

Cleveland, G. and Krashinski, M. (2004) *Financing ECEC services in OECD countries*, Paris: Organisation for Economic Cooperation and Development.

Cleveland, G. and Krashinsky, M. (2009) 'The nonprofit advantage: Producing quality in thick and thin child care markets', *Journal of Policy Analysis and Management*, vol 28, no 3, pp 440–462.

Duncan, S. and Williams, F. (2002) 'Introduction', *Critical Social Policy*, vol 22, no 1, pp 5–11.

Esping-Andersen, G. (1990) *Three worlds of welfare capitalism*, Cambridge: Polity Press.

Esping-Andersen, G. (1999) *Social foundations of post-industrial economies*, Oxford: Oxford University Press.

Friedman, R.R., Gilbert, N. and Sherer, M. (1987) *Modern welfare states – A comparative view of trends and prospects*, Brighton: Wheatsheaf Books.

Harvey, D. (2010) *The enigma of capital*, London: Profile Books. 2nd edition.

Heald, D. (1988) 'The United Kingdom: Privatisation and its political context', *West European Politics*, vol 11, no 4, pp 31–48.

Hendrick, H. (2003) *Child welfare: Historical dimensions, contemporary debate*, Bristol: The Policy Press.

Hill, M. (2007) 'The mixed economy of welfare: A comparative perspective', in: M. Powell (ed) *Understanding the Mixed Economy of Welfare*, Bristol: The Policy Press, pp 177–198.

Kamerman, S. B. and Kahn, A.J. (2001) 'Child and family policies in an era of social policy retrenchment and restructuring', in: K. Vleminckx and T.M. Smeeding (eds) *Child well-being, child poverty and child policy in modern nations: What do we know*, Bristol: The Policy Press.

Kamerman, S.B. and Gatenio-Gabel, S. (2007) 'Early childhood education and care in the United States: An overview of the current policy picture', *International Journal of Child Care and Education Policy*, vol 1, no 1, pp 23–34.

Kamerman, S.B. and Moss, P. (eds) (2010) *The politics of parental leave policies – Children, parenting, gender and the labour market*, Bristol: The Policy Press.

Kazimirski, A., Smith, R., Mogensen, E. and Lemetti, F. (2006) *Monitoring of the reform of the income tax and national insurance rules for employer-supported childcare*, London: HM Revenue Customs.

Lawrence, J. and Starkey, P. (eds) (2001) *Child welfare and social actions in the nineteenth and twentieth century – International perspectives*, Liverpool: University of Liverpool Press.

Le Grand, J. (2002) 'The Labour government and the National Health Service', *Oxford Review of Economic Policy*, vol 18, no 2, pp 137–153.

Leseman, P. (2009) *Tackling social and cultural inequalities through early childhood education and care in Europe*, Brussels: European Commission.

Lloyd, E. (2012) 'The marketisation of early years education and childcare in England', in L. Miller and D. Hevey (eds) *Policy Issues in the Early Years*, London: Sage, pp 107–121.

Lloyd, E. and Penn, H. (2010) 'Why do childcare markets fail? Comparing England and the Netherlands', *Public Policy Research*, vol 17, no 1, pp 42–48.

Mahon, R. (2002) 'Gender and welfare state restructuring: Through the lens of child care', in: S. Michel and R. Mahon (eds) *Child care policy at the crossroads – Gender and welfare state restructuring*, New York and London: Routledge, pp 1–27.

Mahon, R. and Phillips, S. (2002) 'Dual-earner families caught in a liberal welfare regime? The politics of childcare in Canada', in: S. Michel and R. Mahon (eds) *Child care policy at the crossroads – Gender and welfare state restructuring*, New York and London: Routledge, pp 191–218.

Martin, C. and Le Bihan, B. (2009) 'Public childcare and preschools in France', in: K. Schweiwe and H. Willekens (eds) *Childcare and preschool development in Europe – Institutional perspectives*, Basingstoke: Palgrave Macmillan, pp 57–71.

Mathers, S., Sylva, K. and Joshi, H. (2007) *Quality of Childcare Settings in the Millennium Cohort Study*. Research Report SSU/2007/FR/022, London: DCSF.

Meyers, M. K. and Gornick, J. C. (2003) 'Public or private responsibility? Early childhood education and care, inequality, and the welfare state', *Journal of Comparative Family Studies*, vol 34, no 3, pp 379–411.

Michel, S. and Mahon, R. (eds) (2002) *Child care policy at the crossroads – Gender and welfare state restructuring*, New York and London: Routledge.

Noailly, J. and Visser, S. (2009) 'The impact of market forces on the provision of childcare: Insights from the 2005 Childcare Act in the Netherlands', *Journal of Social Policy*, vol 38, no 3, pp 477–498.

OECD (2001) *Starting Strong I. Early childhood education and care*, Paris: Organisation for Economic Cooperation and Development.

OECD (2006) *Starting Strong II. Early childhood education and care*, Paris: Organisation for Economic Cooperation and Development.

Penn, H. (2007) 'Childcare market management: How the United Kingdom government has reshaped its role in developing early childhood education and care', *Contemporary Issues in the Early Years*, vol 8, no 3, pp 192–207.

Penn, H. (2008) *Early childhood education and care in Southern Africa: A perspective report for CfBT Educational Trust*, Reading: Centre for British Teachers.

Penn, H. (2009a) 'International perspectives on quality in mixed economies of childcare', *National Institute Economic Review*, vol 207, no 1, pp 83–89.

Penn, H. (2009b) 'Public and private: The history of early education and care institutions in the United Kingdom', in: K. Scheiwe and H. Willekens (eds) *Childcare and preschool development in Europe – Institutional perspectives*, Basingstoke: Palgrave Macmillan, pp 105–125.

Penn, H. (2011) 'Gambling on the market: The role of for-profit provision in early childhood education and care', *Journal of Early Childhood Research*, vol 9, no 2, pp 150–161.

Plantenga, J. and Remery, C. (2009) *The provision of childcare services: A comparative review of 30 European countries*, Brussels: European Commission.

Prochner, L. and Kabiru, M. (2008) 'ECD in Africa: A historical perspective', in: M. Garica, A. Pence and J.L. Evans (eds) *Africa's future, Africa's challenge: Early childhood care and development in Sub-Saharan Africa*, New York: The World Bank, pp 117–133.

Rauhala, P-L. (2009) 'Child care as an issue of equality and equity: the example of the Nordic countries', in: K. Scheiwe and H. Willekens (eds) *Childcare and preschool development in Europe – Institutional perspectives*, Basingstoke: Palgrave Macmillan.

Scheiwe, K. and Willekens, H. (2009) 'Introduction: Path-dependencies and change in childcare and pre-school institutions in Europe – Historical and institutional perspectives', in: K. Scheiwe and H. Willekens (eds) *Childcare and preschool development in Europe – Institutional perspectives*, Basingstoke: Palgrave Macmillan, pp 1–22.

Sosinsky, L. S., Lord, H. and Zigler, E. (2007) 'For-profit/nonprofit differences in center-based child care quality: Results from the National Institute of Child Health and Human Development Study of Early Child Care and Youth Development', *Journal of Applied Developmental Psychology*, volume 28, no 5, pp 390–410.

Stewart, J. (2007) 'The mixed economy of welfare in historical context', in: M. Powell (ed) *Understanding the mixed economy of welfare*, Bristol: The Policy Press, pp 23–40.

Swank, D. (2005) 'Globalisation, domestic politics, and welfare state retrenchment in capitalist democracies', *Social Policy and Society*, vol 4, no 2, pp 183–195.

Thane, P. (1996) *The Foundations of the welfare state* (2nd edn), London: Pearson Education.

Tronto, J. C. (1993) *Moral boundaries: A political argument for an ethic of care*, London: Routledge.

UNESCO (2006) *Strong foundations. Early childhood care and education*, Education For All 2007 Global monitoring report, Paris: UNESCO.

Warner, M.E. and Gradus, R.H.J.M. (2011) 'The consequences of implementing a child care voucher scheme: Evidence from Australia, the Netherlands and the USA', *Social Policy & Administration*, vol 45, no 5, pp 569–592.

Whitfield, D. (2006) *A typology of privatisation and marketisation*, ESSU Report No 1, London: European Services Strategy Unit.

Williams, F. (1999) 'Good enough principles for welfare', *Journal of Social Policy*, vol 28, no 4, pp 667–687.

Yuen, G. (2010) 'The displaced early childhood education in the postcolonial era of Hong Kong', in: N. Yelland (ed) *Contemporary perspectives on early childhood education*, Maidenhead: Open University Press, pp 83–99.

TWO

Childcare markets: do they work?

Helen Penn

Introduction

This chapter considers the limitations of using the market as a workable model for the organisation and delivery of childcare. It presents a brief overview of the reach of economics as a basis for making decisions about childcare, and describes changes in ideas about the application of market principles to traditional welfare contexts.

It describes the neoliberal view of the market, in which the role of the state is regarded as minimal, and taxation and regulation are viewed as mainly controversial impositions on business. From this perspective individual choice – including the choice of parents seeking to buy childcare – is paramount; and the best placed people to provide childcare are entrepreneurs whose profits depend on their accurate reading of market demand. Entrepreneurs are therefore likely to be more cost effective and flexible in meeting demand than any than any monolithic state provider could be, and are more likely to be able to muster the capital investment to set up the childcare service. The childcare market is a way of describing a situation where the state has relatively little influence on – or interest in – how services for young children are set up, maintained and delivered.

This is contrasted with a social welfare view of the role of the state, in which communal obligations and social citizenship are given greater priority. Prioritising profit over the needs of vulnerable individuals, such as young children or old and frail people is viewed as morally repugnant, and undermining of basic communal solidarity, citizenship and caring. In this view, the state is the best guarantor that childcare services will be reliable and, in particular, will meet the needs of the most vulnerable alongside those of the strongest, each benefiting from each other's participation in the service (Sandel, 2009). Here the key issue is equity rather than choice.

The market model for childcare, as opposed to a state provided and/or a state funded model of childcare, has been adopted with little public discussion in a number of mainly neoliberal English speaking countries and also in many East and South Asian countries (see Yuen, this volume). In Canada there has been a debate about the role of for-profit childcare versus non-profit care, but essentially within a market context. Private for-profit childcare has long been the accepted model of provision in the US, adopted so widely that it is part of the fabric of thinking about childcare; it is rarely considered worthy of investigation concerning its format or impact even although that effect may be profound (see Sosinsky, this volume).

In the 1980s in the UK private centre-based childcare outside that provided directly by local government or childminding/family daycare was unusual; but the private market has been increasing for the past 15 years or so, and its status was consolidated as part of the 2006 Child Care Act, which made local authority or state provision a 'last resort' (Penn, 2007, 2011). As Blackburn (this volume) shows, more than 80% of childcare provision in the UK is now provided by for-profit entrepreneurs, and the market is framed by calculations of 'attractive visible earnings'. The reach of the market paradigm is now extensive in English speaking countries. The unquestioning acceptance of economic simplifications, and *absence* of debate or investigation in those countries, and the relatively unconditional acceptance, even amongst early childhood professionals, or by parents, of the use of for-profit childcare provided by entrepreneurs, is striking.

This chapter considers what is involved when childcare entrepreneurs try to generate profit, in a system which relies on for-profit entrepreneurs competing with one another for a share of the market. It explores the barriers entrepreneurs encounter in search of profitability, and considers how market approaches might differ from those of public or non-profit services. It recognises the importance of entrepreneurial approaches in contrast to the stultification that is sometimes produced by excessive reliance on state services, but the argument presented here is that for-profit care is often exploitative, and distorts or damages quality and equity of access. At the very least, as Blackburn's chapter shows, quality and equality of access do not figure in standard calculations of profitability.

In other countries outside the neoliberal English speaking consensus, there has been considerably more discussion about non-state provision and in particular whether for-profit provision is acceptable, and under what kinds of conditions it flourishes or is ineffective (see Jacobsen and Vollset, this volume). This chapter explores the position that for-profit childcare is a questionable – and reversible – political choice.

Changing views of economics

It is claimed that economics is a quantitative, empirical and scientific way of describing societal transactions, and that is has led to 'a golden age of discovery' (Coyle 2007, p 232). But the discipline of economics is itself under scrutiny. The failure of most economists to predict recent world economic trends has led to some scathing criticism from economists and non-economists alike (Ormerod, 2006; Tett, 2009; Lanchester, 2010; Milanovic, 2010). Harvey (2010) in his analysis of the geography of capitalism is particularly dismissive: 'economists place all economic activity on the head of a pin' (Harvey, 2010, p 154). The World Economics Association (WEA) (http://worldeconomicsassociation. org) is a worldwide group of mainly academic economists who challenge orthodox economics and its teaching and who present alternative scenarios and interpretations of the market. WEA also produces a widely circulated online journal *Real World Economics*. In the UK, organisations such as the New Economics Foundation (NEF) have focused on the links between social and economic values. For example, researchers at NEF undertook an analysis of the social value of the contribution of childcare workers in the UK to the economy and concluded that they contributed more to the economy than did accountants and bankers (New Economics Foundation, 2009).

Yet a downplaying of the role of the state, and a policy of minimal government intervention, known as 'neoliberal economics', has become an economic holy grail. Lanchester (2010) suggests that for nearly half a century after the end of the Second World War, most developed economies were inspired by the idea of a just, fair and equitable society, in which the state played a major role in redistributing wealth through tax and benefits, and in providing universal services for its citizens. Then the neoliberal approach of minimalist state gained impetus from the fall of communism; the counter-arguments of communists for state control and state intervention had been shown to fail spectacularly. Put crudely, the idea of the market is equated by neoliberals with democratic principles. From a neoliberal perspective, anybody can enter and compete in the marketplace and make money without restraint or barriers; or buy commodities in the marketplace without restrictions. Freedom to make and keep money is the essence of free choice and progress. Choice and competition are better guarantors of efficiency and innovation, as opposed to state services which are frequently perceived as inflexible, paternalistic and inefficient.

Recent popular economics books claim that freedom to participate either as a buyer or as a seller in the market is skewed by existing wealth and privilege, and that neoliberals have systematically tilted economic policy making in order to favour the wealthy (Chang, 2010; Dorling, 2010; Quiggin, 2010). As Lanchester (2010, p 365) succinctly remarks: 'capitalism is not inherently fair: it does not, in and of itself, distribute the rewards of economic growth fairly'.

A neoliberal approach then is one in which equality and fairness are no longer overarching goals. Instead, there is rhetoric of equality of opportunity, which in practice means no more than a freedom to compete in an unequal society. Those who fail to compete successfully are less worthy and less deserving individuals, and less, rather than more, entitled to public funds. 'Trickle-down' economics, as it is sometimes called, holds that rewarding those who are rich for their success, through tax breaks and looser regulation, will benefit those who are poor. Chang (2010, p 137) claims that 'pro-rich policies have failed to accelerate growth in the last three decades' and the trickle down is 'meagre', if it exists at all.

Economic rationales then offer a variable take on childcare, depending on the particular stance adopted. Economics as a discipline does not offer, as some of its adherents claim, a coherent and nearly infallible scientific approach which can explain a wide array of events. Nor can it be used for predictive modelling in an unproblematic way, since its theories rely on simplifications of human conduct using aggregate figures. Neoliberal economic theories present a particular slant on the economic organisation of society, and on the emphasis that is given to competition and productivity (Stiglitz, 2009). Some of these contradictions and differences of approach are explored here in relation to childcare.

Working mothers and the expansion of childcare

The childcare market has expanded as women's roles have changed. Governments and supranational organisations such as OECD and the EU have emphasised the importance of women's contribution to labour market productivity and the consequent need to reconcile work and family life (OECD, 2006; EU, 2011).

In most industrialised countries women's participation in the workforce has increased substantially over the past 25 years, and even in non-industrialised countries women are bearing the brunt of any expansion in outsourced production by multinational companies (Harvey, 2010). As a result the demand for childcare has also increased, and the EU, OECD and even UNESCO have recommended in a range of policy documents that governments support the expansion of childcare (OECD 2006; UNESCO, 2010; EU, 2011).

Governments have chosen either a supply side model of expansion, in which money has been given directly to services, or a demand-led model of expansion, in which money is given to parents to buy childcare. In the supply side model, state provision has been modified or expanded to accommodate the needs of working parents; or non-profit organisations have been grant aided to provide services. In the demand-led model, low-income parents have been given the money directly as subsidies, in order to buy childcare at market prices, and it has been left up to entrepreneurs to provide the service. Neoliberal countries have almost all adopted a demand-led model, since it is based on the primacy of personal choice.

Governments, at least those in rich countries (with the notable exception of the US), agree that some kind of subsidy system is necessary to encourage or support mothers, especially mothers on low incomes, to access the labour market. The *amount* of subsidy is important, and crucially affects quality as well as access (OECD, 2006). However, the *means* of subsidy, supply led or demand-led, critically affects the growth of the for-profit childcare market. Supply led subsidies, with a fixed grant system to the provider, offers a steady income, at least for a period of time, to concerned individuals or groups wishing to provide a service for altruistic reasons. In the UK, as well as in Canada, Australia and New Zealand, supply side funding supported many childcare cooperatives, community nurseries and other kinds of self-help groups and charities providing childcare, although it was rarely extensive and systematic funding; rather locally based and ad hoc. But supply side funding is still used systematically in a number of European countries. This for example is still the pattern of services now in Germany, Austria and Nordic countries (Penn, 2012 forthcoming). But in every case where governments have switched from supply side to demand-led funding, and income to childcare organisations is no longer predictable, this non-profit sector has shrunk. This is most notably the case in the Netherlands, where the 2005 Childcare Act produced such changes rapidly (Lloyd and Penn, 2010).

Demand-led subsidies on the other hand incentivise for-profit entrepreneurs. By promoting and successfully selling their services, entrepreneurs can attract more customers, many of whose fees will be in part guaranteed by government; and by running their businesses more efficiently, they have an opportunity to expand and make a profit. This potential for profitable return in response to demand-led subsidies is what has attracted many investors in the past ten years or so, and what led to the rapid growth of big corporate childcare companies such as ABC in Australia (see Sumsion, this volume). As Blackburn illustrates elsewhere in this volume, the potential profitability of the childcare market attracts banks and other investment companies partly because of the guarantee of subsidies. The major childcare chains in the UK are mainly owned by private equity companies. Until the current recession, childcare was seen as an expanding market, generating above average profits for shareholders and for owners of small businesses alike.

Making a profit

What is entailed in running a for-profit childcare business efficiently? The possibility of making a profit attracts investors. But childcare entrepreneurs face serious barriers to profitability. Some of these barriers are considered here.

Labour costs

The most significant cost limitation that entrepreneurs face is fixed labour costs. These usually amount to between 70 and 80 per cent of outgoings. Caring cannot be made more productive; the caring capacities of members of staff can be improved but cannot usually be extended to cover more children. If there are regulatory conditions in place about ratios or qualification levels, then labour costs can be higher. The only way in which labour costs can be reduced is by paying staff less, at or below a minimum wage; employing the least qualified workers who can be paid less; covering ratio requirements with temporary or untrained staff or students on placement; minimising benefits concerning sick leave, in-service training, holidays and pensions; and adopting anti-union policies to minimise resistance to such conditions. The conditions of childcare workers are notoriously bad, as Davis and Fairholme attest (in this volume) in the case of Canada.

Generally there is a consensus that good outcomes for children are related to good child–staff ratios and levels of staff training. Some studies have taken levels of pay as a proxy measure – poorly paid staff tend to be poorly qualified, and have a high turnover (NICDH, 2005). A major study of recruitment and retention of childcare workers in the UK concluded that low pay and poor employment practices led to high turnover in the childcare sector (Rolfe et al, 2003). There is a constant pressure on government from lobbyists representing the childcare industry to reduce regulatory requirements concerning staff ratios and conditions of employment in order to reduce costs.

In state or cooperative-run childcare, the organisation must justify and account for its pay awards and employment conditions, but no such scrutiny is usually required of for-profit enterprises. The entrepreneur has to file financial returns, or report on returns on investment to shareholders, if it is a stock-listed company, but that is a different matter from having accounts scrutinised and influenced by those working in or using the service. Yet such cooperative scrutiny, as opposed to the limited economic concept of 'voice', is regarded as being a key aspect of services in some systems (see Jacobsen and Vollset, this volume).

Property costs

Apart from labour costs, there are substantial capital costs, especially for those entrepreneurs operating in urban areas. The investment required for capital expenditure to set up new services is one of the reasons that demand-led funding is attractive to government – they do not have to raise the money to provide new services but can leave it to private investors. But because of land costs many, if not most, small entrepreneurs are limited in what they can provide. Entrepreneurs are most likely to use or extend existing premises – shop fronts, domestic premises, industrial premises, church halls and so on. Any capital investment is dependent on local property prices, and the investment in a building is covered by the potential sale value of the property if the childcare ceases to be profitable. It is less of a risk to invest in areas where property values are likely to remain stable or to rise, than in poorer areas where property values are more uncertain.

In the UK, there is a significant secondary market in property companies who specialise in buying and selling childcare properties of all kinds. As Blackburn illustrates in this volume, property values underpin childcare profitability, and in the current recession property values have fallen. Many childcare businesses tend to be over-valued as a result, and companies now have many empty properties on their books. This advertisement, from one such company, illustrates how childcare property purchases are hedged.

> T/O £300,000 GP 65%, superbly equipped town centre (children's) activity centre, impressive 13,000sqft property, capacity for 290 + 70 cover cafe, off road parking, licensed premises – potential night club use. (www.daynurseries. co.uk/for-sale)

Bigger companies can provide purpose built childcare, although the long-term viability of land purchase remains a paramount consideration. Companies tend to use commercial prefabricated models, and/or standard designs, easily recognisable, which are a form of branding, rather like a supermarket chain (staff are often required to wear brand uniforms).

In the public sector, or cooperative or non-profit sector, although there are also considerable pressures to use available rather than purpose built premises, fitness for purpose is usually a more important consideration. Fitness for purpose includes the appropriateness of the locality for those being served, especially poor families, rather than the viability of the local property market. Since non-profit services are primarily altruistic, to meet an identified need from a specific group of people, they are more likely to be shaped by an overarching vision of what children and parents using the service might need or welcome in the way of space and facilities, and this usually presumes discussion with and accountability to users.

When public money is invested in a property, if the service closes down, the value of the property reverts to the public authority or charity concerned. If a private company owns the building, even if public money has been directly (through grants) or indirectly (through subsidies) invested in it, then the value accrues solely to the entrepreneur. This question of disposal of assets is not one that is usually addressed as an aspect of childcare markets, but may be critical, given the volatility of the market and the significance of property values.

Technology

Within capitalist enterprises generally, there is a drive to improve technology in order to reduce labour costs and raise profits. Since technology cannot replace human caring, technological improvements in childcare enterprises are limited to more marginal activities, such as administration and management, ordering and supplies and so on. Here the for-profit sector can excel. There are a considerable number of supply companies who specialise in childcare technology. This advertisement from a US firm emphasises how technology can be used to improve marketing and increase recruitment, necessary concerns for a childcare business.

> Child Care Marketing Solutions is excited to announce the launch of their new Child Care Business Success System, a comprehensive toolkit for marketing and enrollment-

building. The system features ten learning modules with ten accompanying audio CDs, designed specifically for early childhood business owners and administrators. By using these innovative, cutting edge, and cost-effective strategies, centers and schools can easily increase their enrollment, improve customer satisfaction, and improve their return-on-investment on marketing and advertising budgets. Includes actual examples, templates, and worksheets. Discover the hidden wealth buried in your child care center! (Childcare Exchange, 2010)

Technological improvements and computerisation can produce considerable gains in efficiency, but again the issue is to what use are these being put. Here it is explicitly in the creation of wealth. There may be less pressure – and less investment available – to introduce technological change in state or non-profit services, but the overriding consideration would again be fitness for purpose – for example keeping parents informed, keeping children's records up to date, keeping accurate staff records, monitoring expenditure, undertaking research through monitoring – innovations which might improve the quality of the service.

Competitive edge

In any market, producers vie with one another to sell their product. Childcare markets are no different. One aspect of competition is guarding a product and the processes involved in making it against competitors who may wish to use or exploit such knowledge. This means that childcare entrepreneurs, too, may be cagey about disclosing information of any kind about their businesses. Expecting business competitors to pool information, or to share resources, especially in times of recession, is like asking the wolf to lie down with the lamb (Penn and Randall, 2005). The confidentiality argument is stated succinctly by this major childcare provider:

> Why give away techniques and confidential information which have taken time, energy and a great deal of expense to develop? In a competitive environment this intellectual property or pool of trade secrets represents one of the most important assets a company owns... this is exactly what the Government is expecting the best nurseries to do in an effort to raise standards... Both the private and

the maintained sector will be expecting to spend time sharing best practice with other nurseries even if they are competitors... this is neither fair nor reasonable (Bentley, 2008, p12)

The business confidentiality approach of private entrepreneurs like this may limit mutual cooperation and learning. But even more so, it militates against transparency and openness. A nursery cannot be run on democratic lines, or engage in open discussions with users, or disclose information that might impact on its profitability without threatening that profitability.

Fee income

The main income of for-profit entrepreneurs is from fees. Parental contributions are high, even if they are supplemented by tax credits and other demand-led subsidies. Blackburn estimates that in the UK as a whole, 60% of the costs of childcare are borne by parents, although there is considerable variability within that figure. In order to make a profit, the fees must be as high as the market will bear. At the time of writing the price for top-end childcare in London is between £80 and £100 *per day* (Daycare Trust, 2011). Even with a childcare subsidy system, this kind of fee cannot be met except by high-income families, and in this sense access to childcare is inequitable.

If parents are able to claim government subsidies, then entrepreneurs can charge a higher fee from them than they might otherwise do. Subsidies may have the effect of driving fees upwards. Fees in the UK are high by OECD standards. The OECD produces comparative figures for gross fees, and for net fees (once tax and benefits have been taken into account) and the UK compares unfavourably with other countries on both counts (OECD, 2011).

Where children require extra help – because of some kind of disability, or for linguistic support for example – this can only be provided at extra cost. Similarly if a childcare facility is to offer more flexible care, such as extended hours or extra holiday care, this too can only be provided at extra cost. Far from being responsive to parental need, entrepreneurs need to standardise their offers to make a profit. The recent London Childcare Affordability Project 2009 (CAP09) project included an attempt to offer parents additional top-up for childcare precisely in order to provide more flexible care for more vulnerable children (Hall et al, 2011).

Businesses also have to be careful about the collection of fees, since the cash flow of the nursery is dependent on prompt payment. In a commodified system, childcare becomes a financial contract between the buyer and the purchaser, subject to legal constraints, rather than a shared care arrangement with 'parental participation'. A recent article in the practitioner magazine *Nursery World* by the managing director of a debt collection agency explains how nurseries should insist on spelling out the details of the contract with each parent and make clear the penalties for breaching it:

> The fact that many nurseries are conducting business without clear accepted terms and conditions from their customers means they could face serious consequences if queries or payment disputes arise... Here are our tips for what to include in your terms and conditions to get quicker and more effective payment of debts and other late payment charges from late payers:
>
> • Clear payment terms, that is the right to recover interest and debt collection charges in securing payment
> • The right to refer disputes to your local County Court if there is a dispute (so it is more convenient for you to give evidence)
> • Make sure that both parents sign and accept your terms and contract details. (Hughes, 2011, p 27)

Market volatility

Successful businesses compete and expand; unsuccessful businesses fail and close. Markets are inherently unstable and businesses, small and large, fail all the time, although failure tends to be minimised or ignored in the economic literature, and success, by contrast, is extolled (Ormerod, 2006; Harvey, 2010). Small entrepreneurs have a very high failure rate. Childcare businesses are no exception, and while there may be many new entrants to the market so total numbers may appear constant, there is likely to be considerable turnover. Kershaw and his colleagues, working in British Columbia, show that even in an expanding market, businesses themselves are fragile (Kershaw et al, 2005). Unlike public services which are intended to provide a consistent service whatever the vagaries of the market or vulnerabilities of the clientele, the private market responds primarily to profit and loss. The balance sheet is necessarily the primary consideration rather than, for example, the wellbeing of poor or vulnerable children. In times of recession the unreliability of the marketplace becomes still more volatile. For instance, childcare markets are contracting in the UK (Laing & Buisson, 2010; Ofsted, 2010). In this scenario, advertising and marketing to attract customers is especially important, from the sophisticated marketing techniques described above by the US company Childcare Marketing Solutions to a basic discount store approach. This leaflet was pushed through my door by a local company Excel Childcare Services Ltd.:

First ever WINTER sale!

6% discount on *all* fees for the first 3 months (12 weeks) for babies and children starting at the nursery before 28th February.

You could be quid's in – saving huge amounts of money and have excellent, homelike childcare.

HURRY! HURRY! HURRY! LIMITED PLACES

The nursery being advertised was rated by OFSTED as unsatisfactory, the lowest rating it could have short of being deemed unfit to open. Marketing is necessarily about successful presentation in order to increase sales rather than about a description of the product which will enable parents to make a considered choice.

The market also consolidates. In the childcare business, smaller operators are swallowed up by bigger companies, and bigger companies themselves are sold on or reorganised. The corporate market in the UK is currently around 8% of for-profit businesses, although these provide 28% of all places. All but one of the 20 largest companies has been taken over or bought out in the past five years (Laing & Buisson, 2010). The biggest childcare company in the world, ABC Learning, based in Australia, which provided 30% of childcare in Australia, and 70% of the provision in the state of Queensland, expanded very rapidly, then spectacularly failed in 2009. The Australian government had to bail out the company, because of the number of childcare places at risk, and spend many millions of dollars in a holding operation, until the assets could be sold on. The affair was so damaging that the government was more or less obliged to resell to a non-profit consortium, and tighten its regulatory procedures (Parliament of Australia, 2009; Sumsion, this volume).

Such market volatility is an obstacle to providing stable and consistent care that young children need for their wellbeing, and for the reassurance mothers need in order to combine work and domestic life.

Regulation

In a neoliberal context, the state is viewed as a liability, in so far as it limits individual choice and seeks to control and thereby distort the market through regulation. But because of the difficulties and inequities in childcare markets, most governments – at least in high income countries – have a raft of policies in place to support childcare markets. Most childcare markets are subject to some kind of government intervention, in the form of regulation, subsidies or price controls.

This section draws on a study I recently undertook for the European Commission (but not published at the time of writing) on regulatory mechanisms for childcare markets in European countries. Three kinds of regulatory control are briefly discussed here; financial controls, quality controls and data collection. There are considerable differences between countries as to how services are financed, and what regulatory controls might cover. The position of a tranche of European countries on these two aspects of regulatory control is presented in Table 2.1 (p 35).

Financial interventions

To compensate for the inherent inequity in the childcare market, many countries have introduced price controls. Parents pay fees on a banded scale related to household income – usually around 15% of net household income. There is also a price ceiling. In other countries, most notably the UK and Ireland, there are no price controls, and parents may pay as much as one third to one half of household income for a childcare place. The effect of introducing price controls is to limit profitability, so that most provision in those countries that legislate for price control tends to be non-profit rather than commercial.

Since childcare is a labour intensive and expensive service to provide, these price controls are invariably underwritten by supply side funding, that is by grants, usually on a per capita basis, given directly to the childcare setting. These per capita grants are usually tied into some kind of quality rating. In a demand led system, where the possibility of profit is a major incentive to providers, and take-up of places cannot be easily tracked, fee-capping would probably be unworkable; the only control government could introduce would be in the subsidy level to parents – but as discussed, that usually has a knock-on effect on fees. Governments may also insist on asset controls, as discussed above.

Quality interventions

Almost all high income countries have introduced regulations on quality (see chapter seven in this volume for a discussion about what happens when regulations cannot be introduced). The introduction of a regulatory system also implies a monitoring system and the ultimate sanction of legal penalties for those childcare businesses that are in breach of regulations.

Quality regulations usually include requirements for health and safety, space, staff training, staff–child ratios and curricula, although these may vary considerably between countries. For example, the space requirements for inside and outside space in Nordic countries are considerably more generous than in the UK, where there are no mandatory outside space requirements. These relatively lax regulations concerning space in the UK enable entrepreneurs to make use of properties that might otherwise be deemed unsuitable for children – converted terrace houses, or shop fronts for example.

Similarly there is considerable variety across Europe in regulations concerning staff training. In some countries, most notably Denmark, there is a requirement that a majority of staff will be trained to postgraduate level, and undertake regular in-service training. In others, again the neoliberal English speaking group of countries, staff qualifications are set low, at two years post-16 vocational training or lower, and there are no mandatory requirements for in-service training.

Where businesses are competing against one another in a fragmented system and do not operate in any networked way, monitoring in itself requires considerable resources. For example, the England monitoring body Ofsted inspects on a four year cycle (and more frequently if there are complaints or other causes for concern) and carried out over 90,000 inspections in a three year period 2005–08 (Ofsted, 2010). This requires a considerable workforce. Inspections are themselves now franchised, and there are questions about the viability and consistency of inspections. However, in those European countries which support childcare markets but impose stringent requirements, having detailed accountability systems in place is a more important regulatory control than an external monitoring system. For example, in Norway nurseries, together with parents and even children, produce annual plans which are approved at a local authority or regional level. Nurseries are also required to network on a local level, and share training (see Jacobsen and Vollset, this volume).

Data collection

There is no standard means of data collection about childcare across Europe, although the EU-SILC database (Standard of Living and Income Conditions data) does provide standardised information derived from household surveys. Partly the difficulty is definitional, concerning the overlap between care and education, and partly it is administrative – since childcare is governed by different administrative arrangements across Europe. If usage, uptake and quality of for-profit care are problematic issues, for all the reasons discussed here, then the data collected should record auspices or type of ownership, if ownership critically affects supply, quality and take-up of provision. A study by Cleveland et al (2008) which compared for-profit and non-profit care, estimated that the difference in quality between the two types of provision ranged from 7 to 22%, the non-profit care achieving the better quality ratings. In most countries where childcare markets are established, these data are not collected; it is assumed that quality of provision can be achieved by any provider, and ownership is irrelevant to quality. But this is a false assumption without evidence.

Summary

This chapter has explored some of the conflicting priorities between childcare by for-profit entrepreneurs and non-profit or state systems. The argument for a childcare market is that it will increase competition and lower prices. Economists argue that a childcare market is the most efficient and cost-effective way of recognising and providing for consumer demand. But 'consumer demand' is a complicated issue, especially since the word 'consumer' applies to the parent who is purchasing the service, not the child who is experiencing it; and because consumer confidence in childcare is partly a reflection of social class (Vincent et al, 2008). Plantenga, in this volume, writing about the Netherlands, also offers a critique of the concept of consumers in childcare.

The key question is whether the childcare market is a reliable and equitable way of delivering childcare. For neoliberal countries, the risks and complications involved in allowing entrepreneurs to provide childcare are either unrecognised or deemed acceptable – or a combination of both. In other countries where there is a childcare market, it is carefully controlled and generously funded, and although there may be many kinds of provider, the type of funding and the regulatory framework means that for-profit companies have limited room to manoeuvre. In yet other countries the childcare market is altogether unacceptable, and the government takes on the responsibility for providing childcare.

Any policy maker has to clarify and weigh the economic advantages and disadvantages of a particular course of action and make some estimate of its costs and benefits. This chapter has considered some of the tensions arising in delivering childcare through the marketplace. It has focused solely on childcare markets, and has not considered the strengths and weaknesses of the public sector or of cooperative and non-profit approaches in providing childcare. But it has indicated that there are considerable – and generally unrecognised – limitations and tensions in relying on the childcare market. Viewing childcare as a commodity to be bought and sold undermines equity and quality, and regulation has to be comprehensive and wide-reaching in order to try and compensate for these failings.

Table 2.1: ECEC Regulatory Framework: an *approximate* overview

Country	Legislation	Date	Derivation	Scope of regulation	Underlying quality principles	Regulatory body or procedures
Belgium	Regional legislation Regional guidance Regional inspection systems	Flemish: 2003 Quality of Health and Welfare Services	Administrative/ Expert	U3 Includes staff qualifications, adult–child ratios, training, access, fees cap, information service, non-discriminatory practices Excludes pay and working conditions Education services are almost all publicly delivered	U3 Child wellbeing and safety, social learning, labour market access 3–5 Education goals	Flemish: Kind en Gezin, an in-house arms length agency oversees all aspects of implementation. French: Office de la Naissance et de L'Enfance
Czech Republic	National Legislation and ordinances. No guidance documents. National or regional inspectorates	1991 Act on Public Health 1991 Act on Sole Trading (private) 2004 Education Act (private kindergartens)	Ministry of Education Youth and Sports, with some consultation of experts	U3: none other than sole trader requirements Education services are almost all publicly delivered. V. small number of private kindergartens are expected to follow official programmes.	U3: n/a Kindergartens education goals leading to school	U3: n/a Kindergartens in house quality evaluation plus occasional inspection visits

Country	Legislation	Date	Derivation	Scope of regulation	Underlying quality principles	Regulatory body or procedures
Denmark	National legislation No national guidance Details left to municipalities	2007 Dagtilbudsloven Act	Parliamentary discussions public debate involving trades unions who have right of comment	Includes working conditions of staff renegotiated at 3 year intervals. Access for parents, qualifications of staff, cap on fees, guaranteed sustainability Applies to all services, whatever the auspices	Improve children's wellbeing; development and learning; to give family flexible choices; to promote inclusion of children with additional needs; to ensure coherence and continuity within services; non-discrimination; child's right to express her view; understanding of democracy	Each provider has annual plan, to be agreed by parent board, including children's 'environmental assessment' No inspectorate Some independent research commissioned
Finland	National legislation, National Curriculum guidelines	1973 Children's Daycare Act, amended 1983 2005 Act on the Professional Qualifications of Social Welfare Personnel 1998 Basic Education Act 2002 Resolution on ECEC	Steering group within the Ministry, with stakeholder representatives, ongoing online consultation, ECEC expert team at Ministry	Includes staff qualifications, curricular guidelines, healthy environments, pay and working conditions through collective bargaining, access, fee caps Mentoring networks at municipal level, 'learning in work'	Play based education, lifelong learning; Non-discrimination and equal treatment; The child's best interest; giving weight to views of the child; own culture, language rights and religion	Municipalities set up their own collaborative networks to review provision Some independent research commissioned No inspectorate

Country	Legislation	Date	Derivation	Scope of regulation	Underlying quality principles	Regulatory body or procedures
France	National legislation and guidance	2005 Childminders Act Education Act 1989 2010 Code de la Sante publique	Administrative / Expert	U3 Includes staffing standards, ratios, qualifications, training, fees Over-3 services are all publicly delivered	Enhancement of cognitive and physical abilities Favouring biological rhythms Social integration, labour market access	U3 Mainly executive board of CNAF Visits from physicians. Kindergartens regional inspection service
Germany	National legislation and guidance Regional legislation and guidance	1990 Child and Youth Services Act modified and amended most recently in 2009 16 Lander provide regional legislation based on act National curricular framework	Research consortium piloted self-assessment and external assessment procedures, plus regional initiatives	At Lander level includes curricular framework, staff qualifications, ratios, access, sustainability, working conditions of employees	Holistic approach Children involved in decision making Intercultural awareness Gender awareness Experiential learning and enquiring disposition towards learning	National Quality Initiative as described Large providers have their own quality frameworks
Greece	National legislation National guidance, very sparse	Joint ministerial decision 2002 for daycare Framework Law 1989, 1985 for kindergartens	Administrative (Lack of consultation strongly criticised by expert)	Minimal requirements	U3 Harmonious psychosomatic development Education curriculum, teacher dominated	Few implementation tools

Country	Legislation	Date	Derivation	Scope of regulation	Underlying quality principles	Regulatory body or procedures
Hungary	National Legislation National and local guidance	1997 Act on the Protection of Children 1993 Education Act	Legislative processes of ministerial and professional consultation	Includes setting criteria for environment, staff qualifications, ratios, access, fees, working conditions, curriculum.	Equal opportunities Freedom of conscience and religion Right of minorities to mother tongue teaching Rights and obligations of children Rights and obligations of parents	Municipal licensing and monitoring through 'methodological' or demonstration nurseries and in service training Variety of inspection agencies
Italy	National legislation Regional or local guidance Public procurement rules apply: services tendered by region mainly to municipality	1971 Créches Act 2000 Act (62/2000) 2000 Welfare Law Regional laws eg Emilia Romagna 2000/2004 on services to U3s 1968 Act on scuole dell'ifanzia	Public professional debates within interested regions	At regional level includes setting criteria for staff qualifications, ratios, premises, access, working conditions, fees, curriculum	Respect for children's rights Solidarity Non-discrimination Accessibility Good governance	Participatory methods involving staff; teams of pedagogic coordinators

Country	Legislation	Date	Derivation	Scope of regulation	Underlying quality principles	Regulatory body or procedures
Netherlands	National legislation and guidance about quality conditions	General Quality Framework introduced in 2004 Childcare Act	Multiple stakeholders involved, including employers and parents	Includes staff qualifications, curricular guidelines, health and safety. Requires service to be delivered in Dutch language. Excludes pay and working conditions, access, fees, closures. Applies only to childcare	Childcare is a business. Parents require choice. Nursery education as aspect of education system	Various self-assessment tools developed but use optional. Parents can complain to national complaints committee via local parents committee
Norway	National legislation on grant eligibility. National legislation and guidance about quality conditions	2005 Kindergarten Act. 2009 Quality in Kindergartens White paper	Public hearings. Sami assembly, various commissions	Includes staff training, curricular guidelines, complaints procedures, pay and working conditions, access, fees cap, closures, annual plans considered by staff/parent committees. Applies to all services, public or private.	Good opportunities for children's development. Lifelong learning. Democracy, tolerance, appreciation of sustainable development	Framework implemented through compulsory self-evaluation: annual plans/review for each provider for all stakeholder groups. National research
Poland	National legislation. Local guidance	1991 Law on Health Care Centres. Education Act	Administrative	Includes staff qualifications, health and safety and premises requirements, ratios	Developing intellectual abilities, building a system of values, health and physical fitness, developing skills	Municipal evaluation teams in compliance with national regulations

Country	Legislation	Date	Derivation	Scope of regulation	Underlying quality principles	Regulatory body or procedures
Portugal	National legislation and guidance	Framework Law for Preschool Education 1997 amended 2007 plus many other laws and joint orders defining specific aspects of provision	Administrative with help of independent experts	Includes premises and equipment, personnel requirements including compulsory in-service training, excludes access, fees, closure	Human dignity, solidarity, user empowerment, transparency, good governance	Licensing compulsory for all provision Self-evaluation systems, questionnaires for levels of client satisfaction at institutional level Training manuals
Romania	National law for crèches No other specific legislation or guidance or codification	2007 Crèche law amended 2009 2006 Social Assistance Act 1995 Education Act includes kindergartens	Municipal Administration	Unclear: mainly health and safety but very little private provision	Uniqueness of child Pluri-disciplinary approaches	Internal kindergarten standards, but no more general provision
UK	National legislation and guidance, extremely detailed and exhaustive Centralised inspection regime (Ofsted) to oversee compliance	2006 Childcare Act 2004 Education Act 2008 Statutory Guidance on the Early Years Foundation Stage	Consultations through White Papers, invited consultancy from the business community Not consensual	Includes staff training, curricular guidelines, ratios, health and safety. Excludes pay and working conditions, fees, closures. Applies only to childcare.	Childcare is a business Parents require choice Wellbeing of child; reduction of risk Good school outcomes	Elaborate complaints procedures, via Ofsted. All initiatives subject to substantial independent research evaluation (often critical)

References

Bentley, A. (2008) 'To the point', *Nursery World*, June, no 10, p 12.

Chang, H-J. (2010) *23 Things they don't tell you about capitalism*, London: Allen Lane.

Childcare Exchange (2010) http://ccie.com/favoritethings_exchange.php

Cleveland, G., Forer, B., Hyatt D., Japel, C. and Krashinsky, M. (2008) 'New evidence about childcare in Canada: Use patterns, affordability and quality', *Institute for Research in Public Policy: Choices*, vol 4, no 12, www.irpp.org/choices/archive/vol14no12.pdf.

Coyle, B. (2007) *The soulful science: What economists really do and why it matters*, Princeton, NJ: Princeton University Press.

Daycare Trust (2011) *Childcare costs survey 2011*, London: Daycare Trust.

Dorling, D. (2010) *Injustice: Why social inequality persists*, Bristol: The Policy Press.

European Commission (2011) *Early childhood education and care: Providing all our children with the best start for the world of tomorrow*, Brussels: Communication from the Commission.

Hall, S., Pereira, I., Darragh, J., Knight, M. and Bridges, L. (2011) *Qualitative research into families' experiences and behaviours in the Childcare Affordability Pilots (CAP09): 100% costs pilot*, Research Report DFE-RR101 London: Department for Education.

Harvey, D. (2010) *The enigma of capital*, London: Profile Books, 2nd edition.

Hughes, C. (2011) 'Recover your debts', *Nursery World*, Febuary, p 14.

Kershaw, P., Forer, B. and Goelman, H. (2005) 'Hidden fragility: Closure among licensed child-care services in British Columbia', *Early Childhood Research Quarterly*, vol 20, no 4, pp 417–32.

Laing & Buisson (2010) *Children's nurseries UK market report 2010*, London: Laing & Buisson.

Lanchester, J. (2010) *Whoops! Why everybody owes everyone and no one can pay*, London: Allen Lane/Penguin. Kindle Edition.

Lloyd, E. and Penn, H. (2010) 'Why do childcare markets fail? *Public Policy Research*, vol 17, no1, pp 42–48.

Milanovic, B. (2010) *The haves and the have nots*, NY: Basic Books.

New Economics Foundation (2009) *A bit rich: Calculating the real value to society of different professions*, London: New Economics Foundation.

NICDH Early Child Care Research Network (2005) *Study of early child care and youth development*, New York: Guildford Press.

OECD (2006) *Starting strong II. Early childhood education and care*, Paris: OECD.

OECD (2011) *Social and family database.* www.oecd.org/els/social/family/database.

Ormerod, P. (2006) *Why most things fail,* New Jersey: John Wiley and Sons.

Office for Standards in Education (OFSTED) (2010 Annual Report London: Ofsted

Parliament of Australia Senate Education, Employment Workplace Relations Committee (2009) *Childcare report,* www.aph.gov.au/SEnate/committee/eet_ctte/child_care/report/c02.htm

Penn, H. and Randall, V. (2005) 'Childcare policy under Labour and the EYDCPs', *Journal of Social Policy,* vol 34, no 1, pp 79–97.

Penn, H. (2007) 'Childcare market management: How the UK government has reshaped its role in developing early education and care', *Contemporary Issues in Early Childhood,* vol 8, no 3, pp 192–207.

Penn, H. (2011) 'Gambling on the market', *Journal of Early Childhood Research,* vol 9, no 2, pp 150–161.

Penn, H. (2012) 'The business of childcare in Europe' submitted to *European Early Childhood Education Research Journal,* 2011.

Quiggin, J. (2010) *Zombie economics: How dead ideas still walk amongst us,* New Jersey: Princeton University Press.

Rolfe, H., Metcalf, H., Anderson T. and Meadows, P. (2003) *Recruitment and retention of childcare, early years and play workers: Research study,* London: National Institute of Economic and Social Research.

Sandel, M. (2009) *Justice: What's the right thing to do?* London: Penguin Books.

Stiglitz, J. (2009) *Report on the commission on measurement of economic performance and social justice,* Paris: French Presidency, www.stiglitz-sen-fitoussi.fr.

Tett, G. (2009) *Fool's gold: How the bold dream of a small tribe at J.P. Morgan was corrupted by Wall Street greed and unleashed a catastrophe,* London: Little Brown.

UNESCO (2010) *World conference on early childhood care and education: Moscow framework for action and co-operation: Harnessing the wealth of nations,* Paris: UNESCO.

Vincent, C., Braun, A. and Ball, S. (2008) 'Childcare, choice and social class: Caring for young children in the UK', *Critical Social Policy,* vol 28, no 1, pp 5–9.

THREE

Future directions for a mature UK childcare market

Philip Blackburn

Introduction

Equitable access to childcare in the UK is largely choreographed by a dominant pay-as-you-go private market, which is now categorised as mature in macroeconomic terms. This chapter concentrates on pertinent issues for childcare providers in sustaining their businesses within a changing economic and socioeconomic demand climate post-maturity. Such concerns are unlikely to centre on equity issues, the topic of this volume, but the sustenance of the private childcare market in the future will crucially highlight the incidence of equity for consumers. Gaining an insight into economic factors determining the likely future of this market should be helpful to the analysis and formulation of wider early childhood education and care policy both in the UK and elsewhere.

Laing & Buisson is a market research company that provides annual reports on the childcare nursery market in the UK using its own survey material as well as government statistical information, in particular Office of National Statistics databases (ONS, 2011a). This chapter draws on the reports to give an overview of market trends, and to make predictions for the future under a new government in a depressed economic climate. The data cited here are taken from these annual reports, in particular the 2011 report, unless otherwise stated.

In 2006 demand for daycare nursery services in the UK (number of children attending) failed to grow for the first time on record and during the following year day nursery supply growth (places available) ground to a halt, following growth which averaged double figures annually in the previous five years (2002–06 inclusive). This was the first sign that the UK's largest paid childcare market had reached a level of maturity; a *mature market* is one where demand and supply has reached an equilibrium characterised by the absence of significant growth or innovation. Trends since reveal market contraction, as supply and demand both fell by over 6% overall during 2008–10 inclusive (Laing & Buisson, 2011). While this contraction was not unexpected during a period of economic recession which saw the UK economy shrink by 5% in real terms in 2009, it was at the same time consistent with market maturity.

This chapter presents a macroeconomic perspective of the key levers which are likely to shape demand and supply for paid childcare in a market that has matured. Its focus centres on prospects in the UK for: childcare demand using data from population trends, demographics and employment dynamics; funding of childcare by private individuals, employers and the government; and the development and structure of supply which has reached maturity. The aim of the chapter is to identify the likely direction of macroeconomic trends for UK childcare markets in the future, especially in a weak economic environment.

Demand in a mature market

The growth of childcare is shaped primarily by three crucial determinants: numbers of children; the need for childcare; and the ability of parents and others to pay for childcare. There are, of course, likely to be important 'one-off' demand developers such as service innovation, regulatory changes, or government policy.

Early years population

Strong growth of UK childcare markets throughout the 1990s and first half of the 2000s took place in the absence of an underlying early years (under 5s) population driver. On the other hand, during this period the early years population headed downwards, falling by around half a million from 3.9 million to 3.4 million, as the UK fertility rate dipped significantly in the 1990s to a low of 1.64. However, childcare demand was still immature during this period, and its growth was crucially driven by trends such as a rise in the average age of mothers having a first child and higher female employment. More recently the birth rate between 2002 and 2009 inclusive has risen from 1.64 to 1.94.

Now that the children's daycare nurseries market has developed and matured, and the trends of age of mothers and female employment participation have levelled off, as will be discussed below, the increase in the numbers of young children is expected to become a much more important driver for childcare. However, longer term during the 2020s the UK early years population is forecast to remain largely static, consistent with a long-term fertility rate assumption of 1.84 from 2015 onwards. However, actual fertility rates measured in 2009 and 2010, available since projections were made, were noticeably above expectations suggesting actual growth in the 2010s is likely to overshoot the 5% projection. In its most optimistic scenario for fertility (high variant projections), based on a long-term fertility rate assumption of 2.04 from 2015, the numbers of young children are projected to increase very strongly (ONS, 2011b).

As noted earlier, a main driver of childcare demand in the recent past was a strong and sustained increase in the proportion of women working, and an upward shift in the average age of women having children. Following a lull during the early 1990s recession, the proportion of women working moved from around 49% of all working aged women to a peak of 54% in 2006, and remained at this peak until the onset of recession in 2008. There was a clear increased preference by many more women to establish an employment 'career' and generate higher household income before starting a family. This was highlighted by increased labour market participation rates for women aged 25–34 years, which moved from 64% in 1992 to 71% in 1999, and then to a high of just under 73% prior to the recession in 2008, and for women aged 35–49 years which moved steadily upwards from 72.5% in the early 1990s to 75% in the late 1990s and to over 76% prior to recession.

As women delay having a family, their propensity to use childcare increases as they have a greater incentive to return to work to a 'career' which can generate disposable resources to fund childcare. A milestone was reached in 2001 in the UK, when the highest proportion of women giving birth shifted from 25–29 years to 30–35 years for the first time, when the average age of mothers having children moved to 29 years, compared with around 27½ at the start of the 1990s. Since then this trend has continued, with latest estimates showing the average age of mothers giving birth is around 29½. However, (2008-based) projections suggest the propensity for women to have children later in life has levelled off, as the average age of mothers giving birth is projected to remain at 29½ until the late 2020s when it is forecast to edge higher, and fertility across all age cohorts will move roughly in line with the downward projection in fertility rate over time.

The need for paid and informal childcare is inherently dependent on the size of the childbearing female workforce, and on the parental workforce as a whole. At the end of the 2000s, a harsh global recession delivered a reversal in male and female employment rates, though the largest falls in participation were for younger men and women (teenagers and those in their early 20s). For the first part of the 2010s the workforce driver is likely to remain subdued as employment rates look to fall back to their pre-recession levels, particularly for younger age groups. As such the need for childcare from the working population is expected to rise only gradually for some time to come. An average of independent medium-term forecasts taken at mid-2011 (HM Treasury, May 2011) projected a gradual modest recovery in UK economic growth from 1.5% in 2011 to 2.5% in 2014 and 2015, accompanied by an 11% drop in unemployment between 2011 and 2015 inclusive. However, expectations for growth in 2011 have since been revised downwards closer to 1% (HM Treasury, July 2011), as the UK economy proved weaker than expected. Government policy to substantially reduce public debt provides a tight fiscal straightjacket up to 2015.

Maternal employment

The most positive long-term underlying driver for childcare demand is employment growth to service a rapidly ageing population, as life expectancy increases. Though the dynamics of economic sufficiency across population ages over time are complex, the trends suggest that workforce output will need to increase strongly in the future to ensure older generations are adequately cared for. A widely used statistic for the EU is that without change, by 2050, the ratio of workers supporting pensioners will fall to near 2 compared with the current 4 (Economic Policy Committee, 2009). In that case, pressures on the workforce are expected to be become visible even in the medium term (10–15 years). As a result one could speculate that female participation would move closer to male participation. Long-term labour market forecasts made prior to the recession estimated that labour market participation of working aged females would move from 70% in the second half of the 2000s to 73% by 2020 (Madouros, 2006). At the same time the participation rate for working age males was projected by Madouros (2006) to remain more or less static at just over 83%.

Figure 3.1 illustrates the gender employment gap by age, and the scope for growth in female employment participation. However, increased female labour participation *per se* is not a certain driver of childcare demand, since a large part of female labour growth is projected to be above childbearing age. Madouros (2006) projected that nearly two thirds of new labour market participants up to 2020 would be over 50 years old. However, a more positive trend for childcare demand was that a quarter of new participants would be aged between 25 and 35. Less positive was a projection for labour market participants aged 35–39 to fall marginally in the long term.

Figure 3.1: UK labour market participation and the 'gender gap'

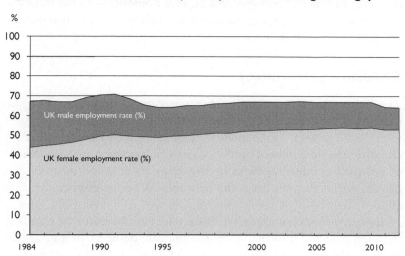

Equally, in another scenario, an ageing population may directly put pressure on fertility across all ages because the UK currently has a sub-replacement fertility rate (below 2.1 children per woman), meaning future generations may face difficulties supporting the economy's population. Magnus (2009) argues that increased labour market participation of childbearing age females in the UK would probably lead to higher fertility, as there is positive causality between female labour market participation and fertility in countries with higher fertility than the UK. But Magnus suggests that there are considerable barriers to increased labour market participation for women of childbearing age in the UK, and that workplaces need to encourage equal pay and equal treatment, more flexible working practices, better access to IT skills and, crucially, for 'more, better and affordable childcare facilities'.

Flexibility in particular is a key factor which will shape childcare preferences in the future. Flexible working conditions covering flexible hours, job share, working from home, amongst others, are likely to widen childcare choices that are available to households, and better enable preferred choices to be met. A growing trend for flexibility in the past ten years is fully expected to continue, and probably accelerate in the next ten years. For instance, new legislation in the UK is set to improve paternity leave and flexible working rights for parents of young children. For the paid childcare demand market, however, employment flexibility is likely to be considered 'double-edged.' While flexible employment conditions are likely to encourage more women and men into employment, as domestic and work commitments can be better managed, flexibility also enables households to use informal or parental childcare arrangements more easily such as parental sharing of childcare responsibilities.

Childcare preferences

The other key factor shaping the need for childcare is childcare preferences of households. Preferences are determined by a range of interrelated factors, which include income levels and ability to pay for childcare, the flexibility of household working practices, the availability of informal childcare options such as grandparents and relatives, and parents' belief about what is the best early years experience for their child.

Ability to pay is a crucial determinant which orchestrates the trade-off between paid and informal/parental childcare demand. In itself ability to pay is determined not only by the level of household income, but also by levels of government childcare subsidy and assistance from employers. Over the next ten years, the level of funding available for formal childcare will shape the trade-off for future generations, as will be discussed later.

The use of informal childcare, and its relationship as a market substitute to paid (formal) childcare, is generally not well understood. It is often assumed that households' use of informal childcare options – grandparents, relatives and friends, and also, in its broadest definition, childcare provided by parents themselves – has a strong positive correlation with the price of formal childcare. That is, as the (real) price of formal childcare increases, more households seek informal childcare, which is generally free at the point of delivery, or look to supply more parental care. It would then appear crucial for the paid childcare sector to keep price increases in line with economy inflation at the least to prevent a shift towards informal/parental care.

The informal versus paid relationship is more complex, however. Recent research from Rutter and Evans (2011) indicated that a significant proportion of parents preferred informal childcare because they believed it offered the best experience for their child in the most secure environment. Ofsted has been critical of some day nursery care, especially in poor areas (Ofsted, 2010) and some parents may be wary of current standards of nursery provision (see Penn in Part One of this volume). Other important demand factors for informal childcare are its flexibility and convenience. A study by Viitanen and Chevalier (2003) found that many women may take care of children themselves rather than relying on any kind of care, formal or non-formal.

Recent trends confirm that the use of informal care has been rising strongly at a time when use of daycare nurseries has decreased. The Department of Work and Pensions' regular *Families and Children Study* (Maplethorpe et al, 2010) confirmed a clear rise in the use of informal childcare between 2005 and 2008. In particular, significantly more working and non-working mothers used grandparents. For instance, use by working mothers with 3- and 4-year-olds increased from 42% to 49%, and use by non-working mothers with children under 3 years rose from 19% to 25%. More ex-partners provided childcare for single parents, and mothers not working had a stronger tendency to use relatives for childcare than previously. At the same time, coverage of day nurseries across working mothers with 3- and 4-year-olds fell sharply from 14% to 10% between 2005 and 2008, and moved from 5% to 4% for non-working mothers with children under 4 years.

A key limiter on informal childcare, however, may be the wider participation in the UK labour market in the future, as the population as a whole may need to increase its workforce output to meet higher costs of society. Such increased participation may reduce the availability of suitable informal childcare labour. For instance, grandparents may need to work for more years before retirement, and, therefore, have less time available to provide informal childcare when working parents are looking for this option.

Paying for childcare

In the UK, childcare markets are financed by a mixture of funders, though private individuals paying for their own care remain the largest funders by some way. For the UK children's day nursery market, valued at £4.1 billion in 2010, an estimated 60% of total fee income generated by nurseries came directly from the pockets of individuals, and a further 14% represented childcare vouchers funded by individual employees through salary sacrifice. That said, a significant proportion of self-pay individual funds are supported by tax credits. In 2010 at least a quarter of self-pay (non-voucher) spend was funded by childcare tax credits (see Figure 3.2). The remainder of market fee income for day nurseries comprised 13% funded by employers through direct subsidy or vouchers, 10% spent by local government to fund sessions for 2-, 3- and 4-year-olds, and 2% by other miscellaneous sources such as charity and grants. In a climate of weak economic growth and fiscal austerity pursued by the UK's Coalition government, funding pressures are likely to become more acute across all sources.

Figure 3.2: Who pays? Funding split for UK day nursery market

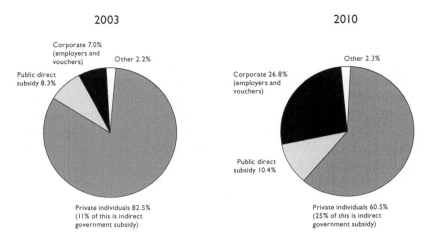

2003

Corporate 7.0%
(employers and
vouchers)
Other 2.2%
Public direct
subsidy 8.3%

Private individuals 82.5%
(11% of this is indirect
government subsidy)

2010

Other 2.3%
Corporate 26.8%
(employers and
vouchers)

Public direct
subsidy 10.4%

Private individuals 60.5%
(25% of this is indirect
government subsidy)

The price of childcare is increasingly likely to be a crucial lever determining demand and market prosperity. In particular, evidence of real price inflation (increase in prices over and above economy inflation) on a consistent basis in the future is likely to weaken demand, as demand for paid childcare has probably become more sensitive as markets have matured. A comprehensive study of the relationship between price and use of paid childcare by Duncan et al (2001) concluded that price had a significant negative effect on use of paid childcare in Great Britain. In addition the propensity to use paid childcare is dependent on the supply of informal childcare, and affordability amongst other factors. Other studies by Blau (2000) and Viitanen (2001) have found that labour market participation is significantly dependent on childcare prices.

Macroeconomic evidence suggests real price inflation for childcare has been a feature in the past, but less so recently as childcare markets have matured, while demand has been vulnerable. Annual survey estimates of price changes across childcare markets by the Daycare Trust (2011) suggest that prices grew consistently above economy inflation in the 2000s, with particular strong growth in the early 2000s when growing by at least double the rate of inflation. Laing & Buisson's estimates of price inflation in the daycare nursery market since 2002 also provide evidence of real price inflation in the first half of the 2000s, but little evidence of real inflation in the second half, with the exception of 2009, when marginal price deflation in the economy did not stop price increases being implemented. Proxy evidence from the regular *Families and Children Study* (Maplethorpe et al, 2010) funded by the Department for Work and Pensions during the 2000s provides some support for a real increase in childcare prices over time as the number of families with young children reporting childcare to be 'not at all affordable' increased from 30% in 2002 to 32% in 2008.

The key driver for higher prices in childcare markets is cost plus wage inflation. Like prices, wages for nursery staff were estimated to have increased in real terms in the first half of the 2000s, and moved closer in line with economy inflation in the second half of the 2000s (Laing & Buisson, 2011). This took place during a period when average qualifications of early years childcare staff were on a clear upward trend (Phillips et al, 2011), suggesting that a better qualified early years workforce has not received a real pay uplift on average for this attainment. In the future, however, the greater penetration of (graduate level) early years professionals across childcare markets may be expected to put upward pressure on wage costs. Latest Laing & Buisson estimates indicate that these professionals are paid around 30% more than other (non-managerial) qualified childcare practitioners.

A risk for childcare funding in future is a reduction in public subsidies for childcare payments from a Coalition government looking to make large-scale cuts to its welfare spend. The government has so far selected to cut childcare tax credits by 10% (of childcare costs) and also reduce relief on corporate childcare for higher taxpayers (to receive basic rate relief only). In both cases these cuts provide 'one-off' increases in childcare prices for claimants which appear likely to put downward pressure on the demand for childcare. However, there is an absence of empirical evidence to provide clear insight on changes in likely behaviour. On the surface, statistics appear to confirm that the childcare tax credit (within the Working Tax Credit) has significantly encouraged labour participation from low income households since its introduction, as the number claiming has risen from just over 300,000 in 2004 to just under 500,000 in 2011 (HMRC, 2011). However, its actual impact on labour participation and childcare use is not well known. A recent qualitative survey of 2,000 mothers claiming the credit (Resolution Foundation, 2011), suggested the 10% subsidy cut from April 2011 would see more than two thirds of claimants either reduce their working commitments and/or childcare use.

Corporate funding has been an engine of growth for UK childcare markets in recent years, as its funding share quadrupled from 6–7% in 2005 to over 28% in 2009 (Laing & Buisson, 2011). Generally employers have been willing to fund increasing amounts of childcare for their employees through the 2000s, but the trigger for increased corporate funding was primarily the introduction of tax relief on childcare vouchers from April 2005. However, corporate funding in the future is far from certain to display the same strength. In 2010, corporate growth stalled, as its proportion of nursery market funding dropped to 27%. While this probably reflected a lagged downward impact from continued high levels of unemployment post-recession, it may also reflect a flattening in corporate support for childcare. Employee benefits survey research confirms that penetration may have levelled off, as just over half (55%) of employers surveyed offered vouchers as a core benefit in 2011, the same as in 2010, and only 17% of employers offered vouchers as a voluntary benefit, down from 22% (*Employee Benefits Magazine*, 2011) .

A political risk is that tax relief on corporate childcare, a key demand lever, is reduced further to limit costs to the Exchequer. Previously in autumn 2009 the Labour government announced plans to phase out tax relief on childcare vouchers, but a public backlash saw this overall policy shelved. However, maximum relief was capped at the basic tax rate of 20%, which meant a reduction in relief for higher rate taxpayers from April 2011. While reductions in relief are clearly politically unpopular, gradual reductions in the future may be seen as palatable.

Of all funding trends, part-time early education places subsidised directly by government appear to be the most transparent despite widespread cuts to public spending taking place. The Coalition government has recently committed to a universal extension from 12.5 hours to 15 hours per week during term time for 3- and 4-year-olds, and to 15 hours per week for 40% of the most deprived 2-year-olds. While much of this provision (60%) is available within the state education sector, the rest of the places are provided by private nurseries in the childcare market, and the government pays providers a fixed subsidy to cover the cost. This funding remains contestable with private/third sector providers of childcare. Qualitative surveys of nursery providers (Laing & Buisson, 2011; NDNA, 2011) continue to report that for a majority of providers fixed subsidies do not adequately meet unit costs of provision. However, despite sustained lobbying of government by providers over a number of years, there has been little change in this funding (Laing & Buisson, 2011; NDNA, 2011). Despite protests, the vast majority of nursery providers have remained committed to subsidy provision.

Supply in a mature market

Growth in UK childcare market capacity took place largely in the 1990s. For instance, daycare nursery places more than tripled from around 100,000 to well over 300,000 in a ten year period. This day nursery capacity was built by private enterprise, and supported by third sector organisations. The public sector had no part in this development and its supply share dwindled during the period.

The building of capacity by private enterprise was generally fragmented across the country, as most new nurseries were set up by self-interested local individual investors and partnerships, which were creating supply in their localities for the first time. The 1990s also saw the rise of corporate nursery groups, many of which, backed by private equity investors, sought to build up nursery businesses with a brand identity, mostly focusing on local or regional markets only. Around two thirds of the largest 40 nursery groups in operation in 2011 began operations in the late 1980s and first half of the 1990s. During this time, nursery groups were able to take advantage of scale economies at the nursery level (by developing large facilities), and expanded through a mixture or organic purpose built development and small or medium scale acquisitions.

There were great expectations by market investors for the UK children's nursery sector at the start of the 2000s, following the earlier rapid expansion. This prompted a number of large business transactions at the time which established the sector's major groups. For the first half of the 2000s, supply grew at a strong rate, averaging in the region of 10–15% each year. An additional driver during this time was supply-side expansion under the Labour government as it sought to intervene in market allocations to bring childcare to disadvantaged children, most notably through its Neighbourhood Nurseries initiative to provide childcare provision in poor areas (NNI Research Team, 2007). In 2005, however, supply growth fell to single figures, and by 2007 sector growth had stalled. In 2008 and 2009, day nursery sector capacity started to fall for the first time on record (Laing & Buisson, 2011). The stall prior to economic recession, and decline during recession suggested that supply had matured in the children's day nursery market.

The economic recession led to the closure of nurseries which were no longer sustainable under market conditions. The most vulnerable were those in areas where unemployment rose sharply, and, therefore, the number of families using paid childcare decreased significantly. Regional trends confirm that the most acute rises in unemployment rates in 2009 were spread throughout the UK, being in the North East, West Midlands, London and the South West. In addition net losses to the childcare sector in 2009 and 2010 appeared to confirm that a large number of small-scale providers had closed (and/or were deregistered) during the period, as the average capacity of deregistered establishments was significantly below the average for registered establishments (Ofsted,

2009, 2011). This may suggest that small nurseries, which are not able to generate scale economies at the nursery level (scale economy is achieved when average unit costs of production decrease as capacity increases), may be more vulnerable to business downturns than large nurseries, though empirical evidence to support this is not conclusive.

The Coalition government is highly unlikely to follow the expansionary supply-side childcare strategy of the previous Labour government. On the contrary, public sector cuts confirm that a significant proportion of existing public sector nursery supply (10% of market supply), and initiatives supported by local government may be vulnerable in the next few years as local authorities look to make efficiency savings and discontinue uneconomical subsidised care. As such the volume of daycare offered by these nurseries could be cut back, funding may be withdrawn, or public owned day nursery services may be increasingly outsourced. Government support for early childhood provision is likely to focus on targeted interventions for the poorest families.

Identifying scope for growth

The third sector (non-profit) perhaps offers the greatest scope for market supply growth. It currently accounts for around 13% of children's nursery places. The Coalition government is strongly promoting an increased third sector presence in key community services such as childcare, as part of its 'Big Society' concept. It is hoped that parents will influence the development of local services in partnership with third sector organisations (Teather, 2010). At the time of writing, the Localism Bill proposes new rights to make it easier for non-profit groups to become service providers in the community. Longer term, this may see third sector organisations take over a larger amount of childcare provision which is currently supplied and/or owned by local government, which includes local authority nurseries, Children's Centres and-school based childcare.

A popular prediction for the children's nursery market at the start of the 2000s was for corporate nursery groups to have a much more significant market share, both collectively and individually. Corporatisation in reality has been less than spectacular. At the start of 2002, nursery groups collectively accounted for 14% of places, and the largest group could boast a market share of 1.3%. By 2011 this share had increased to 21% collectively, and 1.8% for the largest nursery group (Laing & Buisson, 2011). The total number recorded rose from around 125 to over 300. On average, however, the size of corporate nursery groups has not increased. The number of places for the average group has moved from 455 to 470 in the course of the past ten years.

There has been some consolidation at the top end of the corporate market, which has seen most of the largest nursery businesses outgrow the market. The top ten nursery groups increased their share from 6.3% to 7.7%. However, corporatisation within the children's nursery market remains modest, and there are no UK nursery groups which are widely recognised as national brands. However, the maturity of supply may precipitate stronger consolidation in the childcare market.

The care home industry, which is structurally similar to childcare, has much wider corporate penetration, as care home groups now account for 55% of UK care home supply, with the top ten care home groups holding a 28% market share. Care home corporatisation has been on a stronger upward trend than childcare rising from just over a third (34.5%) some six years earlier.

There are a number of factors keeping corporatisation at a modest level in the nursery market. Firstly childcare is not an easy service to brand and corporatise. It is a staff based service with limited scope for differentiation from other competitors since all providers must follow the welfare and learning and development requirements stipulated by the regulatory framework, the Early Years Foundation Stage (DCSF, 2008). Also because it is a staff intensive service, it is difficult to homogenise service standards and quality across the corporate group. Secondly, as nurseries must follow strict staff/child ratios, staffing costs are relatively inflexible, and profit margins relatively narrow for all providers. Despite these issues, however, similar intensive staffing characteristics within the UK care home sector have not been a barrier to greater corporatisation in recent years.

Most nursery groups are not geared up to operate nationwide, since they are local/regional outfits with relatively small scale management resources. Wider expansion for many groups would probably involve a significant upscale in corporate management. And the incentives for nationwide operations are also not wholly clear. While some scale efficiencies are on offer, such as bulk purchasing, common systems and management, shared strategies and recruitment, and brand recognition, additional operating costs from central management may be a barrier to greater expansion.

There has been only modest interest from investors in recent years as UK market scope has been less favourable, and other large corporates operating outside the sector have had little interest in diversifying into childcare. Investor confidence was also dented by the collapse of the largest global nursery provider, Australian based ABC, which accumulated massive unsustainable debt through rapid expansion within several global markets, as discussed by Sumsion in this volume.

Conclusion

For the reasons discussed earlier, significantly greater corporate penetration of children's nursery supply in the future in the UK now looks less likely. The nursery market remains highly fragmented. However, there is a healthy appetite for corporate expansion, particularly by small nursery groups which are performing well in the current business climate. But acquisition activity is generally slow at this time as business conditions post-recession remain vulnerable, access to debt funding is difficult for many operators, and there is a shortage of businesses which are considered high quality (Christie & Co, 2011).

Longer term, it remains to be seen whether a childcare business in the UK grows large enough to be considered a national brand. No established corporate brand has been interested in developing a large-scale childcare business in the UK to date, though incumbent nursery groups may grow sufficiently in the long term to be nationally recognised. Busy Bees and Bright Horizons perhaps have the largest scope as they are owned by global specialists. Busy Bees has Knowledge Universe as its parent group, which includes as its sister company KinderCare Learning Centers, the largest childcare provider in the United States, as described by Sosinsky in this volume. And Bright Horizons Family Solutions, based in the United States, is the largest global corporate childcare provider. However, there remains a question mark on whether there is an appetite for childcare corporatisation by UK users, and whether corporate groups can generate sufficient scale economies that can support the costs of operating a national-based corporate structure.

In general, supply in the childcare nursery market is likely to grow only gradually in the next ten years, in line with modest gains in demand. Although growth is certain to be a key strategy for childcare providers, there is likely to be increased focus on developing existing services to add (actual or perceived) value, and/or develop new specialised services to differentiate from competitors. Developments include the increased use of technology in settings to improve security (such as fingerprint recognition), and aid learning (such as ipads and interactive white-boards), and examples of new specialised services include activity studios, sports and educational classes, outdoor pursuits, organic food, on-site paediatric and wellbeing services, and uniforms for children attending.

Growth in the children's nursery market to date has been largely facilitated by private investment including large-scale private equity and small-scale individual savings. Private equity was attracted to the nursery market in the second half of the 1990s and early part of the 2000s as the market was characterised by high growth, strong demand dynamics, attractive visible earnings, rising business asset values, and positive early years policy from government. However, towards the mid-2000s, investment became less appealing, as supply growth decelerated, and positive demand trends levelled off. At this time, private equity-backed nursery groups consolidated through acquisition, as deal values reached high levels (ten times underlying profit/cash flow). Deal values at high profit multiples were driven by 'bull market' expectations for future valuations, which were proved to be misplaced when the global credit crunch in 2008 and acute economic recession in 2009 led to a sharp downward revision of business values, in line with a slump in property prices. There was also a significant downward revaluation of future profits for childcare businesses due to less optimistic expectations for economic prosperity.

In the near term, investment activity in the nursery market is likely to be subdued as business asset values are below trend, and credit markets are only gradually opening up. More cautious future market expectations mean investors are looking to secure only high quality businesses at realistic prices. This selective activity is reflected in the nursery business property market, where a large number of properties are listed but the number of transactions is currently low as investors have been more restrained (Christie & Co, 2011). It is also low because business expectations of many sellers do not match buyer valuations. Most investment in the near term is likely to come from strong businesses which are using organic profits and/or small-scale bank debt funding to expand. Although private equity is likely to be modest in the near term, below trend business values are likely to encourage equity investment on a larger scale sooner rather than later.

Investors in UK children's nurseries are now investing in a relatively mature market where returns are less spectacular than the past, but probably more stable. As such large-scale investment is likely to focus on market consolidation to achieve the growth potential which private equity seeks.

In summary, mature markets present new considerations for the key determinants of demand and supply for childcare. Maturity, in essence, indicates that trends which have underpinned childcare growth in the past have either levelled off or changed direction, and, from a macroeconomic perspective, new demand and supply relationships are emerging.

The onus on private individuals to pay for childcare is likely to increase, as childcare tax credits and corporate childcare relief are reduced by a government intent on shrinking welfare spend, and further growth in employers' funding of childcare, an engine of growth in the recent past, is held back by a weak economy and high unemployment. As such, individuals are likely to become increasingly resistant to increases in childcare prices. Latest trends confirm increased usage of informal childcare in recent years.

The childcare market supply will continue to be dominated by private enterprise and private investment. However, investment in childcare has also matured, as investors are more cautious, and expectations for investment returns are more grounded than in the past. There may be some market consolidation of childcare groups, though significantly greater corporate penetration, above the current 20%, is less likely.

References

Blau, D. (2000) 'An economic perspective on child care policy', *Journal of Population and Social Security (Population)*, Supplement to Volume 1, pp 426–445.

Christie & Co (2011) *Business outlook 2011*, London: Christie & Co Business Intelligence.

Daycare Trust (2011) *Childcare costs survey 2011*, London: Daycare Trust.

Department for Children, Schools and Families (2008) *Statutory framework for the Foundation Stage*, London: DCSF.

Duncan, A., Paull, G. and Taylor, J. (2001) 'Price and quality in the UK childcare market', Discussion Paper 01/13, University of Nottingham.

Economic Policy Committee (2009) *The 2009 ageing report - Economic and budgetary projections for the EU-27 Member States (2008–2060)* Working document, Brussels: European Commission and the Economic Policy Committee.

Employee Benefits Magazine (2011) *Employee benefits – The benefits research 2011*, London: Centaur Media.

HM Revenue and Customs (2011) *Child and working tax credits statistics - April 2011*, Newport: National Statistics.

HM Treasury (2011) *Forecasts for the UK economy: A comparison of independent forecasts*, No 289 & No 291, London: HM Treasury.

Laing & Buisson (2011), *Children's nurseries – UK market report 2011*, London: Laing & Buisson Ltd.

Madouros, V. (2006) *Labour force projections 2006–2020*, London: Office for National Statistics.

Magnus, G. (2009) 'Top economist predicts that ageing societies are going to need more and better childcare', *Nursery Management Today*, vol 8, no 1, pp 26–27.

Maplethorpe, N., Chanfreau, J., Philo, D. and Tait, C. (2010) *Families with children in Britain: Findings from the 2008 Families and Children Study (FACS)*, Research Report no 656, London: Department for Work and Pensions.

NDNA (2011) *Free entitlement funding – 2011 survey of members*, Huddersfield: National Day Nurseries Association.

NNI Research Team (2007) *National evaluation of the Neighbourhood Nurseries initiative: Integrated report*, Research Report SSU/2007/FR/024, London: DCSF.

Office for National Statistics (2011a) *Database of statistics*, www.statistics.gov.uk.

Office for National Statistics (2011b) *Statistical bulletin: Annual mid-year population estimates, 2010*, Newport: National Statistics.

Ofsted (2009) *Database of registered childcare providers in England*, www.ofsted.gov.uk.

Ofsted (2010) *The annual report of Her Majesty's chief inspector of schools, children's services and skills 2009/10*, London: Ofsted.

Ofsted (2011) *Database of registered childcare providers in England*, www.ofsted.gov.uk.

Phillips, R., Norden, O., McGinigal, S. and Oseman, D. with Coleman, N. (2011) *Childcare and early years providers survey 2009*, Research Report DFE-RR012, London: Department for Education.

Resolution Foundation and Netmums (2011) *Childcare tax credit survey*, Briefing paper, London: The Resolution Foundation.

Rutter, J. and Evans, B. (2011) *Informal childcare: Choice or chance? A literature review*, London: Daycare Trust.

Teather, S. (2010) 'The minister's view – To each child a fair start', *Nursery World*, 27 October.

Viitanen, T. (2001) 'Cost of childcare and female employment in the UK', *Labour*, vol 19, no S1, pp 149–170.

Viitanen, T. and Chevalier, A. (2003) 'The supply of childcare in Britain: Do mothers queue for childcare?' Royal Economic Society Annual Conference 2003, 211, St Andrews: Royal Economic Society.

Part Two

Explorations in childcare markets

Local providers and loyal parents: competition and consumer choice in the Dutch childcare market

Janneke Plantenga

Introduction

Throughout Europe, an important policy shift in recent years concerns the introduction of market forces in sectors that have traditionally been organised as a public responsibility. Relevant examples in this respect are the energy market and health insurance (Cutler, 2002; Giulietti et al, 2003). The main reason for the transition of public to private is the assumption that the market will create a more efficient incentive structure, as the market driven approach will increase competition and force suppliers to increase internal efficiency, resulting in lower prices. In addition, the introduction of market forces may lead to a better balance between supply and demand. Consumers are expected to select the provider that offers the best price/quality ratio and the sector may adapt quicker to changing circumstances. The introduction of market forces should therefore increase both internal as well as external efficiency.

In line with this overall trend, the Dutch childcare sector was completely reorganised by the introduction of the 2005 Childcare Act. This Act was perceived as a thoroughly modern piece of legislation, because financial support is redirected from the local authorities to the parents with the aim to increase parental choice. The explicit objective of this childcare reform was to stimulate the operation of market forces, so that childcare providers would respond to parental wishes in an efficient way. The government no longer set the targets, for instance 'an increase of 20,000 childcare places in 2010', but the consumer was supposed to persuade the supplier by the laws of supply and demand. As a result of the change towards a demand driven financing system, publicly provided childcare in the Netherlands disappeared. Instead only private for-profit (60% of all Dutch childcare organisations) or not-for-profit providers (the remaining 40%) are now operating and competing in the childcare market (Noailly and Visser, 2009).

The introduction of the Childcare Act did not go unnoticed. All conditions for extensive media coverage were present: a recognisable and sensitive product, a large number of parents affected (most of them well educated) and a clear shift in policy. Five years after its introduction, however, most of the dust seems to have settled and the childcare sector and childcare consumers seem to have got used to the new opportunities and responsibilities. Against this background, an important question arises as to the implications of the introduction of market forces in the childcare sector. What are the effects for providers and consumers of the transition from supply to demand financing? Are there signals of increasing internal and external efficiency within the childcare market? Is there indeed more competition, more choice and more quality?

These questions will be answered in this chapter with reference to the concepts of exit, voice and loyalty as introduced by Hirschman (1970). According to Hirschman, economists tend to concentrate on the exit option when describing the relations between a firm and its customers in competitive markets; dissatisfied customers simply stop buying the firm's product and shift towards an alternative supplier. Yet, in real life, the exit option may not always be accessible and dissatisfied customers can also raise their voice. Voice can have different forms, like formal complaints or consumer involvement in managerial decisions. The voice and exit options may strengthen, but also undermine, each other. The threat of exit, for example, may increase the effectiveness of the voice option. At the same time, the voice option may become less relevant, if the number of dissatisfied customers decreases because of an effective exit option. The costs and benefits of the two strategies may also differ. Exit seems a relatively easy way to change an unsatisfactory situation. In contrast, the voice option implies costs in the short run while the long-term benefits are uncertain. Yet in the long run voice may have important benefits as it provides direct information on the causes of customers' dissatisfaction. Besides exit and voice, Hirschman also introduces the concept of loyalty. Loyalty refers to a certain attachment of the customer to a product or organisation. Loyalty may explain why a customer has not used the exit option even if better alternatives are available. Loyalty may also increase customer willingness to use the voice option. Introducing the concepts of exit, voice and loyalty within the context of childcare markets, facilitates the analysis and understanding of actual customer behaviour within a context in which personal relations play an important role, both between supplier and customer, and between supplier and child.

This chapter will first describe in more detail the introduction of the Dutch Childcare Act. Next it focuses on recent developments in the childcare market, followed by some theoretical considerations. Finally, the policy implications of the transition from welfare to market are considered and some conclusions are drawn. The results of our analysis indicate that market competition in the childcare sector is almost by definition imperfect. Parents have difficulties in assessing quality, while high switching costs also stand in the way of a well-functioning market. This is not to say that the introduction of market forces in the Dutch childcare market will by definition lead to inefficiencies. Rather that the positive impact of parental choice on internal and external efficiency of the childcare market should not be overestimated.

The introduction of the Dutch Childcare Act

The organisation of childcare in the Netherlands has never been particularly transparent. At the end of the 1980s, the Netherlands had, alongside Ireland and the UK, the lowest level of institutionalised childcare facilities in the European Union (Moss, 1990). It was only during the 1990s that the number of places started to increase (Plantinga 2006; Noailly and Visser, 2009). At that time the importance of strong market structures and deregulation were emphasised. For the childcare sector this implied that policy was targeted towards public–private partnerships; employers were expected to share childcare costs with central government. It was argued that childcare provision promoted female labour supply, while by investing in childcare employers could lower the costs of recruitment, absenteeism and training of new staff.

The emphasis on benefits to employment also implied that childcare policy became part of labour market policy; the main focus was on increasing the female participation rate. By implication, early childhood education is not included; all 4-year-olds are entitled to free and full-time early education delivered in primary schools. In the Netherlands 5 years is the compulsory school starting age. Also, programmes for disadvantaged children are mainly organised within educational settings and are financed differently.

The involvement of employers in financing childcare has been unique for the Netherlands and made it possible to realise a large increase in childcare at a time of budget constraints. However, this also led to a complex and fragmented financing structure. At the end of the 1990s, the formal childcare sector consisted of subsidised, employer financed and privately financed places, each with their own financing structure. Employer financed childcare places, bought from a childcare provider, were the most numerous. Part of the employer's expenses was repaid by the parents, who paid a means tested fee. Employers also received a corporation tax rebate for every childcare place they subsidised. The result was a tripartite financing structure (OECD, 2002; Plantinga, 2006).

This system contained several bottlenecks (MDW, 1998; WBK, 2002). It was, for example, not clear who was responsible for the necessary increase in childcare provision. Was it the government, the childcare providers or the social partners who could determine the growth of employer financed childcare places by collective labour agreements? Moreover, the patchwork of financial arrangements was considered too complex; there were fiscal arrangements for parents and employers, specific arrangements for single mothers and specific arrangements for local government. Indeed, according to OECD in its analysis of Dutch childcare policy, the financing structure was 'a complicated set of public funding arrangements, bound to involve administrative waste' (OECD, 2002, p 93–94). Another problem concerned inequity in the availability and cost of childcare places. Some parents both received employer support with childcare; others could claim support only from one parent's employer or none at all. Local government policies also diverged. Some municipalities targeted their childcare subsidies at certain groups; others had a more general policy. Finally, parental costs varied in different municipalities. Each year, the Ministry of Social Affairs and Employment published guidelines for parental contributions to childcare fees, but these guidelines had only advisory status; local policy could vary. Hence access to childcare services was not uniform or equitable. Finally, there were bottlenecks with regard to quality and inspection. Despite a national system concerning basic quality, local inspection employed different foci, criteria and scope.

In order to solve these problems, the new Childcare Act was introduced on 1 January 2005 (Wet Kinderopvang, WK). With the introduction of this new Act the financial organisation of the childcare sector changed from a system of supply financing to one of demand financing. Working parents now in principle pay full childcare costs and are then compensated directly by the tax authorities and the employers. The financing is thus again on a tripartite basis. In principle, employers pay one third of the actual childcare costs. In addition, parents receive a payment by the tax authorities based on their income and the costs of the childcare. At the lower income level the state takes over most of the remaining childcare costs and the fiscal refund will cover 63%

of the childcare bill, leaving 3.5% to be paid by the parents. Beyond certain, higher, income levels the state does not pay and parents pay the remaining 67%. When the Childcare Act was introduced, the employer contribution was not mandatory; employers were supposed but not obliged to pay one third of employee childcare costs. Since this resulted in some degree of inequity, the employer contribution became mandatory from 1 January 2007.

As for childcare quality, the Act only contained a broad outline, stating that the provider is supposed to supply 'sound' childcare services. This is understood to mean 'that the service will contribute to a good and healthy development of a child in a safe and healthy environment' (Article 50). Within the context of self-regulation, further details were left to the childcare sector itself. The sector in 2004 agreed an annually renewable compact, stating the minimum quality requirements with regard to accommodation, pedagogical policy, group size, and staff–child ratios. This compact has been translated into non-binding policy guidance providing a benchmark for local government, which is charged with registration and inspection. The policy guidance also provides information for parents on the minimum quality standards of registered formal childcare provision. The Childcare Act also contains information on the role and responsibilities of parent committees. In a market driven approach, dissatisfied customers should be able to opt for an alternative supplier. The legislator stated that this control mechanism should be complemented with formal parent participation, mainly because of the specific nature of the product. As parent committees are mandatory, this regulation has created a formal voice option. Each parent committee can advise on a number of quality and safety issues, in addition to opening hours and hourly prices.

In summary, a major advantage of the introduction of the 2005 Childcare Act appears to be that access to childcare services is now standardised in all municipalities and that national regulation replaces guidelines previously administered at a local level. In addition, the role of parents has been strengthened. The system of demand financing enables parents to choose childcare with the optimal ratio of price and quality (the exit option), while parent committees also represent an institutionalised voice option. For providers, demand financing represents a direct financial relationship with the customer, although this is mediated by parental tax credits, which will lead to a growing emphasis on internal and external efficiency. By the laws of the market, providers will be forced to adjust quality, quantity and prices in response to parental preferences, leading to a perfect match between supply and demand.

Of course, this is how it works in theory. The question arises: does it also work this way in practice? What has the Dutch childcare market come to look like after the introduction of the Childcare Act?

The Dutch childcare market since 2005

A well-functioning market has enough exit options; there are enough suppliers to compete, and to bring innovative products on the market at the lowest possible price. It follows that the market has limited entry barriers and is accessible to new suppliers. Likewise, the demand side has to comply with certain conditions. Consumers need to be well informed about prices and quality, and should be able to respond on the basis of the available information. To what extent does the Dutch childcare market reflect this profile?

Supply side developments

Just before the introduction of the Childcare Act, in 2004, the number of childcare places was estimated at just below 113,000 for children aged 0–4 (the age at which most Dutch children enter primary school) and 62,000 for school-age children. Since children usually do not need full-time childcare, the number of children using formal childcare services is much higher than the number of places. Estimating the average number of children per childcare place at 1.8, there were approximately 25% of children under 4 benefiting childcare in 2004 and 7% of children aged 4–12.

Soon after the Act's introduction, a slight dip in demand occurred. Demand was reduced because of higher prices, especially for medium and higher income groups and parental aversion to the increased paperwork required. After the first year, however, demand picked up again, partly because of increased subsidies, resulting in lower prices, partly because providers took over some of the administrative costs, and partly because of the improved economic situation. As a result, within three years of the Act's introduction, uptake for the youngest children had increased from to 25% to 36%. Growth has been particularly strong in out-of-school school care; between 2004 and 2008 uptake increased from 7% to 18%. The growth in provision resulted partly from autonomous growth and partly from new businesses entering the market. In 2003, approximately 1,200 providers were active in the field; in 2008 this number had increased to more than 1,800 (Paulussen-Hoogeboom and Gemmeke, 2009). From a parental point of view, the growing number of childcare providers seems positive, as it indicates that parents still have choice; although there are strong local providers, covering a large part of the local market, in most instances there are also a few small companies which provide an alternative option.

Despite the positive growth in childcare provision, the situation seems less favourable in terms of quality. In fact, a recent report reporting on a longitudinal study of quality in Dutch childcare services indicates that the quality of childcare is quite low (NCKO, 2009). In this study 'process quality' is investigated by a representative sample of 200 groups belonging to 200 separate childcare organisations. Process quality refers to health and safety issues, but also to the interaction skills of childcare staff; how they interact with children and how they stimulate their development. None of the groups studied received a good score: 51% received a mediocre score, 49% an insufficient score. Moreover, process quality seems to have decreased, compared with findings from 2005 and 2001. According to the researchers, possible explanations are the strong growth rates within the sector, and their association with shortages of suitably qualified staff and increased work pressures.

All these developments illustrate the dynamism of the Dutch childcare market during the past decade. Overall growth may be consistent with a better balance between demand and supply, yet the score on quality seems to be less favourable.

Demand side developments

The growth in childcare provision over the past couple of years translates into a growing number of childcare services near to where parents live. Research on the number of childcare settings at ten minutes' distance, indicated that in 2004 parents had on average six settings in the immediate vicinity, compared to more than eight in 2008. The research also indicated that there are rather large differences by level of urbanisation. Yet, even in the less urbanised areas the average number of nearby locations has increased (Berden and Kok, 2009).

Despite this strong growth in childcare locations and places, choice for parents remains limited, as demand seems to have increased even faster. In 2008, for example, approximately 31,000 children remained on waiting lists (Van Beem and Wever, 2008). Reflecting the high female part-time labour market participation rate, waiting lists seem especially long for Monday, Tuesday and Thursday. Indeed, waiting time for a full-time childcare place for the youngest children seems to have increased in the period of 2004–08. In contrast, waiting lists for out-of-school care seem to have shrunk during the same period (Berden and Kok, 2009).

It can be argued that even if parents do have choice, their agency is limited as consumers find it difficult to make an informed decision and to respond smoothly to changes in prices and quality. Quality in particular can only be judged to a certain extent by parents; they have limited insight into pedagogical principles, or health and safety issues (Walker, 1991; Mocan, 2007). To complicate things even further, it seems that parents find certain characteristics more important than experts do. For parents, active play with the children and activities for children from different ages is of great importance. Another important aspect from their perspective is a pleasant centre ambience and short travel distance between home and centre (Kok et al, 2005; Berden and Kok, 2009). A pedagogical plan, qualified leaders and a quality kite mark seem less important to parents than to providers and experts. Because of the divergence between the parents' perception of quality and the experts' evaluation, a real risk exist that parents overestimate the quality (Mocan, 2007). Indeed, parents are in general very satisfied about the quality of childcare: on a scale from 0 to 10 the average mark given is higher than 8 (Kok et al, 2005; Vyvoj, 2005; Berden and Kok, 2009).

Another typical feature of the childcare market is that parents rarely switch, once they have opted for a certain childcare provider. This low propensity to switch may either be explained by an almost perfect match between demand and supply or by high switching costs. Table 4.1 indicates that switching costs do indeed play an important role in the childcare market. When a 2008 survey asked under which conditions parents would consider a switch to an alternative provider, 32% stated 'never'. Only 7% would consider switching when the alternative offered more quality and only 10% if the alternative was cheaper. Apparently, consumer choice in the childcare market is limited to the entry decision; after the initial choice, consumers do not change easily to another provider. Of course, this 'status quo bias' generates market power on the supply side of the market. If consumers do not base their choices on differences in price and quality, competition between firms may be weak. By implication, the benefits of the transition from welfare to market system in terms of internal and external efficiency may be limited.

Theoretical considerations: the impact of loyalty

The childcare market is an unusual and atypical market. Although at the time of writing more than 1,800 childcare providers offer services to at least 300,000 parents, market competition does not seem to matter much. The supply side is characterised by strong local players; the

Table 4.1 When would parents consider switching to an alternative provider? (n=821)

	2004	2008
Never	55%	32%
When the alternative is (much) cheaper	11%	10%
When the alternative offers more quality	5%	7%
When the alternative is more closer to home	4%	6%
When my employer offers child care facilities	11%	–
When my (private) child minder is no longer available.	6%	39%
Other reasons	8%	6%

Source: Berden and Kok, 2009, Table 5.1

demand side by loyal parents. Of course these findings are influenced by the fact that market competition in the childcare sector is a quite recent phenomenon and that demand and supply have not yet fully adjusted to the new regulatory framework. Conversely, several elements seem to be structural in this particular market, like the high switching costs on the demand side; apparently childcare is not just like any other commodity.

According to Klemperer, a leading theorist in the field, switching costs results from:

> a consumer's desire for compatibility between his current purchase and a previous investment. That investment might by a *physical investment* in (a) equipment or in (b) setting up a relationship, an *informational investment* in finding out (c) how to use a product or (d) about its characteristics, (e) an *artificially created investment* in buying a high priced first unit that then allows one to buy subsequent units more cheaply or even (f) a *psychological investment*. (Klemperer, 1995, p 517; original emphasis)

Applying Klemperer's categories to the Dutch childcare market, switching costs appear to be due to several of these reasons. Physical investments, for example, play a role in the sense that there are transaction costs involved in switching suppliers. Firms may offer identical services, but it takes time and effort to finalise one (long-term) contract and negotiate another. There may also be informational investments. Learning to use a particular 'brand' creates a strong incentive to continue to use those particular services. In the childcare market these learning costs may range from the careful adjustment of travel and working arrangements to the settings' opening hours, to familiarity with other customers (parents) who in case of an emergency, such as a traffic jam or a late-night board meeting, can collect the child before closing time. Yet another category of switching costs refers to uncertainty about the quality of untested brands. In service markets in particular, where quality is highly important but at the same time difficult to observe beforehand, consumers may refrain from any gamble of trying an alternative supplier. Finally, there may also be a kind of non-economic brand loyalty, referring to the psychological costs of switching. Customers may initially be indifferent between competing providers, but the fact of using one brand may change their relative preferences in favour of the chosen provider.

Switching costs in the childcare market may be particularly high, because the service is provided for parents as well as for children. For example, the informational investment in finding out how to use a new brand or discovering its characteristics not only holds for the parents, but also for the children. It is the children who have to familiarise themselves with the other children in the group and who have to adapt to the characteristics of the childcare staff or the setting's programme. These informational investments by children themselves no doubt add to the switching costs perceived by parents, because they now have to rationalise the change not just for themselves, but also for their child. Even when problems arise, such as a dirty setting, price increases or dissatisfaction with the management, parents may still not want to stop the pleasant contact the child has with the staff or the other children in the group. Parents thus display a high level of brand loyalty, because of the specific nature of the sector, but also because of loyalty to their children.

It is important to emphasise that this *status quo bias* in the childcare market is perfectly consistent with rational decision making. The high switching costs, because of physical and informational investments, and because of parental loyalty towards their children, translate into a long-term contract which to a certain extent is resistant to change in the relative prices and/or quality. Moreover, the length of the contract deepens the investment; the longer a particular childcare service is used, the more familiar and safe parents and children feel in the organisation and the closer they feel to staff, other children and their parents. Therefore the costs of switching are likely to get consistently higher compared to the benefits associated with a superior alternative, especially if the maximum contract length of four years is taken into account. When parents do change, it is likely that they will do so at the beginning of the contract period. After some time, the effort (in costs and/or time) will no longer offset the benefits of a new relationship.

Policy implications

High switching costs have a major impact on market competition. In the perfect model, the search by the consumer for a better price encourages competition between firms. In a market with high switching costs, however, the consumer is to some extent locked in to repeat purchasing from the same firm and will therefore not respond very rapidly to market signals. Switching costs are thus a real obstacle to perfect competition. If consumers do not switch, the introduction of market forces may lead to more market power for the providers, higher prices and/or lower quality.

There may be an exception to this general conclusion; some markets may benefit from high switching costs and loyal consumers. This applies particularly if the prospect of a long-term relationship induces the provider to certain investments which would be unprofitable if the relationship between provider and consumer could be terminated at any moment. An often quoted example in this respect refers to the market for health insurance where providers may be inclined to cut back on their investment in prevention activities, if consumers frequently switch to another health insurer. This analysis may be partly relevant for the childcare market, in as much as the prospect of a long-term relationship might stimulate providers to organise their services in such a way that they contribute to children's safe and healthy development. Yet, in contrast with the healthcare market, this long-term relationship only creates the opportunity, not the implicit incentive to invest in high quality childcare. In the childcare market a high quality strategy does not pay back in terms of lower costs at the other end of the spectrum. Rather, the benefits, in terms of a happy, settled and healthy child, are at the level of children, parents or society as a whole. In short, the argument that high switching costs, via long-term contracts, translate into high quality childcare services reflects considerable confidence in the sense of responsibility of the provider. If there are indications that this confidence is not warranted, additional policy measures may be necessary to counter the adverse effects of high switching costs. In principle there are two possible policy options in this case. The first policy option concerns measures aimed at lowering switching costs; the second concerns measures aimed at lowering the adverse consequences of high switching costs (CPB, 2005).

Measures aimed at lowering the switching costs vary from improving market transparency, for example by publishing information on prices and quality, to campaigns to convince consumers that shopping around makes sense, as well as specific forms of regulation, like prohibiting firms from setting up unnecessary administrative hurdles to switching, forms of standardisation or prohibiting long-term contracts (CPB, 2005). In the childcare market, however, switching costs are not the result of restrictive contract terms at provider level, but are related to the physical, informational and psychological costs of making a switch at consumer level. In fact, the very nature of this service makes frequent shifts less optimal; a high quality childcare system is simply not compatible with parents shopping around until they have found the optimal match between price and quality. It is therefore not the switching costs as such that should be lowered, but rather the negative consequences in terms of higher market prices and/or lower quality.

A relevant policy option aimed at lowering the adverse consequences of high switching costs would be trying to enhance market competition. If firms compete for market shares, this might lower prices far enough to compensate customers for price rises after purchase. An example is the mobile phone market, where deregulation of entry has promoted fierce competition, resulting in a large drop in prices (CPB 2005, p 28). This strategy is likely to be more successful when entry costs are relatively low. In addition, deregulation of entry may lead to an increased focus on price, to the detriment of other characteristics, such as quality. This strategy may thus be rather dangerous, especially when the product quality cannot be easily assessed by customers. Another strategy to alleviate the negative consequences of high switching costs involves enabling parents to make an informed choice when entering the market, thereby lowering the probability of regret. This calls for increased market transparency. At this moment, childcare setting inspection reports are available online and provide important information on health and safety. A quality report card for childcare services could also be considered. Such a card might enable parents to benchmark nearby services, selected on basis of the postal code, on a number of quality criteria. More far reaching policy measures under this heading would include forms of regulation like imposing minimum standards, such as those employed in the UK and discussed by Moss in his chapter elsewhere in this volume.

Until now, demand for more childcare market transparency or quality control has been limited. Apparently the transition from a public to a private system has not yet caused much concern with regard to prices and/or quality of the childcare services. Given our analysis, there is reason to believe, however, that the market power of the providers is indeed quite substantial, even if we take into account that the Dutch childcare market is still developing. This raises two questions. The first question concerns the estimated magnitude of the inefficiencies due to high switching costs. The second question is a more political one and considers whether the customer, or indeed the child, has a right to be protected from the negative consequences of high switching costs. Currently we appear to presume that the answer to the second question is no. This means we appear to assume implicitly that the inefficiencies of high switching costs in the childcare market are fairly small. Future developments will reveal whether this is a tenable position in the longer term.

Conclusion

The introduction of the Dutch 2005 Childcare Act implied a real policy shift. Because of national legislation, parents now not only have equal access to childcare services, but their position has been strengthened by the switch from supply-side to demand-side subsidies. Yet the analysis presented here indicates that market competition is almost by definition imperfect, that parents have difficulties in assessing quality and that high switching costs stand in the way of a well-functioning market. This is not to say that the introduction of market forces in the Dutch childcare sector will by definition lead to lower quality or higher prices, rather that market control by parents will always be limited, as a result of which the provider carries extra responsibility. If a strategy of self-reliance is thought of as too risky, an appropriate policy response should aim at measures to alleviate the negative consequences of high switching costs.

Of course, high switching costs are not typical for the childcare market alone. In the whole service sector it is perceivable that loyalties between providers and consumers translate into a low price elasticity of demand. A typical feature of services is that they are used at the same time as they are produced. This distinguishes services from commodities like steel and strawberries (Begg et al, 1997, p 2). As a result of this particular feature, it is usually assumed that services cannot be stored. In some cases, however, this particular feature also implies a personal relationship between the provider and the consumer. Even more important: the quality of the product may depend directly on the personal relationship. In such cases, raising efficiency by the introduction of market forces is almost impossible, because the client does not fit into the idealised image of a mobile, detached consumer. This conclusion may be even more relevant if the service is provided to a third party, as is often the case with care and welfare services.

It is quite conceivable that this different perspective on childcare services will also generate a different view on the optimal division of responsibilities between the market and the state. Local providers and loyal parents do not by definition generate efficient markets. The very nature of this provision may lead to additional market regulation, aiming at steering and perhaps limiting the choices of providers and parents.

References

Begg, D. K. H., Fischer, S. and Dornbusch, R. (1997) *Economics*, London: McGraw-Hill.

Berden, C. and Kok, L. (2009) *Ontwikkelingen op de markt voor kinderopvang 2004–2008*, Amsterdam: SEO economisch onderzoek.

CPB (Centraal Plan Bureau) (2005) *Switch on the competition. Causes, consequences and policy implications of consumer switching costs*, no 97, The Hague, NL: CPB.

Cutler, D.M. (2002) 'Equality, efficiency and market fundamentals: The dynamics of international medical-care reform', *Journal of Economic Literature*, vol. XL, pp 881–906.

Giulietti, M., Waddams Price, C., and Waterson, M. (2003) *Consumer choice and industrial policy: A study of UK energy markets*. Center for the Study of Energy Markets, working paper series (CSEM WP 112), Los Angeles: University of California Energy Institute.

Hirschman, A.O. (1970) *Exit, voice and loyalty: Responses to decline of firms, organizations and states*, Cambridge: Harvard University Press.

Klemperer, P. (1995) 'Competition when consumers have switching costs: An overview with applications to industrial organization, macroeconomics, and international trade', *Review of Economic Studies*, vol 62, no 4, pp 515–539.

Kok, L., Groot, I., Mulder, J., Sadiray, K. and Ham, M. van (2005) *De markt voor kinderopvang in 2004*, Amsterdam: Stichting Economisch Onderzoek.

MDW (MDW Werkgroep kinderopvang) (1998) *Rapport van een werkgroep in het kader van het project Marktwerking, deregulering en wetgevingskwaliteit over de kinderopvang in Nederland*, Den Haag.

Mocan, H.N. (2007) 'Can consumers detect lemons? Information asymmetry in the market for child care. An empirical analysis of information asymmetry in the market for child care', *Journal of Population Economics*, vol 20, no 4, pp 743–780.

Moss, P. (1990) Childcare in the European community. *Women of Europe*, supplement no 31, Brussels: European Commission Childcare Network, August.

NCKO (2009) *Pedagogische kwaliteit van de opvang voor 0- tot 4-jarigen in Nederlandse kinderdagverblijven in 2008*, Amsterdam: Universiteit van Amsterdam/Nijmegen: Radboud Universiteit Nijmegen.

Noailly, J. and Visser, S. (2009) 'The impact of market forces on childcare provision: Insights from the 2005 Child Care Act in the Netherlands', *Journal of Social Policy*, vol 38, no 3, pp 477–498.

OECD (2002) *Babies and bosses: Reconciling work and family life, vol 1: Australia, Denmark and the Netherlands*, Paris: Organisation for Economic Cooperation and Development.

Paulussen-Hoogeboom, M.C. and Gemmeke, M. (2009) *Monitor capaciteit kinderopvang 2008–2011. Capacititeitsgegevens in het voor 2008*, regioplan publicatienr. 1806a, Amsterdam: Regioplan.

Plantinga, M. (2006) *Employee motivation and employee performance in child care. The effects of the introduction of market forces on employees in the Dutch child-care sector*, Enschede: Febo druk.

Van Beem, M. and Wever, Y. (2008) *Wachtlijsten en wachttijden buitenschoolse opvang en dagopvang (2e meting)*, Den Haag: B&A Consulting bv.

Vyvoj, B. (2005) *De klant in beeld. Wet kinderopvang en de gevolgen voor ouders. Concept rapportage nul-meting gevolgen Wet Kinderopvang voor de gebruikers*, Paterswolde: Vyvoj.

Walker, J.R. (1991) 'Public policy and the supply of child care services', in: D. M. Blau (ed) *The economics of child care*, New York: Russell Sage foundation, pp 51–77.

WBK (Wet Basis voorziening Kinderopvang) (2002) *Regeling met betrekking tot tegemoetkomingen in de kosten van kinderopvang en waarborging van de kwaliteit van kinderopvang (Wet Basisvoorziening Kinderopvang)*, Memorie van Toelichting. Tweede Kamer, vergaderjaar 2000–2002, 28447, nr. 3.

FIVE

Tinkering with early childhood education and care: early education vouchers in Hong Kong

Gail Yuen

A story to begin

On 11 October 2006, the chief executive of the Hong Kong Government announced the introduction of a voucher scheme which was intended to make affordable and quality early education more accessible to children aged 3 to 6. The announcement sparked heated debate about which children should and which should not be included in the scheme (Yuen, 2007). In the following months, local news switched focus to the confusion over how the scheme was to be operated in the school year 2007–08. As issues relating to the new policy gradually unfolded, the concerns were brought to the attention of the government and a mid-term review of the first five-year policy cycle was requested.

On 24 May 2009, more than 4,000 educators, parents, advocates and legislators took to the streets to press the government for immediate action. Mounting discontent finally led to the formation of a working group to conduct a policy review (Information Services Department, 2009b). On 23 January 2011, another public rally was mobilised in response to the report of the Working Group on Review of the Pre-primary Education Voucher Scheme (2010). This time not just educators, parents, advocates and legislators, but also many more young children, were involved. Their demands were no longer focused on the voucher scheme. It was instead a demand for 15 years of universal education, i.e. free early education for 3- to 6-year-olds plus nine years of compulsory education and three years of free senior secondary education. The rally, unfortunately, did not lead to the passing of a pertinent motion at the Legislative Council. Attempting to respond to public demand, the government issued a press release on the same day, stating that the proposed governance structure of universal provision could possibly constrain parental choice and the flexible development of the sector; therefore, it was not advisable to simply borrow overseas experiences for direct use in the local context (Information Services Department, 2011).

Early childhood education and care in a market context

The market approach to early childhood education and care services, either before or after the introduction of the voucher scheme, is a policy direction long adhered to by the British colonial administration before the sovereignty of the city reverted to China in 1997 (Yuen, 2010a). In Hong Kong, these services for children from birth to 6 are fully privatised, but mostly non-profit making. Kindergartens provide early education for children aged 3 to 6 and in some cases as young as 2, the latter known as kindergarten–cum–childcare centres. Childcare centres, which may include crèches for the first two years of life, serve children under 3. In contrast with standalone childcare centres, kindergarten–cum–childcare centres take up a sizeable market share of services for children aged between 2 and 3.

By comparison, the early education market is much bigger than the childcare market. As at September 2009, 134,293 children aged 3–6 were enrolled in 872 local kindergartens and kindergarten–cum–childcare centres, 774 of which were non-profit with the rest being for-profit providers (School Education Statistics Section, 2010). The enrolment rate for this age group is over 90%. According to official statistics, only 5.3% of the population aged 15 and over did not have any schooling or pre-primary education in 2009 (Census and Statistics Department, 2011). In contrast, there were only 12 non-profit childcare centres providing 682 places (97% utilisation rate) for children under 3 in 2008–09. Of these ten were crèches, with the other two providing services across the three years. Another 22,800 places (56.7% utilisation rate) were available in kindergarten–cum–childcare centres (Social Welfare Department, 2009). In addition, there are 14 childcare centres, almost all for-profit, that offer 1,353 places for children aged 2–3 (Social Welfare Department, 2011).

Although both part-time (half-day) and full-time services are available, kindergartens are predominantly bi-sessional operations. Full-time services constitute around 25% of the early education market (School Education Statistics Section, 2010). Most non-profit childcare centres, on the other hand, offer full-time services. Historically, these services started out under the Social Welfare Department as a form of family support. Many children who use full-time services also come from families with limited resources and with both parents in work (Social Welfare Department, 1992; Yuen and Yu, 2012). As a result of the latest effort to harmonise early childhood education and care services in 2005, provision for children aged 3–6 has been transferred to the Education Bureau. Still, two separate sets of ordinances and regulations remain in use for the two types of services. Conceivably, younger and older children using the same kindergarten-cum-childcare centres are subject to different policy impacts.

So, broadly speaking, the Hong Kong early education and childcare markets stay as a split system. Such a policy trajectory can be traced back to the 1981 Education White Paper which defined early childhood services on the basis of age (Hong Kong Government, 1981). In the face of growing concerns about the issue of equality for children across the ages, an official recommendation addressing the ceaseless demand for unifying early education and care eventually arrived in the mid-1990s. Contrary to expectations, the recommendation changed policy direction from unification to harmonisation (Reconstituted Working Party on Kindergarten Education, 1995). The response to a further push by the Education Commission (2000) to examine the unification issue was the same; unification remained a longer-term goal (Working Party on Harmonisation of Pre-primary Services, 2002).

According to Kaga et al's cross-national study on the integration of early education and care services within education (Kaga et al, 2010, p 17), 'Differences between services in welfare and education in key areas such as access, regulation, funding and workforce' often lead to 'inequalities, discontinuities and problems for children, parents and workers'. In effect, the voucher scheme has worsened the split early childhood education and care system in Hong Kong. Which providers, parents, children and teachers are subsidised and how, have proved extremely contentious issues. As will be discussed, the rationale and assumptions underpinning the scheme need to be carefully deconstructed in order to expose not only the embedded inequalities and inequities, but also the technology of control over young children and women in early education and care services.

Fitting the voucher scheme into the market

In the 2006 policy announcement by the chief executive, the voucher scheme was described as a new initiative for 'cherishing the family'. Since considerable investment had gone into developing kindergartens, a refocusing of resources would lead to the provision of quality early education becoming an integral part of family support. The official positioning of the voucher scheme is quite revealing in showing how the government justifies policy attention to young children's development and learning with reference to the family. The government viewed the voucher scheme as a means to ensure access to affordable and quality early childhood education by all eligible children aged 3–6. It is achieved through providing a direct subsidy to parents, increasing operational transparency, strengthening the quality assurance mechanism, as well as upgrading professional qualifications of teachers and principals to diploma and university degree levels respectively (Education and Manpower Bureau, 2006).

The new policy was intended to benefit 90% of all eligible children and attract the participation of 80% of kindergartens in the scheme. By 2009–10, a total of 119,000 (85%) of children and 800 (84%) kindergartens had joined the scheme (Working Group on Review of the Pre-primary Education Voucher Scheme, 2010). Eligibility applies to children enrolled in a non-profit kindergarten implementing the official curriculum guide (Curriculum Development Council, 2006). For kindergartens to join the scheme, their tuition fees cannot exceed the maximum levels predetermined for part-time and full-time services. The annual voucher value increases from HK$13,000 (£1,040) per child in the first year to HK$16,000 (£1,280) in the scheme's fifth year. The actual amount of money received by each family is less than the voucher value, because the subsidy for professional upgrading (£160 to £240) has been included in all but the fifth year. Parents can apply for additional financial assistance, that is, the fee remission scheme, as needed (Education and Manpower Bureau, 2006).

The direct subsidy provided to parents in the form of a voucher serves not only to lessen their financial burden, but also to maintain and enhance flexibility, vibrancy and diversity within the private early education market (Information Services Department, 2011). It explains why officials have cogently argued against universal provision as an overseas experience not suitable for direct application to the local context. To enable kindergartens to exercise full autonomy in the market, the government initiated two other policy changes alongside the voucher scheme: one the withdrawal of the direct subsidy scheme from non-profit kindergartens (but not non-profit childcare centres), the other the removal of the recommended teacher salary scale. The former was intended to provide eligible kindergartens with financial assistance to enhance teacher qualifications without substantial tuition fee increases (Education and Manpower Bureau, 2006).

Additional problems with the voucher scheme

Considering part-time early education provision adequate for children aged 3–6, the government based the voucher value on a part-time operation irrespective of parental preferences. This is a critical concern noted from the early policy debates because full-time tuition fees are double those for part-time services. In its report, the Working Group on Review of the Pre-primary Education Voucher Scheme (2010) argues that there is no conclusive evidence showing differential effectiveness between part-time and full-time provision. It reiterates the primary responsibility of the family to facilitate child development in the early years. Worth noting here is that Sylva et al (2004) also found no differences in developmental outcomes between half-day and full-day attendance in their longitudinal study on effective pre-school education in Britain.

Regardless of the inconclusive findings on differential impacts, a legitimate question remains concerning the intention of the voucher scheme to support the family. It relates to the evidence that children using full-time provision are likely to come from families with fewer resources or with both parents working. Also being ignored is the reverse trend of workforce participation between women and men in the past decade, with women's participation rising from 45.6% in 1998 to 49.7% in 2008 and men's decreasing from 74.5% in 1998 to 69.7% in 2008 (Women's Commission, 2009). Studies by Peyton et al (2001), Noble (2007) and Kim and Fram (2009) all suggest that parents' choice of early childhood services is complex, involving pragmatic reasons combined with specific considerations regarding their child and family. Finally, Yuen and Yu (2012) found a strong parental preference for full-time provision, because of the unique learning opportunities it offers children to develop independence and social skills.

Due to the per-head and part-time basis of calculating its value, the voucher scheme has inevitably disadvantaged full-time provision. Part-time services are attended by two different groups of children, in morning and afternoon sessions, unlike full-time provision. Thus, full-time providers receive fewer subsidies not only from parental vouchers, but also for teacher development and other setting improvements. As a result, they have experienced difficulties in sustaining a stable operation and workforce. In some kindergarten-cum-childcare centres, the turnover rate of teachers became as high as 50% (Council of Non-profit-making Organisations for Pre-primary Education, 2010). From the government's point of view, this instability is merely transitional, and would be resolved upon the completion of professional upgrading in 2011–12 (Legislative Council Secretariat, 2009).

Stable relationships and positive interactions between adults and children have been well documented as an important aspect of quality provision, which is even more crucial to children with additional needs (European Commission Network on Childcare, 1996; McCartney, 2004; Sylva et al, 2004; OECD, 2006). It seems that neither the Working Group nor the government recognises how such a process-oriented aspect is connected to the development and learning of young children, not to mention early childhood teachers' wellbeing and work environment.

A majority of teachers in one recent study of their work and professional development cast doubt on the voucher scheme being a reflection of an official commitment to the sector. Hectic work schedules, workload increases caused by regulatory measures, pressures associated with professional upgrading, difficulties in hiring substitute teachers and frequent staff changes, together with the removal of the recommended salary scale as well as a lack of salary adjustments after upgrading (Yuen et al, 2010), have combined to create an 'exploitative' work environment for teachers in the early education market.

Thus far, the Working Group on Review of the Pre-primary Education Voucher Scheme (2010) has largely refrained from commenting on these fundamental issues associated with or exacerbated by the voucher scheme. Instead it recommended the establishment of a consultative group to examine issues pertaining to the sector's long-term development and quality. Frequent delays to address concerns about the sustainability of the workforce seem to point to an intentional neglect of consistent evidence on quality matters (e.g. McCartney, 2004; Sylva et al, 2004; OECD, 2006). Later in this chapter it will be discussed how the process of 'othering' along bodily terms, as noted by Tronto (1993, p 114), has enabled a vicious cycle to persist in which 'care is devalued and the people who do caring work are devalued'.

The new curriculum guide (Curriculum Development Council, 2006) issued after the recent harmonisation effort, has inserted the word 'teacher', as opposed to 'pre-primary educator' in the previous curriculum guide (Curriculum Development Institute, 1996), to describe those working with children aged 2–6. Under the voucher scheme, teachers of 2-to 3-year-olds in kindergarten-cum-childcare centres are being excluded from this definition, because they are in effect 'childcare workers' under the remit of the Social Welfare Department. In its report, the Working Group on Review of the Pre-Primary Education Voucher scheme (2010) has ignored the professional needs of this particular group of workers. Similar disparities occur with regard to childcare centres. While kindergarten teachers are required to attain a diploma level qualification and some are already working towards a university degree voluntarily, childcare workers need only to possess a qualification equivalent to one year's initial training. Those working with very young children are clearly being positioned less favourably by the voucher scheme, suggesting the operation of a hierarchy of caring work.

The new fee hikes caused initially by the withdrawal of the direct subsidy scheme from kindergartens and annually by rising operational costs, have continued to attract public criticism, with some questioning whether the new policy does actually reduce parents' financial burden (Tai Kung Pao, 2008, 2010). The voucher value and predetermined fee caps for part-time and full-time services were said to have taken into account adjustments such as regular salary increments, inflation, salary increases for professional upgrading and so on (Education and Manpower Bureau, 2006). The Working Group on Review of the Pre-primary Education Voucher Scheme (2010) also insists that the current fee levels reflect actual operational costs. In reality there has never been any official acknowledgement or genuine examination of the costs of high quality provision for young children (Yuen, 2010a). The withdrawal of the recommended salary scale is a case in point.

Furthermore, the government planned to keep the maximum caps of the fee remission scheme for the five-year policy cycle, while counting the voucher value as part of any fee remission granted to parents, arguing this avoids double benefiting (Working Group on Review of the Pre-primary Education Voucher Scheme, 2010). Consequently, some parents needing additional financial assistance cannot benefit from the scheme at all, because the voucher and fee remission subsidies basically cancel each other out.

Parents using full-time provision who need additional finance are the hardest-hit group. The annual fee increases of full-day services exceeded the maximum cap of the fee remission scheme soon after the new policy was implemented. Many parents who had applied for financial assistance were forced to absorb the difference in fees and pay more than they used to pay under the same fee remission scheme before the introduction of the new policy (Council of Non-profit-making Organisations for Pre-primary Education and Hong Kong Council of Social Service, 2009). It is important to note here the difficulty for parents using full-day services to apply for extra financial support. In addition to being means-tested for their financial needs, parents have to demonstrate their social needs for using full-time services. Stringent assessment criteria are set, for example one parent having to work full time and the other 104 hours or more in a month; parents with chronic illness or disability; children from single parent families, problematic family situations or large families (Working Party on Harmonisation of Pre-primary Services, 2002). This social needs assessment was initially set up by the Social Welfare Department, before the transfer of responsibility for services for children aged 3–6 to the Education Bureau.

Urgent calls for justice by educators, parents, advocates and legislators have at last led to an official change of mind; the annual adjustment of the fee remission caps has been resumed (Information Services Department, 2009a). But the government remains silent about the Working Group's recommendations on changing the method of calculating the voucher and fee remission subsidies, as well as removing the social needs assessment.

Recent local studies indicate parents not in need of additional financial support, particularly those of higher socioeconomic status, tend to be more positive about the voucher scheme, suggesting a lessening of their financial burden. They plan to spend the money saved from the scheme mostly on enrolling their children in special interest classes or other activities (Yuen, 2010b; Yuen and Yu, 2012). Moreover, parents endowed with more cultural and social capital, as described by Bourdieu (1986), know how to act autonomously as informed consumers (Yuen, 2010b). They are conscious about constructing the middle-class child and eager to respond to the call of education reform that positions early childhood education as a foundation for lifelong learning (Yuen and Grieshaber, 2009). A study by Choi (2011) notes the practice of intensive parenting among middle-class parents, who attempt to reflect in their interactions as 'good parents' with their children the government's promotion of parental involvement. Vincent and Ball (2006) make similar observations of middle-class parents in the United Kingdom. From the perspective of these parents, education extends beyond formal settings to include all kinds of extra-curricular activities. The active engagement of their children in a wide range of experiences is thought to help shape the middle-class child and assure future success in education markets.

An analysis from an ethic of care perspective

How the needs of young children are perceived and how these needs are to be met can greatly influence early years policy planning. It is almost impossible to answer these questions without touching on how children and women, that is mothers and teachers, are seen and how their needs are constructed. Working with young children is often thought of as 'natural' for women and related to caring and nurturing. Probably a common phenomenon in paternal societies, women also happen to be the less powerful and well resourced. Hong Kong is by and large a Westernised city. Nevertheless, the Chinese idea that women should be responsible for the household, the private, while men are working outside, the public, continues to set the tone for the division of labour in the modern city (Women's Commission, 2011). As Tronto (1993) explains from her feminist perspective:

> Care conjures an association with the private, the emotional, and the needy; thus a concern about care is a sign of weakness. Both the devaluation of care as work, and the location of care within trivial, private, and emotional states, making understanding of the broader social, moral, and political ramifications of care difficult. (Tronto, 1993, p 112)

Tronto (1993, p120) problematises the common view that care is individualistic, confined to dyadic relationships only, and that neediness is 'a threat to autonomy' as opposed to the fact that all humans have needs at various points of life. This dominant thinking is evident in the consultative documents produced for harmonising the early education and care services in Hong Kong (Reconstituted Working Party on Kindergarten Education, 1995; Working Party on Harmonisation of Pre-primary Services, 2002). They argue that diverse services with varying emphases on early education and care can meet the needs of children at different stages as viewed from a developmental perspective. Because of their unique characteristics, for instance the need for constant individual attention from adults and the fact that they are not mature enough for unsupervised socialisation with peers, very young children, especially from birth to age 2, are best looked after by their parents at home. Parents also play an important role in 'the most critical and vulnerable time in a child's development' (Working Party on Harmonisation of Pre-primary Services, 2002, p 15). The learning of this age group should take place in an informal setting, just like the one provided by childcare centres. Through separating the informal from the formal, 'a clear signal' can be sent to 'parents that pre-primary education does not start until the age of three' (Working Party on Harmonisation of Pre-primary Services, 2002, p 14).

There is apparently a keen desire to avoid 'over-education' of young children, in particular, those under the age of 3, in the light of the prevailing cultural emphasis on academic achievement. To rationalise the exclusion of children under 3 from the voucher scheme, officials add that there is 'no educational basis for children below the age of three to receive formal education which underpinned the pre-primary years' (Legislative Council Secretariat, 2010, p 4). As for children aged 3–6, they also need to spend more time with their parents and family at home (Legislative Council Secretariat, 2010), thus suggesting a preference for part-time services. The question then arises who is expected to perform the ideal parent's role by staying at home to attend the child.

More than a decade ago, the declining utilisation of childcare services became a concern to the government. Such a decline may be linked to the dropping birth rate and availability of alternative options like hiring domestic help (Legislative Council Panel on Welfare Services, 2000). Since 1998, the government has reduced crèche provision (Social Welfare Department, 1998) by more than 50%. In the meantime, non-institutional care to support atypical parental working patterns or other family needs, for instance childminding and non-profit mutual help childcare centres, was explored (Legislative Council Panel on Welfare Services, 2000). The low uptake of childcare, as discussed earlier, does not necessarily indicate the absence of demand. A simple cost comparison between using a crèche service and hiring a domestic helper tells part of the story. The former costs more than the latter. When the government views children of very young ages as extremely weak and immature, care of the kind provided by mothers, domestic helpers or other adults, can be seen as optimal.

According to Tronto (1993), the process of 'othering' along the line of neediness assumes that all humans are autonomous and equal beings. Immediately, this assumption puts young children in an unequal position, because they are exceedingly needy and dependent. To challenge this assumption, Tronto argues that being in need of care from others is to be situated in a state of vulnerability. Vulnerability, as Tronto (p 135) explains, 'belies the myth that we are always autonomous, and potential equal, citizens'. In this respect young children in early education and care services are considered to be extremely vulnerable. The younger the age, the more vulnerable the children and the less likely they are seen by adults as equal citizens.

If young children are not given an equal status, because of their physical constraints, for instance their limited mastery of language, having their needs or responses to the care process noted or interpreted accurately by adults is potentially in doubt. This is in fact the fourth phase, that is responsiveness or 'care-receiving, the response of that which is cared for to the care', of an integrated process of care Tronto (p 127) proposes to advance her political arguments for an ethic of care. The other three phases are: attentiveness or 'caring about, noticing the need to care in the first place'; responsibility or 'taking care of, assuming responsibility for care'; and competence or 'care-giving, the actual work of care that needs to be done' (p 127).

Tronto (p 101) believes that only if care is conceptualised in an integral manner, can a shift from 'the dilemma of autonomy or dependence to a more sophisticated sense of human interdependence' be instigated. Interestingly, the first two phases of the care process tend to be at the discretion of the powerful (in the public sphere where *thought* is made), whereas the third and fourth phases are disproportionally represented by the less powerful (in the private sphere where *action* is taken). Being in a privileged position, the powerful often do not have direct involvement with care-giving and care-receiving. The provision of good care can thus become questionable. Meanwhile, conflicts within and between the four phases, limited resources and fragmentation within the process of care, are likely to make integration less of a reality. The discussion in this chapter so far demonstrates how these issues unfortunately play a role in the policy process governing the introduction of early education vouchers for young children in Hong Kong.

Conclusion

It appears that the voucher scheme has delivered its promise to those who are better equipped and more independent, but has disappointed those who are more needy and dependent on the government for family support and access to quality provision. Market forces are likely to impose continuous constraints on professional practices and militate against enculturating teachers as intellectual workers, and thus the development and learning of young children in early childhood settings (Yuen and Grieshaber, 2009).

The market approach to education never promises equity. Often in conflict with professional values, the market approach is built on performativity, competition, a focus on customer services, a prioritisation of resources for those who are more able to pay, a narrowly defined knowledge base for assessment and most of all, the idea that education is conceivable in terms of how much it costs and can produce (Ball, 2006). Dahlberg and Moss (2005) point out the increasing blurring of 'the boundaries between the economic and the social' as a result of the political partnership of economic neoliberalism with advanced liberalism.

> The ideal citizen and ideal worker also merge, becoming one and the same: an autonomous subject, in no way dependent, with rights but also matching responsibilities, self-governing and responsible for managing his or her risks through making market choices. (Dahlberg and Moss, 2005, p 44)

Education markets, highly regulated in nature, achieve control from a distance through decentralisation. In the markets, social relationships between parents and professionals as well as between teachers and students are being reshaped. So are those between the state and its citizens. An 'individualistic conception of democracy and citizenship' is thus constructed (Ball, 2006, p 121). As a technology to 're-privatise' the sector, the Hong Kong voucher scheme has made it much harder to change these relationships and reconstruct the dominant images of children and women. Rather than redistributing power in the society, it sustains the existing power structures and legitimatises their existence. The voucher scheme has just made the inequalities and inequities that should have been addressed sooner more publicly visible.

For a society to become caring and socially just, Tronto (1993) suggests interweaving morality with politics to bring about change. Instead of confining care to the private or the individual sphere, care as a practice puts thought and action on equal terms. It offers a standard to evaluate how well needs are met through an integrated process of care. As discussed previously, young children in Hong Kong are increasingly being pushed into the private sphere by the voucher scheme and existing welfare policies, making the ethical dilemmas and moral issues that emerge from the market contexts of early education and care services a responsibility of those who actually do the work.

The market approach, which is grounded in the notions of individualism, autonomy and independence, offers a self-regulatory force that manages how care is provided and distributed (Tronto, 1993). By focusing on the able and 'othering' those who are not, binary categories are constructed or maintained among children, parents and workers in the early education and childcare markets along gender and class lines. In the light of the current policy direction, early childhood education and care in Hong Kong will continuously be constrained by the construction of its being a private place in which women take care of children. Care and the people who do caring work will remain devalued.

The market approach privileges the interests of adults or institutions over those of children. It reinforces the assumption that children's needs are same as those of parents or families (James and James, 2004). When children's needs are commodified and privatised, it renders it more difficult for parents and other adults to see the social benefits associated with early childhood education and care and to recognise children of very young ages as equal citizens in society. Several historical opportunities have been missed to unify the early education and care services. How early education and care can be truly integrated to become 'educare' for the benefits of local young children and their inclusion in the lifelong learning movement is a topic that deserves adults' serious attention.

The Gini coefficient of Hong Kong has already crept up to 0.53, surpassing all Asian countries (United Nations Human Settlements Programme, 2009), to show the widening of the income gap at a startling rate. It is high time to expand the notion of social needs beyond the modernist and technocratic realm of thinking to unlock new possibilities. Good care 'requires a deep and thoughtful knowledge of the situation, and of all the actors' situations, needs and competencies' (Tronto, 1993, p 136). Tronto (p 139) claims that 'only in a democratic process where recipients are taken seriously, rather than being automatically delegitimised because they are needy, can needs be evaluated consistent with an ethic of care'. The rallies for improving the voucher scheme and providing 15 years of universal education highlight the top-down, undemocratic practice of policy planning. To continue the existing ways of meeting the needs of young children in Hong Kong is to continue to desensitise oneself from seeing their needs and to reproduce one's privileged position.

References

Ball, S. J. (2006) *Education policy and social class: The selected works of Stephen J. Ball*, London: Routledge.

Bourdieu, P. (1986) 'The forms of capital', in J. G. Richardson (ed) *Handbook of theory and research for the sociology of education*, New York: Greenwood Press, pp 241–257.

Census and Statistics Department (2011) *Hong Kong: The facts*, www.gov.hk/en/about/abouthk/factsheets/docs/population.pdf

Chief Executive (2006) *The 2006–07 policy address*, www.policyaddress.gov.hk/06–07/eng/pdf/speech.pdf

Choi, W. Y. (2011) 'Happy childhood and happy family: The micro-politics of Hong Kong middle-class parenting', in T. L. Lui, C. H. Ng and K. W. Ma (eds) *Hong Kong, living, culture*, Hong Kong: Oxford University Press, pp 251–275.

Council of Non-profit-making Organisations of Pre-primary Education (2010) *Review of the pre-primary education voucher scheme: A position paper* (in Chinese), Hong Kong: Council of Non-profit-making Organisations of Pre-primary Education.

Council of Non-profit-making Organisations of Pre-primary Education and Hong Kong Council of Social Service (2009) *Voucher failing poor school children: Organisations demand amendment of calculation methods* (in Chinese), www.hkcss.org.hk/cm/cc/press/detail.asp?id=358

Curriculum Development Council (2006) *Guide to the pre-primary curriculum*, www.edb.gov.hk/FileManager/EN/Content_2405/pre-primaryguide-net_en.pdf

Curriculum Development Institute (1996) *Guide to the pre-primary curriculum*, www.edb.gov.hk/FileManager/EN/Content_2903/kg_guide_eng.pdf

Dahlberg, G. and Moss, P. (2005) *Ethics and politics in early childhood education*, London: RoutledgeFalmer.

Education and Manpower Bureau (2006) *Item for Finance Committee*, www.legco.gov.hk/yr06–07/english/fc/fc/papers/f06–29e.pdf.

Education Commission (2000) *Learning for life. Learning through life: Reform proposals for the education system in Hong Kong*, www.e-c.edu.hk/eng/reform/annex/Edu-reform-eng.pdf

European Commission Network on Childcare and Other Measures (1996) *Quality targets in services for young children: Proposal for a ten-year action programme*, www.childcarecanada.org/pubs/other/quality/Qualitypaperthree.pdf.

Hong Kong Government (1981) *White paper on primary and pre-primary services*, www.edb.gov.hk/FileManager/EN/Content_689/pried_e.pdf.

Information Services Department (2009a) *Fee remission ceilings to be adjusted annually for kindergarten education*, www.info.gov.hk/gia/general/200906/17/P200906170192.htm.

Information Services Department (2009b) *LCQ12: Review of the pre-primary education voucher scheme*, www.info.gov.hk/gia/general/200912/09/P200912090145.htm.

Information Services Department (2011) *Legislative Council: Response to the 15-year universal education motion debate by the Secretary for Education* (in Chinese), www.info.gov.hk/gia/general/201102/16/P201102160197.htm.

James, A. and James, A. (2004) *Constructing childhood: Theory, policy and social practice*, Basingstoke: Palgrave Macmillan.

Kaga, Y., Bennett, J. and Moss P. (2010) *Caring and learning together: A cross-national study of integration of early childhood care and education within education*, Paris: UNESCO.

Kim, J. and Fram, M. S. (2009) 'Profiles of choice: Parents' patterns of priority in child care decision-making', *Early Childhood Research Quarterly*, vol 24, no 1, pp 77–91.

Legislative Council Panel on Welfare Services (2000) *Childcare services*, www.legco.gov.hk/yr99–00/english/panels/ws/papers/b1943e04.pdf.

Legislative Council Secretariat (2009) *Pre-primary education voucher scheme*, www.legco.gov.hk/yr08–09/english/panels/ed/papers/ed0320cb2–1077–2-e.pdf.

Legislative Council Secretariat (2010) *Pre-primary education voucher scheme*, www.legco.gov.hk/yr09–10/english/panels/ed/papers/ed0111cb2–665–6-e.pdf.

McCartney, K. (2004) *Current research on childcare effects*, www.child-encyclopedia.com/documents/McCartneyANGxp.pdf

Noble, K. (2007) 'Complexities and compromises: Understanding parents' experiences and choice of early childhood education and care services', *Australian Journal of Early Childhood*, vol 32, no 1, pp 24–29.

OECD (2006) *Starting strong II: Early childhood education and care,* Paris: OECD.

Peyton, V., Jacobs, A., O'Brien, M. and Roy, C. (2001) 'Reasons for choosing child care: Associations with family factors, quality and satisfaction', *Early Childhood Research Quarterly*, vol 16, no 2, pp 191–208.

Reconstituted Working Party on Kindergarten Education (1995) *Report of the reconstituted working party on kindergarten education*, www.edb.gov.hk/FileManager/EN/Content_689/kg_rpt_e.pdf.

School Education Statistics Section (2010) *Student enrolment statistics 2009–10*, Hong Kong: Government Printer.

Sing Tao Daily News (2010) *Eighty percent of kindergartens have applied for tuition fee increases*, 21 July (in Chinese), www.singtao.com/yesterday/edu/0721go06.html.

Social Welfare Department (1992) *Study of children attending day crèches 1992*, Hong Kong: Government Printer.

Social Welfare Department (1998) *Review – Significant development 1997–98*, Hong Kong: Government Printer.

Social Welfare Department (2009) *SWD review 2007–08 & 2008–09*, www.swd.gov.hk/doc/annreport0800/pdf/report_2008_en_low.pdf.

Social Welfare Department (2011) *Childcare services*, www.swd.gov.hk/en/index/site_pubsvc/page_family/sub_listofserv/id_childcares.

Sylva, K., Melhuish, E., Sammons, P., Siraj-Blatchford, I. and Taggart, B. (2004) The Effective Provision of Pre-School Education (EPPE) Project: Findings from pre-school to end of Key Stage 1, London: DfES.

Tai Kung Pao (2008) *Inflation dampens kindergarten voucher scheme: 97% kindergarten fees higher than fee remission maximum caps*, October 20 (in Chinese), Hong Kong: Tai Kung Pao (Hong Kong) Ltd.

Tronto, J. C. (1993) *Moral boundaries: A political argument for an ethic of care*, London: Routledge.

United Nations Human Settlements Programme (2009) *State of the world's cities 2008/2009: Harmonious cities*, www.unhabitat.org/downloads/docs/presskitsowc2008/PR%201.pdf

Vincent, C. and Ball, J. S. (2006) *Childcare, choice and class practices: Middle-class parents and their children*, London: Routledge.

Women's Commission (2009) *Hong Kong women in figures*, www.women.gov.hk/download/research/HK_Women2009_e.pdf.

Women's Commission (2011) *Part three: What do women and men in Hong Kong think about the status of women at work?*, www.women.gov.hk/download/research/WoC_Survey_Finding_Economic_E.pdf

Working Group on Review of the Pre-primary Education Voucher Scheme (2010) *Report on review of the Pre-primary Education Voucher Scheme*, www.e-c.edu.hk/tc/WGPEV%20Report%20Eng.pdf

Working Party on Harmonisation of Pre-primary Services (2002) *Consultation document*, www.edb.gov.hk/FileManager/EN/content_713/consult_doc_eng.pdf

Yuen, G. (2007) 'Vouchers in Hong Kong: A milestone of early childhood education?', *Contemporary Issues in Early Childhood*, vol 8, no 4, pp 355–357.

Yuen, G. (2010a) 'The displaced early childhood education in the postcolonial era of Hong Kong', in N. Yelland (ed) *Contemporary perspectives on early childhood education*, Maidenhead: Open University Press, pp 83–99.

Yuen, G. (2010b) 'Early childhood education development in Hong Kong: The market model and the voucher scheme' (in Chinese), *Hong Kong Journal of Early Childhood*, vol 8, no 2, pp 11–16.

Yuen, G. and Grieshaber, S. (2009) 'Parents' choice of early childhood education services in Hong Kong: A pilot study about vouchers', *Contemporary Issues in Early Childhood*, vol 10, no 3, pp 263–279.

Yuen, G. and Yu, W. B. (2012) *Report on parents' choice in the use of full-day early childhood education service* (in Chinese), Hong Kong: Education Policy Forum, Hong Kong Institute of Education.

Yuen, G., Lai, K. C. and Law, K. Y. (2010) *Report on the work of early childhood teachers after the implementation of the pre-primary education voucher scheme* (in Chinese), Hong Kong: Strategic Planning Office, Hong Kong Institute of Education.

SIX

Markets and childcare provision in New Zealand: towards a fairer alternative

Linda Mitchell

Introduction

Early childhood education and care (ECEC) policy designs reflect views about young children, about the roles and responsibilities of parents, community and the state, and about the value and purposes of early childhood education (OECD, 2001, 2006; Rigby et al, 2007). Roles that the state chooses to play have consequences for the nature of early childhood provision and the experiences of children and families. These roles include whether to directly provide ECEC services or allow the market to provide, what standards to set in regulation, and how to deliver funding.

A useful categorisation of state support, developed by New Zealand's Royal Commission on Social Policy (1988), distinguishes between a minimal state and a supportive state. In a situation of minimal state involvement the family is largely responsible for dependants, and the state intervenes only where the family cannot provide. Where children are viewed as dependants and the upbringing of young children is regarded as a private responsibility, governmental responsibility is often limited to the 'needy' and 'disadvantaged'. A minimal state approach favours market provision, targeted funding and low regulated standards. In a supportive state, ECEC is seen as a cooperative effort between the family and the state. Policies are developed around the idea that children are a distinct social group who are citizens with their own associated rights. These ideas are in keeping with those of the OECD (2001, 2006) which has argued that a systematic and integrated approach to policy development and implementation calls for a vision for children, from birth to 8 years, and coordinated policy frameworks: a supportive state.

New Zealand governments have never played a direct role in fully supporting ECEC, and no services are state owned. Nevertheless, a transformation to a more supportive state (Mitchell, 2005) which began during the 1980s, had starts and setbacks during the 1990s and emerged strongly under a Labour-led government from 1999 to 2008. In that decade, fundamental shifts occurred in government resourcing of early childhood education and in policies to support a coherent national framework of curriculum, regulations and funding. At the same time legacies from the neoliberal reforms of the 1980s and 1990s remained, and a market approach to ECEC planning and provision still predominates today, with some exceptions.

This chapter draws on a recently completed longitudinal policy evaluation of New Zealand's strategic plan for early childhood education (Mitchell et al, 2008, 2011) and other policy research (Mitchell and Brooking, 2007; Robertson, 2007; Mitchell, 2008a) to examine the consequences of ECEC policy approaches for children, families and services. The chapter argues that a universal and integrated supportive state approach has contributed much to strengthen quality and access to ECEC. On the other hand, the market approach to provision has not been able to realise early childhood education's full potential to cater equitably for all children and families.

Recently new players in the form of the Quality Public Early Childhood Education (QPECE) coalition of early childhood organisations came together to reconsider the contribution and role of community based ECEC services that are prohibited from making financial gains for members (May and Mitchell, 2009). The project group aimed to reposition these services in the landscape of early childhood education and to develop possibilities for realigning the partnership between the government, community and *whānau* (extended family) in the provision of ECEC services. This chapter ends by discussing the QPECE's alternative model for provision. It argues that a model of state and community partnership in the provision of early childhood services can build services that are responsive to the wider context of children's lives and support a stronger sense of community at local level. In addition, more stringent regulatory standards for staffing and government intervention in negotiating teacher pay and conditions would diminish variability that exists between non-profit community-based and for-profit services in service quality and could deter the for-profit sector growth.

Early childhood education and care in New Zealand

Early childhood education and care in New Zealand is characterised by its variety of service types. There are more than seven distinctive

ECEC service types, each of which has features that can be traced back to the social and political context in which they developed (Smith and May, 2006).

Recently, for policy purposes, ECEC services have been categorised broadly as teacher led and parent/*whānau* led to differentiate between how they operate and are funded. A teacher-led service is one where one or more qualified teachers are responsible for the overall programme in the service. They are required to have a person responsible who is a registered early-childhood-education qualified teacher and to meet the government's teacher registration targets. These services are education and care centres (childcare centres), kindergartens, home-based services and some *kōhanga reo* (Māori immersion language nests). Education and care centres provide all-day, sessional or casual services and cater for children of all ages from birth to school starting age. Kindergartens, historically, were sessional based and catered for 3- and 4-year-olds, but many of these are now shifting to longer sessions, school day or full day and taking younger children (Davison et al, 2012). Kindergarten teachers are recognised as state employees under the 1988 State Sector Act and the Secretary of Education is currently party to its national Collective Employment Agreement. This relationship to the state was severed in 1997 and reinstated in 2000 (Davison and Mitchell, 2009). Home-based services offer flexible provision in the caregiver's or child's home to suit family needs. The home-based educators are supported by an ECE qualified coordinator. Children from birth to school age may attend.

A parent/*whānau*-led service requires parents and/or *whānau* (*whānau* is the Māori word for extended family) to be involved in providing education and care for children. It does not have to meet the teacher registration requirements.

- Playcentres are parent collectives in which parents train as educators and collectively undertake education, management and administration roles (Hill et al, 2000).
- Playgroups are also run by parents and their main aim is to have 'parents providing a play and learning environment for their children' (Robinson, 2002, p 12). However, unlike playcentres, playgroup parents do not have to be trained. Social support for parents is seen as important.
- *Kōhanga reo* offer total immersion in *te reo* Māori (Māori language) and are run by their *whānau*. Their philosophy centres on fostering Māori language and cultural identity, and self-determination (Mitchell et al, 2006).

• Pasifika centres and groups also have a language and culture base, offering bilingual or immersion ECEC in their home Pacific language.

Early childhood policy context

New Zealand is recognised as a world leader in its policies to integrate care and education within policy and curriculum. The development of a national bicultural curriculum, *Te Whāriki* (Ministry of Education, 1996), provides an integrated curriculum framework for all children from birth to school starting age.

Nevertheless, as well as producing *Te Whāriki*, the 1990s were a time of cuts in funding and government support. This period of New Zealand education has been called a 'decade of marketisation' (Nash and Harker, 2005, p 201). Within education, early childhood education was the most extreme, operating within the community and business sphere, with the state playing a limited role. This was a 'minimal state' that relied on the operation of the market to provide ECEC, some of which was of scandalously poor quality.

The election of a Labour-led government in 1999 heralded a transformation in the role of the state. In 2002, the government published *Pathways to the Future: NgāHuarahi Arataki. A 10-year strategic plan for early childhood education* (Ministry of Education, 2002). The plan represented a marked shift away from minimal state involvement during the 1990s to a supportive state that set higher regulated standards for teacher qualifications, offered enhanced professional support and funding, and developed greater policy cohesion.

The government's vision was for all children to participate in quality early childhood education no matter what their circumstances. The strategic plan was framed by goals of increasing children's participation in quality ECEC, improving quality, and promoting collaborative relationships between ECEC services and parents, *whānau*, health and social services, and between ECEC services and schools. This collaborative relationships goal recognises the importance of responsive and reciprocal relationships among education institutions and their communities. In effect it extended the concept of integration into specific policy goals.

Many of the strategic plan actions were aimed at improving the quality of education. The policies together made for a coherent set that were intended to reinforce each other. They were sustained through the funding policies. In particular, a large investment was placed on setting targets to increase the percentage of registered teachers staffing teacher-led services from one 'person responsible' in 2004 to 100% of regulated staff by 2012. Targets were supported by qualification incentives (grants, scholarships, allowances and resources). While most providers were in agreement, private providers, through their national organisation, the Early Childhood Council, have been strong opponents against high regulated standards for qualified teachers.

In parallel, an historic pay parity settlement with school teachers was achieved for kindergarten teachers in 2002 through the negotiation of a national collective employment agreement to which the Secretary of Education became a party. But the settlement was inequitably applied and teachers employed in education and care centres and as coordinators for home-based networks, who are not employees under the 1988 State Sector Act, were not party to it. The pathway to pay parity for these teachers has been slow and is occurring mainly through a voluntary employment agreement (the Early Childhood Collective Agreement) between employers and the union. This covers less than an eighth of the 17,000 teachers in these services. There is a long way to go to reach a unified pay scale for all qualified teachers, and old divisions between the pay of teachers in kindergartens and education and care centres remain. Past experience has shown that unless the government has a direct role in negotiating and funding teachers' pay, inequities and variations in pay and conditions and associated teacher turnover will continue. Such a negotiating role for the government has been fiercely resisted by the Early Childhood Council.

The Ministry of Education published a series of assessment resources starting in 2005 (Ministry of Education, 2005a) and other professional resources (Ministry of Education, 2005b, 2006) congruent with a sociocultural framing of outcomes in *Te Whāriki*. Associated professional development around assessment was also funded. A programme was developed of Centres of Innovation (COI), selected by application to work for three years with research associates to build their use of innovative approaches to teaching and learning based on *Te Whāriki* and share their models of practice with others in the ECEC sector.

Substantial funding and Ministry of Education support accompanied each strategic plan action. A revised funding formula more closely reflecting costs services was implemented. The phasing in of requirements for teacher-led services to employ registered teachers was linked to additional funding roughly linked to teachers' pay rates. The funding increases alone have been almost fourfold, increasing from NZD356,968k [184,843,564 GBP] in 2002 to NZD1,194,314k [618,082,210 GBP] in 2010 (Ministry of Education, 2011).

The most significant ideological shift in government thinking about ECEC as a public good and a governmental responsibility was the implementation in July 2007 of '20 hours free ECE'. This provided higher funding rates for 3- and 4-year-olds up to 20 hours per week. Initially it was intended to be only for community based teacher-led services. The president of the Early Childhood Council, which represents private education and care centres, argued that 'private centres would be forced to close' and that the then Minister of Education's 'socialist finger prints were all over the plan' (May, 2009, p 290). By the time of implementation the government had acceded to this pressure from the for-profit sector and extended '20 hours free ECE' to these services. The nominally 'free' provision was not an entitlement, but was available only to services that opted into the scheme. Services could still ask for optional fees and voluntary donations.

The universal and integrated approaches to staffing and funding contributed to shifts that have occurred in New Zealand's ECEC pedagogical landscape towards more open and democratic ECEC provision. By contrast, the market approach is described as an Achilles heel that is characterised by growing private ownership, and continuing duplications and gaps in ECEC provision, and inequities in access particularly for low income, ethnically diverse and rural families.

Universal approaches to staffing and funding lifting quality and access

The longitudinal evaluation of the strategic plan (Mitchell et al, 2011) measured changes for ECEC services and parents on indicators of the intended outcomes of the strategic plan. In 2004, 2006 and 2009, full data were gathered from a sample of 32 ECEC services in eight localities. Patterns of change were analysed in relation to data from participants about supports and barriers to improvement, and in relation to strategic plan initiatives and service uptake of opportunities afforded by these. In this way, the impact of government policy initiatives could be gauged.

The integrated set of policy initiatives aimed at improving teacher qualifications, pedagogical practices and assessment, and the boost in funding levels and incentives had a striking impact in improving the quality of provision for those ECEC services in the study that took up the opportunities afforded by the policy initiatives. Qualification levels, which were regulated to increase over the time, showed change for teacher-led services nationally and in the study. But usage of professional resources and professional development, which was voluntary, did not occur in services where management did not offer supportive conditions. One message is that policy instruments in themselves may be admirable, but implementation through voluntary uptake will bypass services where management does not support staff to make use of the initiatives. In the strategic plan evaluation such services consistently proved to be centres provided by a for-profit chain.

A key finding of the strategic plan evaluation was that high ratings on indicators of teaching and learning processes interconnected and supported each other. High ratings were directly linked to continuing take-up and usage of the assessment and self-review resources, professional development, COI publications and workshops, and employment of registered teachers. In turn, high indicator ratings were associated with high ratings of observed process quality, derived from observations using a process quality rating scale developed for New Zealand's social and cultural context. Governmental commitment and a willingness on the part of service providers and teachers to take up opportunities offered were both needed to bring about change. Returning to the idea of a 'supportive state', the government was taking on a supportive role through a mix of setting high standards in regulation and providing incentives, resources and opportunities for teachers' education and professional growth.

In the first month of '20 hours free ECE', costs to parents fell by 34% nationwide and even influenced a drop in the Consumer Price Index for Education (Statistics New Zealand, 2007). Mitchell and Hodgen's (2008) evaluation found that in 2004 and 2006 low income families in particular experienced difficulties in affording ECEC costs. These were largely dispelled by 2009.

The introduction of '20 hours frees ECE' led to considerable increases in numbers of 3- and 4-year-olds attending. The number of hours per week that 3- and 4-year-old children attended also increased in line with new operating times. Across all income groups and especially for low income families this policy contributed to parents' decisions to use ECEC provision. Of all parents in the evaluation 17% overall and 30% of low-income parents reported having decided to participate in ECEC because of this policy (Mitchell et al, 2011, p 54). By removing financial barriers, this policy has promoted participation for 3- and 4-year-old children from all income groups. This universal investment in ECEC helped to diminish inequalities in access and enabled more children irrespective of their family circumstances to participate.

An Achilles heel: markets and ECEC provision

In general, successive New Zealand governments have assumed that the non-profit community or for-profit private sector will provide ECEC. There has been only some limited targeted support for planning and capital works and initiatives aimed at increasing participation in areas where many children are not attending ECEC before starting school. This market approach to early education is based on assumptions that children are the responsibility of parents, parents are consumers of education, and markets encourage consumer needs to be met. The power for making decisions is left to the parent consumers. Competition between providers is supposed to contribute to efficiency, cost effectiveness and higher quality. Under this paradigm, it is assumed that parents will not use services that are not meeting their needs, are too costly or are of poor quality.

The New Zealand government has no direct responsibility for the provision of ECEC services, except for the Correspondence School and some services in hospitals. All other services are community based or privately owned, distinguished by the distribution of financial gains to members and the ownership structure. A community based service is an incorporated society, a charitable, statutory, or community trust, or owned by a community organisation, for example a city council, church or university. By contrast a private service may be owned by a private company, publicly listed company, private trust, partnership or an individual. Private services are able to make financial gains and distribute these to their members (Ministry of Education, 2010). Privately owned ECEC services exist in the education and care and home based sector only. These services are most likely to cater for families in paid employment, to offer full-day ECEC, and to charge fees.

The past two decades have seen a substantial rise in the number of education and care and home based services and of children enrolled in them. This has paralleled a trend for women with preschoolers to participate in paid employment. Education and care services (not in homes) cater for the most children using ECEC, from babies to school starting age (usually 5 years). From 852 education and care services in 1992, the number almost trebled to 2,419 in 2010. This increase was accompanied by a burgeoning of the percentage of education and care services that are privately owned. The percentage rose from 41% in 1992, to 51% in 2001, 57% in 2007 and 64% in 2010. Home-based services also grew significantly over this time. In 2010, they are mainly the preserve of the private sector with 74% of the 307 privately owned. Privately owned centres attract the same government funding as those that are community based. The rise in the private-for-profit sector coincided with the exponential increase in government funding available for ECEC children and operations. Other service types, all of which are community owned, have had slower rates of growth and the number of *kōhanga reo* have declined.

Traditionally, most private centres have single owner operators. However, one corporate company, Kindercare, has operated since 1972. In 2002, three new international companies that had bought ECEC centres in New Zealand, Macquarie Bank, Kidicorp and ABC, were listed on the stock market. Consistent with developments in other countries that share a market approach, corporate ECEC has expanded rapidly in the past decade. By 2008, ABC owned 123 centres, following an aggressive campaign to purchase existing centres. It had also bought a College of Early Childhood Education. Kidicorp owned 100 centres, but is no longer a publicly listed company. Macquarie Bank owned 20 centres in New Zealand. Corporate childcare represents 13% of education and care services in New Zealand.

Privately owned services in New Zealand (Mitchell and Brooking, 2007) are more likely to be found in high income communities than are community based services, a finding that is replicated in the Netherlands (Noailly et al, 2007) and Canada (Cleveland and Krashinsky, 2004). The OECD (2006) argued that a reliance on privatised provision of ECEC will almost certainly lead to inequities in provision in poorer communities, because commercial providers are reluctant to invest in such communities. ABC itself has admitted targeting high income communities and those low income communities where government is investing most money, that is areas where profits were easier to make. Its 2007 half yearly results stated that ABC centres in the US were 'located primarily in upper income areas where unemployment remains lower', and that ABC would 'aggressively pursue funding at lower income levels that is designed to mitigate economic circumstances' (ABC Learning, 2007, p 35). The first duty of directors of a publicly listed company under the 1993 Companies Act is not to children and their families, but to absent shareholders. Profits for owners and shareholders are in direct competition with investing fully in the service.

Quality differentials exist between community based and privately owned services on measures of structural and process quality, favouring community based services. Compared with community based services, privately owned services have been found to employ a lower percentage of qualified teachers (Mitchell, 2002); staffing is the biggest cost in teacher-led services. Two national surveys (Mitchell and Brooking, 2007; Mitchell, 2008b) found that private services held less frequent staff meetings, were more likely to have only the statutory minimum annual leave entitlement and had higher rates of teacher turnover. Staff were more likely to describe their workload as excessive and were less likely to regard themselves as part of the decision making team in relation to teaching and learning and policy.

Two New Zealand studies (Smith, 1996; Mitchell et al, 2011) have analysed evidence of differences between privately owned and community based services on measures of process quality. Smith's (1996) study of 100 infant childcare centres found poorer quality in private centres. The strategic plan evaluation (Mitchell et al, 2011) offers a compelling case study of persistent low quality in three teacher-led services where teacher qualification levels were low, employment conditions were unsupportive of teaching and learning, and professional development opportunities were meagre. These were all education and care centres owned by the same publicly listed corporate chain. Two of these were bought by the chain during the evaluation period.

> The 'poor' or 'fair' ratings of overall quality were paralleled by 'poor' or 'fair' ratings on each of the quality dimensions, except for resources, which were rated as 'good'. Routines cut across children's play. For example, in one centre children's names were called for toileting or nappy changing, with no explanation included of the purpose of the call out. In another centre, rules were asserted without explanation ("You're not allowed to snatch. Get listening.") The education programme was limited, for example stories were not read or told during the observations, or told only at mat time. Adult-led art activities (for example stencil pictures, templates) were common. One centre had small broken crayons and blunt pencils for children's writing. Outdoor space in one centre was a large area with no small spaces and shared by 16 under-2-year olds. In another, children were prevented from coming inside when they were outside and vice versa. Children sat by the door. Children sat in high chairs for long periods with limited interaction at times. (Mitchell et al, 2011, p 73)

Only one of the for-profit centres was meeting the requirement of 50% registered teachers in 2009. In this centre, staff were 'juggled', that is moved from centre to centre, to ensure requirements were met. Opportunities for professional development were not offered or were restricted to qualified teachers only, so the many unqualified staff missed out. Staff meetings were held only monthly and there was little non-contact time. With minor individual exceptions, these centres rated poorly on measures of assessment, planning, evaluation and self-review processes.

Parents in these centres were critical of the high fees charged for the '20 hours ECE' and the focus on profit.

> [Corporate company] owns it now. [Corporate company] is a $ making business who don't look after the children and teachers. A barcode to scan your child in and out says it all (Centre A). (Mitchell et al, 2011, p 75)

The market approach to planning and provision affects opportunities for all children to have access to early childhood services that cater for families' circumstances. Ministry of Education statistics show that children from low income communities compared with higher income communities, and children of Māori and Pasifika ethnicities, are less likely to attend an early childhood service before starting school than those of European/pākehā descent. A study of parent decision making in relation to ECEC use (Robertson, 2007), found limited choice for families in rural communities. Anecdotally, there appears to be some oversupply and underutilisation of services, because provision is not strategically planned.

Operating hours may be inflexible and not suited to family circumstances. Robertson's (2007) study found a gap between the hours a child is in ECEC and the hours mothers work. New Zealand studies have consistently found a very high incidence (around 25%) of children attending more than one ECEC service (Department of Labour and National Advisory Council on the Employment of Women, 1999; Mitchell and Brooking, 2007; Mitchell, 2008b; Mitchell et al, 2011). Provision is not attuned to many families' needs, especially those where both parents work. This situation is likely to remain unchanged in the absence of any formal planning requirement, since many ECEC services seem to hold fast to preserving the status quo of their operation. It has been the private sector that has largely filled the need for all day provision.

Towards a fairer alternative

Private providers have access to commercial funding which is not available to community based services. This key reason for discrepancies in growth rates was articulated by the Quality Public Early Childhood

Education project (QPECE). This group was set up to appraise the impact of government policies on community-based organisations and services (May and Mitchell, 2009):

> ... community-based early childhood services and organisations had been ill-placed in the policy environment of the past two decades to respond to the need for the expansion of provision in the sector and the increased participation of children in Aotearoa New Zealand. This was because they were not set up to raise funds in the same way as private companies and are reliant on limited government grants and community funding. The provision of new services had been more possible for private and increasingly corporate providers. (May and Mitchell, 2009, p 2)

Without access to commercial funding, the main form of support for capital works for the community based sector has been through a Ministry of Education discretionary grants scheme. It offered planning and capital grants for eligible community based services or organisations which met criteria set by the Ministry of Education annually. The fund was capped, and many services missed out each year. In 2011 the discretionary grants scheme was replaced with a 'Targeted Assistance for Participation' initiative. Private owners can access this fund, making New Zealand one of the few countries where taxpayers can fund capital assets of private business. So in 2011, the balance has shifted further in favour of the private sector.

Another model for childcare provision, one that is premised on the idea that ECEC is a public good that should be provided as 'a partnership between Government, community, *whānau* and ECE services' was promoted by QPECE. The group decided on the following vision and goals:

Vision

- Every child has a right as a citizen to participate in free early childhood education.
- Every family that wishes to can access high quality, community-based early childhood education.

Goals

- promotion of community based services through development of a national plan for all ECE provision through Aotearoa/New Zealand;
- provision of appropriate services to ensure every child can participate in free high quality ECE;
- robust accountability to Government, parents, whānau and communities linked to indicators that demonstrate high quality ECE. (May and Mitchell, 2009, p 4)

The QPECE project group emphasised democratic processes of decision making where collaborative relationships in planning for ECEC provision occur locally and nationally. Such an approach would open spaces for community participation in shaping the nature of provision and contributing to it. Planning provision, rather than funding any service that meets regulatory requirements, as is currently the norm, offers the opportunity to develop new and responsive forms of provision, with a genuine sense of local commitment to the quality of a community's early childhood education services. A model of mutually supportive state and community partnership in the provision of early childhood services could build services that are responsive to the wider context of children's lives and support a stronger sense of community at local level.

Interestingly, the current government has recently embarked on a number of 'Intensive Community Participation Projects' that will involve the establishment of a local action group to work with ECEC services and local families and develop community plans for ECEC provision. Existing ECEC services themselves need also to examine and adapt their own provision so that they offer a comprehensive package of services for families. The history of provision suggests that this would be hard for them to do without external incentives and support, since most service types have held fast onto their habitual modes of operation despite changes in society.

It is unrealistic to expect the current government to bring in measures to favour the community based sector since its actions, right-wing ideology and market philosophies are inconsistent with these aims. Already it has extended its capital grants scheme to the for-profit sector. Even under a centre-left Labour-led government in the past decade, the pressures exerted by the for-profit national lobby group were too great for that government to withstand. For political reasons, the Labour-led government withdrew from positively discriminating in favour of community based provision in its '20 hours free ECE' policy.

Another way to deter growth in the for-profit sector and address quality differentials that exist between for-profit and community based services is through higher regulated standards for teacher qualifications, teacher–child ratios, group size and professional development requirements, and through direct government intervention in negotiating teacher pay and conditions. Such measures would not allow the leeway that enables some providers in the for-profit sector to operate with minimum standards, cut costs and return profits.

It is through collective advocacy that most of the gains in ECEC policy in New Zealand have been won, often 'against the odds' (Wells, 1991). The 'fairer alternative' and the advantages of a planned community based and state supported ECEC sector and the benefits of high regulated standards will require a long-term campaign.

Postscript

The landscape for such a campaign is changing. Already the national government has removed funding for professional resources and COIs. It has reduced the required targets to 80% registered teachers in teacher-led services. It cut funding for employing higher levels of registered teachers and stopped funding for professional development for about 6 months for review. ECEC centres are now able to operate with 150 children over 2 years and 75 children under 1 year, replacing maximum centre sizes of 50 and 25 children respectively. There is no regulated group size in New Zealand, so the maximum centre size has been the only regulated way in which numbers of children in a group have been constrained.

An Early Childhood Education Task Force (ECE Taskforce, 2011) charged with undertaking a full review of the value gained from different types of government investment in early childhood education, has proposed targeted funding for low income groups, and Māori and Pasifika children, while retaining fiscal neutrality. The proposal would inevitably undermine the '20 hours ECE' policy, with families outside the 'priority groups' paying more.

References

ABC Learning (2007) *Half yearly results*, Brisbane, Australia: ABC Learning.

Cleveland, G. and Krashinsky, M. (2004) *The quality gap: A study of non-profit and commercial child care centres in Canada*, Toronto: University of Toronto at Scarborough, Division of Management.

Davison, C. and Mitchell, L. (2009) 'The role of the state in early childhood education: Kindergartens as a case study of changing relationships', in I. Livingstone (ed) *New Zealand annual review of education. Te arotake a tau ao te matauranga i Aotearoa*, vol 18, Wellington, New Zealand: School of Education, Victoria University of Wellington.

Davison, C., Mitchell, L. and Peter, M. (2012) *Survey of kindergarten provision. Results of a 2010 survey of New Zealand Kindergartens Inc kindergarten associations*, Hamilton, New Zealand: Wilf Malcom Institute for Educational Research, University of Waikato.

Department of Labour and National Advisory Council on the Employment of Women (1999) *Childcare, families and work. The New Zealand childcare survey 1998: A survey of early childhood education and care arrangements for children*, Wellington, New Zealand: Labour Market Policy Group.

ECE Taskforce (2011) *An agenda for amazing children. Final report of the ECE Taskforce*, www.taskforce.ece.govt.nz/

Hill, D., Reid, R. and Stover, S. (2000) 'More than educating children: The evolutionary nature of playcentres philosophy of education', in S. Stover (Ed) *Good clean fun: New Zealand's playcentre movement*, Wellington, New Zealand: Playcentre Federation, pp 30–38.

May, H. (2009) *Politics in the playground. The world of early childhood education in New Zealand*, Dunedin, New Zealand: Otago University Press.

May, H. and Mitchell, L. (2009) *Strengthening community-based early childhood education in Aotearoa New Zealand*, Wellington, New Zealand: NZEI Te Riu Roa.

Ministry of Education (1996) *Te Whāriki*, Wellington, New Zealand: Learning Media.

Ministry of Education (2002) *Pathways to the future: Ngā Huarahi Arataki*, Wellington, New Zealand: Ministry of Education.

Ministry of Education (2005a) *Kei Tua o te Pae. Assessment for learning: Early childhood exemplars. Books 1–10*, Wellington, New Zealand: Learning Media.

Ministry of Education (2005b) *Foundations for discovery: Supporting learning in early childhood education through information and communication technologies: A framework for development*, Wellington, New Zealand: Ministry of Education.

Ministry of Education (2006) *Ngā Arohaehae whai hua. Self review guidelines for early childhood education*, Wellington, New Zealand: Learning Media.

Ministry of Education (2010) *The ECE funding handbook*, Wellington, New Zealand: Ministry of Education.

Ministry of Education (2011) *Government expenditure on early childhood education*, Wellington, New Zealand: Ministry Of Education.

Mitchell, L. (2002) *Differences between community owned and privately owned early childhood education and care centres: A review of evidence*, Wellington, New Zealand: NZ Council for Educational Research. www.nzcer.org.nz.

Mitchell, L. (2005) 'Policy shifts in early childhood education: Past lessons, new directions', in Codd, J. and Sullivan, K. (eds) *Education policy directions in Aotearoa New Zealand*, Southbank, Victoria: Thomson Learning.

Mitchell, L. (2008a) *Assessment practices and curriculum resources in early childhood education. Results of the 2007 NZCER national survey for ECE services*, Wellington, New Zealand: NZ Council for Educational Research.

Mitchell, L. (2008b) *Provision of ECE services and parental perceptions. Results of the 2007 NZCER national survey of ECE services*, Wellington, New Zealand: NZ Council for Educational Research.

Mitchell, L. and Brooking, K. (2007) *First NZCER national survey of early childhood education services*, Wellington, New Zealand: NZ Council for Educational Research.

Mitchell, L. and Hodgen, E. (2008) *Locality-based evaluation of Pathways to the Future: Ngā Huarahi Arataki*. Stage 1 report, Wellington, New Zealand: Ministry of Education.

Mitchell, L., Royal Tangaere, A., Mara, D. and Wylie, C. (2006) *Quality in parent/whanau-led services*. Wellington, New Zealand: Ministry of Education.

Mitchell, L., Wylie, C. and Carr, M. (2008) *Outcomes of early childhood education: Literature review.* Report to the Ministry of Education. Wellington, New Zealand: Ministry of Education.

Mitchell, L., Meagher Lundberg, P., Mara, D., Cubey, P. and Whitford, M. (2011) *Locality-based evaluation of Pathways to the Future - Nga Huarahi Arataki. Integrated report 2004, 2006 and 2009*, www.educationcounts. govt.nz/publications/ece/locality-based-evaluation-of-pathways-to-the-future-ng-huarahi-arataki.

Nash, R. and Harker, R. (2005) 'The predictable failure of school marketisation: The limitations of policy reform', in J. Codd and K. Sullivan (eds) *Education policy directions in Aotearoa New Zealand*. Southbank, Victoria: Thomson Dunmore Press.

Noailly, J., Visser, S. and Grout, P. (2007) *The impact of market forces on the provision of childcare: Insights from the 2005 Childcare Act in the Netherlands*, CPB Memorandum 176, The Hague: CPB/Netherlands Bureau for Economic Policy Analysis.

OECD (2001) *Starting strong I. Early childhood education and care*, Paris: Organisation for Economic Cooperation and Development.

OECD (2006) *Starting strong 11. Early childhood education and care*, Paris: France, Organisation for Economic Cooperation and Development.

Rigby, E., Tarrant, K. and Neuman, M.J. (2007) 'Alternative policy designs and the socio-political construction of childcare', *Contemporary Issues in Early Childhood*, vol 8, no 2, pp 98–108.

Robertson, J. (2007) *Parental decision making in relation to the use of early childhood education services*, Wellington, New Zealand: Ministry of Education.

Robinson, C.-L. (2002) *Playgroup paper*, Wellington, New Zealand: Early Childhood Development.

Royal Commission on Social Policy (1988) *The April Report*, vol 111, *Future Directions*, Wellington, New Zealand: The Royal Commission on Social Policy.

Smith, A. B. (1996) 'The quality of childcare centres for infants in New Zealand', *State of the Art Monograph no 4*, Palmerston North, Massey University: New Zealand Association for Research in Education.

Smith, A. B. and May, H. (2006) 'Early childhood care and education in Aotearoa-New Zealand', in E. Melhuish (ed) *Preschool care and education: International perspectives*, London: Routledge.

Statistics New Zealand (2007) *Consumer price index: September 2007 quarter*, Wellington, New Zealand: Statistics New Zealand.

Wells, C. (1991) 'The impact of change: Against the odds', Paper presented at the Early Childhood Convention, Dunedin, New Zealand.

SEVEN

Publicly available and supported early education and care for all in Norway[1]

Kari Jacobsen and Gerd Vollset

Introduction

In this chapter the authors describe the current situation and the recent development of the early childhood education and care (ECEC) sector in Norway, focusing on more recent history. In particular the chapter focuses on the introduction of a legal right to a place from the age of one in 2009 and the change of the financing schemes in 2011 which have supported the Norwegian childcare market. The authors have been working in ministries responsible for kindergartens since the 1970s. The references are mainly publicly available documents. Vollset (2011) describes the development of the Norwegian kindergarten sector as part of national family policy up to the transfer of the sector to the Ministry of Education and Research in 2006. The first Stoltenberg government, a red–green coalition, came to power in autumn 2005. This government aimed to see kindergartens as the first step in lifelong learning, to increase the number of places, to introduce equal treatment of municipal and non-municipal kindergartens in relation to public grants, to reduce parents' fees and to introduce a legal right to a place for all children from the age of one (the Soria Moria Declaration 2005). This was a follow-up of a broad political settlement in the Norwegian Storting (parliament) in 2003.

'Kindergarten' (*barnehage*) is the common term for different types of early childhood education and care institutions. The first Act on Child Day Care Institutions came into force in 1975. The 1975 Norwegian Kindergarten Act with later amendments, is used to cover the age group 0–5 years; compulsory school age is 6. As paid parental leave is about one year, there is little need for care for children under the age of one. Since 2009 children from the age of approximately one year have a legal right to a place.

Kindergartens may offer full-time or part-time services. In addition there are 'family kindergartens' with small groups of children cared for by assistants with teaching guidance from a qualified preschool teacher or 'open kindergartens' where the children attend with one of their parents (or another person), who takes care of them under the leadership of a preschool teacher. Kindergartens may be non-municipal or municipal owned and run.

Unlike many other European or OECD member countries, legislation concerning ECEC covers both non-municipal and public institutions. This chapter describes the growth of non-municipal childcare and the societal pressures and regulatory framework which has shaped it, and the caution with which private childcare has been introduced.

Norwegian kindergartens today

In the 2005 Kindergarten Act the Norwegian Storting has established the current regulatory framework governing the kindergarten sector. The Act has sections concerning the purpose of kindergartens, and on the content of what is offered to children; on parents' and children's rights to participation; on approval of and supervision of kindergartens by the local authorities; and on staff competencies. Staffing at kindergartens must be sufficient for the staff to carry out satisfactory pedagogical activity.

The new rationale of the 2010 Kindergarten Act and the curricular framework (Norwegian Ministry of Education and Research, 2010) incorporate the social and educational mandate of kindergartens in today's society. The rationale is as follows:

> The kindergarten shall, in collaboration and close understanding with the home, safeguard the children's need for care and play, and promote learning and training as a basis for an all-round development. The kindergarten shall be based on fundamental values in the Christian and humanist heritage and tradition, such as respect for human dignity and nature, intellectual freedom, charity, forgiveness, equality and solidarity, values that also belong to other religions and beliefs and that are rooted in human rights.
>
> The children shall be able to develop their creative zest, sense of wonder and need to investigate. They shall learn to take care of themselves, each other and nature. The children

shall develop basic knowledge and skills. They shall have the right to participate according to their age and abilities. The kindergartens shall treat the children with trust and respect, and acknowledge the intrinsic value of childhood. They shall contribute to wellbeing and joy in play and learning, and shall be a challenging and a safe place for community life and friendship. The kindergarten shall promote democracy and equality and counteract all forms of discrimination. (Section 1, first and second paragraph)

This rationale follows the tradition laid down in the first Act on Child Day Care dated 1975, but it is much broader. On 1 March 2006, the Norwegian Ministry of Education and Research laid down regulations which provide a Framework Plan for the Content and Tasks of Kindergartens. This Framework Plan is a revised version of Norway's first Framework Plan, established by the Ministry of Children and Family Affairs in 1995. The Framework has a holistic approach to children's learning, and takes a broad view on what experiences children should be acquainted with in kindergarten, over and above preparation for school. The regulations came into force on 1 August 2006 and are legally binding for all kindergartens in Norway. Due to the amendments of the rationale, the current Framework Plan was amended in 2011 in accordance with the new rationale.

The Kindergarten Act requires head teachers and pedagogical group leaders to be qualified preschool teachers with a bachelor's degree. There must be one qualified preschool teacher per 7–9 children under the age of 3 and one teacher per 14–18 children over the age of 3. In family kindergartens there must be one qualified preschool teacher per 30 children. Approximately a third of the staff must be qualified preschool teachers, the rest being assistants and child and youth workers.

All sorts of kindergarten fall under the legislation of the Kindergarten Act, but not private childcare arrangements such as babysitting or nannies. If a service operates on a regular basis where one or more children spend more than 20 hours per week, and if there are ten or more children over the age of 3 present at one time, or five or more present under the age of 3, and the activity is carried out in return for remuneration, the service is obliged to seek approval as kindergarten and conform to the Kindergarten Act and its Regulations, provided in accordance with the legislation.

By the end of 2009 there were 6,675 kindergartens in Norway, 3,096 public kindergartens and 3,579 private. At the same time there were 270,174 children in kindergartens, about 80,000 more than in 2000.

A total of 88% of all children aged 1–5 had a place in a kindergarten. Of children aged 1 and 2 years, about 79% attended kindergarten; 96% of children aged 3–5 attended (Statistics Norway, 2010).

There are 429 municipalities in Norway. Given that about 4.9 million people live in Norway, many of the municipalities are small. The municipalities play an important role in the kindergarten sector. According to national legislation, the municipalities are the local authorities which regulate all kindergartens, both municipal and non-municipal. Owners of kindergartens must apply to the local authority for approving their service in accordance with current rules, and are obliged to run their service in accordance with current statutes and rules. The municipalities must supervise the kindergartens. They are responsible for meeting the need for kindergarten services demanded by their inhabitants and for ensuring children's legal right to a place in kindergarten. However, the municipalities are not obliged to run the kindergartens themselves. The municipalities must, from 2011, administer the block grants from the state for kindergartens, both the municipal and the non-municipal establishments (Ministry of Local Goverment and Regional Development).

Kindergarten owners are by law obliged to state the operating conditions of their kindergartens. Admission criteria should be part of the conditions. Approved kindergartens are required to cooperate with the admission of children. The municipality must facilitate a coordinated admission process, taking account of the diversity and distinctive character of the kindergartens. Great importance is attached to the wishes and needs of users in connection with the actual admission. The coordinated admission process is intended to ensure equal treatment of children and equal treatment of municipal and privately owned kindergartens. Since spring 2009 the municipalities are obliged to offer all children a place in kindergarten, municipal or private, if they reach one year of age before September and their parents apply for a place in the spring admission procedure, which is an annual procedure.

Kindergartens also have to comply with other legislation. One of the most important regulations is that of environmental healthcare in kindergarten and school, which has to be complied with if the service is regularly provided for more than ten hours weekly and three or more children are attending at the same time. This regulation also applies to childminders if they meet the criteria mentioned (Norwegian Ministry of Health and Care, 1995).

Finance

Since the first Act on Child Day Care in 1975 before the 'kindergarten settlement' in the Norwegian Storting in 2003, kindergartens were financed by a division of the costs between earmarked state grants, the municipalities and the parents' fees. All approved kindergartens received a state grant, but many of the non-municipal kindergartens were run without economic subsidies from the municipalities. These private kindergartens had relatively high parental fees. The state grant varied according to whether the children were under or over 3 years of age, and their attendance hours.

In 2003, a reform of the financing of the kindergarten sector took place. It originated from an agreement between the majority of political parties in the Norwegian Parliament. As a result of the agreement, the Kindergarten Act was amended, and several new regulations were adopted. The goal was to ensure equal economic treatment for non-municipal and public kindergartens, affordable prices for parents and full coverage of high quality kindergarten places for all children whose parents so wished. From the outset, it was recognised that a system where the majority of the costs were to be borne by the central state budget had to take into account the substantial cost differences relating to kindergartens in the different municipalities. Furthermore it became clear in the legislative procedure that the municipalities had higher costs than the non-municipal kindergartens (85% of the costs of the municipal kindergartens in 2003). Non-municipal kindergartens were given a legal right to grants from the municipalities through the adoption of regulation number 539 of 19 March 2004 on equivalent treatment of kindergartens with regard to public subsidies (Norwegian Ministry of Children and Family Affairs 2004).

Another major change was the introduction of a maximum price ceiling on parental fees, both in municipal and non-municipal kindergartens, to obtain the goal of capping parents' fees at 20% of the costs of the service. This implied that the non-municipal kindergartens could no longer charge parents fees at their own discretion. As of 1 January 2006, the applicable rate was fixed at NOK2,250 per month. The parents' fees at the time of writing in 2011 are NOK2,330 (approximately GBP260) per month and NOK25,630 (approximately GBP2830) per year. The government decided to freeze the parents' fees at this rate until NOK1,750 at 2005 value is reached. This was a promise in the election campaign in 2005. Parents with more than one child would benefit from a fee reduction of a minimum of 30% for the second child and a minimum of 50% for the third child or subsequent children. There would also be free places or lower fees for children from low-income families (announced in the Soria Maria Declaration, which laid the foundation for governmental cooperation between the Labour Party, the Socialist Left Party and the Centre Party, 13 October 2005).

Another main change was the introduction of a new obligation for the municipalities to cover operational costs of non-municipal kindergartens. To enable the municipal sector to finance its public responsibilities, a new state grant scheme for kindergartens was introduced. Until the end of 2010 the kindergarten sector in the municipalities received earmarked grants, calculated on the basis of the number of children in the kindergarten and depending on age of the children and their attendance hours. The scale of these grants was set by the Storting annually.

The Norwegian Storting has decided that the financing of the sector should be changed from 2011. A new Section 14 in the Kindergarten Act came into force on 1 January 2011, when the state grants to kindergartens were included in the General Purpose Grant Scheme for municipalities (*rammetilskudd til kommunene*, Ministry of Local Government and Regional Development). From the same date new regulations regarding equivalent treatment pursuant to the new legislation entered into force. Municipal kindergartens in general have been and are still organised like other municipal activities. As such, the financing of the municipal kindergartens is a part of the general budget of the municipality.

The new financing scheme is designed to ensure that each non-municipal kindergarten receives at least the same level of public funding as under the former financing system, but it can be reduced if the municipalities reduce the costs in their own municipal kindergartens. Through the new financing scheme all grants will still be paid to the kindergartens by the municipality. To secure further running costs of non-municipal kindergartens, the municipalities have a duty to finance existing non-municipal kindergartens that were approved and established before 31 December 2010. The municipalities can consider whether non-municipal kindergartens established after 1 January 2011 should receive municipal financing. Non-municipal kindergartens must still be treated equally with regard to public grants. Regulations concerning financing of non-municipal kindergartens are adjusted to this change.

The Kindergarten Act and current regulations do not regulate profit. The municipalities' responsibility for the non-municipal kindergartens and whether it should be possible to extract a profit from them has been politically discussed on different occasions. In White Paper no 27 (1999–2000), *Barnehage til beste for barn og foreldre* (the best kindergartens for children and parents), the former Ministry of Children and Family Affairs described and discussed this topic:

> Non-municipal kindergartens have a long tradition in Norway, and they have made an important contribution to the coverage attained in many municipalities.... From the purpose of the running of kindergartens one can distinguish between three types of kindergarten in a varied kindergarten sector: first, kindergartens with an alternative pedagogical profile, for example the Steiner and Montessori kindergartens. Secondly, kindergartens with a specific religious basis.... A third important group is kindergartens owned and run by parents or voluntary organisations, with the primary purpose to provide more places because of unmet need. The Government intends that non-municipal kindergartens must be part of an integrated and equal part of the supply of kindergartens in the municipalities, with one exception: in the past ten years some kindergartens have been established with the intention of giving the owners the highest possible profit. The Government does not wish these kindergartens to be supported by public money. The Kindergarten Act gives all kindergartens who meet the legislative demands the right to be approved. In the yearly [governmental] budget decisions, all approved kindergartens will have the right to state grants. The Government will consider a change to prevent these [kindergartens] from getting state grants from 2001. (Norwegian Ministry of Children and Family Affairs, 1999, pp 37–8)

The majority in the Storting was of another opinion:

> The majority in the Committee [The Norwegian Storting's standing committee on family, cultural and public administration affairs], all except the one member from the Socialist Left Party, disagrees that there has up till now been unreasonably high profit in the non-municipal kindergartens. The majority also draws attention to the fact that the incentive for extracting profit will be restricted with full coverage. Large profits due to high parental fees will only be possible when the lack of places is acute. Another

majority, all except the members of the Liberal Party, means it is not advisable that private kindergartens receiving state grants make a profit. This majority endorses the White Paper's positive approach to non-municipal kindergartens except for those kindergartens making a profit for the owner. This majority supports this view, but disagrees that there have been large profits earned in kindergartens until now. Yet this majority asks the Government to monitor the development closely. (Innst. S nr. 207, 1999 – 2000, p 23)

Recently the Ministry of Education and Research has seen more cooperatives and commercial owners running kindergartens. The Ministry found it important to ensure that public grants and parents' fees benefit children in kindergartens and are not used to accumulate private wealth. If a kindergarten owner runs the kindergarten more efficiently than the municipality, or with lower quality, it is possible to make a profit. The Ministry is currently considering legislation concerning profit.

The development of the early childhood education and care (*barnehage*) sector

A detailed history of Norwegian childcare is offered in the *Norwegian Background Report to the OECD* in connection with the *Thematic Review of Early Childhood Education and Care Policy* published in 1998 (Norwegian Ministry of Children and Family Affairs, 1998). The tipping point came with women's emancipation. In the 1960s and 70s women's situation in Norway changed rapidly. Women themselves wanted liberation, and established different sorts of liberation movement. They wanted education and work on an equal footing with men, and they wanted daycare institutions for their children. As there were very few daycare institutions, in spite of public initiatives, many children were cared for by childminders in the informal market with no public support or supervision or by other private arrangements, without other control mechanisms than parents' own satisfaction or needs.

At the start of the 1970s, gender eq The majority in the Storting was of another opinion uality became an important political premise for the development of what at the time was called a modern and new Norwegian family policy. In light of international political trends and the education explosion in the 1960s that affected both men and women, it was no longer possible to pursue a policy that reinforced the image of Norway as the foremost nation of housewives in the

Nordic region. There was a strong cross-political consensus on this issue, particularly among women. The Social Democratic governments of the 1970s pursued an increasingly active policy in this field, under the slogan of 'freedom of choice', meaning freedom for women to choose to work outside the home even if they were also mothers.

Before this, family policy had largely been concerned with the financial situation of families with children. The goal was to ensure that children also shared in society's growing prosperity. Child benefit, family taxation issues and food subsidies were important elements of this policy. The new political instruments consisted of adapting working life to accommodate the needs of workers with parental obligations and developing a system of high quality, publicly subsidised childcare, which was virtually non-existent around 1970.

> The most important and most costly single measure was the introduction of pregnancy leave with full pay. This was later renamed 'birth leave' and is today called 'parental leave'. Giving working parents – both fathers and mothers – the right to take shorter leaves of absence related to parenthood, enabling parents to work part time without blocking career paths and introducing other initiatives to ensure job opportunities for women were also important components of this policy. The second key area was the increased provision of quality daycare centres for children at a price that families could afford.... Both daycare and working-life policy have been important elements of family policy throughout the three decades. (Vollset, 2011, pp 283–7)

Women's participation in the labour market increased massively from the middle of the 1970s to the middle of the 1980s. The establishment of new kindergarten places could not cope with parents' needs for care for their children. Families and friends came up with their own solutions. In the middle of the 1980s the number of children who were cared for by 'day mothers' increased from 30,000 to 60,000 during a four year period (Vollset, 2011). National and municipal authorities knew little or nothing about these private care solutions. Some of them were in the 'informal market economy', others were more formal. As places in kindergartens were not available and parents wanted to work outside home, they had to find solutions themselves.

In a White Paper from the late 1980s, *St. meld. nr 8 (1987–88)*, *Barnehager mot aar 2000 (Kindergartens towards the year 2000)* (Norwegian

Ministry of Consumer Affairs and Government Administration, 1988), the Labour government presented a financing plan with a sharing of running costs with 40% from the state, 30% from the municipalities and 30% from the parents in a future kindergarten sector. For the first time the government presented the goal that kindergarten costs should be affordable for all (Vollset, 2011).

When the White Paper was presented, there were both municipal and non-municipal kindergartens. The non-municipal owners were usually local associations, non-profit organisations and parents groups running kindergartens, usually with municipal economic support in addition to the state grants. None of these groups had much in the way of economic resources. The municipalities supported the non-municipal kindergartens in different ways. It was quite common to cover the shortfall for the non-profit organisations. It was also common to buy some places for prioritised children on the municipal waiting lists. The municipalities guaranteed loans in the Norwegian Housing Bank or gave providers premises to run their kindergartens in. If the municipalities gave economic or in-kind support, they could set up conditions for this support, for example a right to use some of the places or that the organisation should use the municipal social admission criteria. But many of the non-municipal kindergartens decided their admission criteria themselves, for example parents groups establishing kindergartens for their own children (Vollset, 2011).

It never was a prerequisite that a kindergarten should have municipal support to be eligible for state grants. All kindergartens approved in accordance with the Child Day Care Act had a right to state grants. The owners had the freedom to decide admission criteria and parental fees. When the state grants increased in accordance with the White Paper's signal of the need for establishment of kindergartens rapidly in response to increasing demand for places, the authorities created the conditions for the commercial operation of kindergartens (Vollset, 2011). Parents who could afford it were willing to pay quite a lot for a place. It was common that for instance 'day mothers' and childminders charged the same amount of money from parents as kindergartens did.

However, more recently the authorities' main political aims for the kindergarten sector have been full kindergarten coverage, lower parental fees and high quality on kindergarten services. As Vollset points out:

> Towards the end of the 1980s, it became increasingly obvious that realising the goal of daycare for every family that wanted it at an affordable price was unrealistic until the turn of the millennium at the earliest. This was the case

even though two political moves were made that reduced the queue for a daycare place by as many as two cohorts – the introduction of the one year of maternity leave and lowering of the school starting age to six.... On the other hand, the general approach to achieving sufficient daycare capacity remained unchanged; the model still consisted of municipal responsibility for the provision of daycare facilities coupled with a relatively high central government subsidy per place.... In the 1990s, private daycare centre owners operated their centres solely on the basis of government grants and high parental fees. While the economy underwent a downturn in 1988–89, bringing harder times, concern was focused on families with small children. They still had no access to childminding at a reasonable price; on the contrary, parental fees had increased substantially even in municipal daycare centres, and efforts to expand capacity had not yet benefited the youngest children. (Vollset 2011, pp 285–6)

All significant changes that have been introduced in recent decades have been made to help achieve these paramount objectives and have led to a substantial increase in the state's costs. However, in spite of public efforts, achieving the full goal of kindergarten coverage has taken a long time. The two main problems were a shortage of kindergarten places and the fact that the available places were too expensive for parents to constitute a real alternative for many families.

Owners and ownership in the kindergarten sector

There is a large variety of kindergarten owners, but there are more similarities between their services than differences, because of tight legislation. There might also be greater differences within the different kindergartens of one owner than between those of different owners. The Kindergarten Act does not legislate for ownership. The different owners may organise their ownerships in different ways. Table 7.1 shows the total numbers of kindergartens and children in 2003 and 2008. Table 7.2 illustrates the percentages in different private ownership in 2003 and 2008.

New kindergartens after the Kindergarten Settlement in 2003 were to a great extent created by the establishment of large kindergartens by municipalities or by private enterprises. The smaller kindergartens established and run by parents, local communities and different types of non-profit organisations have lost influence over recent years. There

Table 7.1: Kindergartens and children in kindergartens 2003 and 2008, by public or private ownership

	Kindergartens		Children	
	2003	2008	2003	2008
Total	5,924	6,705	205,172	261,886
Public	52.5%	46%	57.8%	54%
Private	47.5%	54%	42.2%	46%

Source: Statistics Norway

Table 7.2: Private ownership: kindergartens 2003 and 2008 and children 2008, percentages

	Kindergartens 2003	Kindergartens 2008	Children 2008
Total	3,013	3,623	120,384
Congregations	9.5	7.1	6.4
Parents	29.2	21.9	27.9
Associations of housewives, social welfare etc.	2.5	1.3	1.0
Enterprises	7.2	15.1	21.2
Pedagogical/ideological organisations	2.8	3.5	4.2
Single persons	34.5	34.0	16.8
Others	14.3	17.1	22.5

Source: Statistics Norway

has also been a clear change in direction towards non-municipal establishments rather than municipal enterprises. The majority of kindergartens are now in non-municipal ownership while the majority of children attend municipal kindergartens, even if the proportion is decreasing. The increase in public support in recent years has made it more 'attractive' or economically profitable for non-municipal enterprises to establish kindergartens.

Types of private kindergarten ownership

It is not possible to present all the different types of kindergarten ownership. An example of a non-profit private kindergarten owner is the Kanvas Foundation. Kanvas was established as a membership organisation in 1986, named Barnehageforbundet (Union of Kindergartens) as an initiative by parents. In 1992 it was converted into a non-profit foundation. All surplus income is reserved for the benefit of their purpose: kindergartens. All funds of Kanvas are reserved for strengthening the competence of their employees, to continuously improve their institutions and to develop and build new kindergartens. The kindergartens have non-economic goals; any surplus income remains with the kindergarten concerned and is used to improve quality or held back as an economic reserve.

Since the conversion into a non-profit foundation in 1992 Kanvas has focused on building, owning and operating kindergartens in Norway. Kanvas has a central administration in Oslo offering financial, administrative and educational services. The administration provides service, support and advice to the employees of their kindergartens, enabling them to satisfy the needs and expectations of their customers. Kanvas currently runs about 55 kindergartens in ten different municipalities across southern Norway. They employ more than 900 professionals taking care of approximately 3,000 children.

According to their website Kanvas is one of Norway's largest non-municipal actors within development and management of kindergartens. Based on a vision of 'everyday engagement' Kanvas is advocating and providing services that improve everyday life for both children and parents. They regard kindergarten as the first step in a child's lifelong education. In their care children develop safely through play until they reach the age of primary school.

Trygge Barnehager AS (Safe Kindergartens, a joint stock company) was established in 1987. According to their website they have established about 380 kindergartens all over the country. Most of these kindergartens are organised as parent cooperatives, but they have also established kindergartens for foundations, associations, enterprises, private persons and municipalities. Recently they have also established and run their own kindergartens through their running company FUS as joint stock companies. Today there are about 125 FUS kindergartens, which are organised as independent companies with great freedom to manage their own business. FUS kindergartens have non-economic goals; an economic surplus is used to improve quality or held back as an economic reserve if the decision is made to allow the surplus to remain with the kindergarten concerned (see Trygge Barnehager's website).

Norway's oldest and largest chain of private family kindergartens Noetteliten og Hakkebakkeskogen familiebarnehage was established in Oslo in 1996. They have now 31 family kindergarten units in private homes, where they rent the ground or first floor to use as family kindergarten. They have eight or nine children under the age of 3 in each department together with two assistants, and a staff of ten qualified preschool teachers to supervise each group once a week. These family kindergartens are owned and run as a business owned by a sole owner. The greatest difference between these family kindergartens and ordinary kindergartens for this age group is that there is no preschool teacher available in the groups on a daily basis (see website). This way of running kindergartens is less expensive than if there were preschool teachers available daily.

Parents' satisfaction with ECEC services

In the past 20 years surveys and evaluations have shown that parents with children in kindergartens are satisfied with the service and experience good cooperation with the kindergartens (Gulbrandsen and Sundnes, 2004). As a whole it seems as if parents with children in private kindergartens are more positive on questions about cooperation than parents with children in public kindergartens, but the differences are small. Parents with low income are less content concerning cooperation with staff than parents with higher income (TNS Gallup, 2008).

Conclusions

The provision of kindergarten services in Norway has never been a typical economic activity. The kindergarten sector has for several decades been defined as part of the public sector, even if not directly provided by them, and has been financially dependent upon the municipal and public authorities, with the state fixing parents' fees from 2004.

When it comes to the increase in non-municipal services and social entrepreneurs, we see parallels in several parts of the Norwegian public welfare services, but not within the education sector, as most children in Norway attend state school. As we have seen, the Norwegian kindergarten sector has always had a large element of private actors. The lack of kindergarten places in the 1990s gave rise to high parental fees, while the fees cap, the maximum fees policy, prevents such prices today. The strong regulation of all kindergartens, independent of ownership, means that there are few systematic differences between municipal and non-municipal kindergartens. The exceptions are the few who offer, for instance, Montessori pedagogy or have a specific religious content. Families' freedom of choice is emphasised. Surveys among users show that most families want a kindergarten close to where they live. It is obvious that both the non-municipal and the public kindergartens have the possibility of delivering equal and equitable services. The childcare supply in Norway is of a very different kind compared with the reliance on for-profit care which exists elsewhere.

Note

[1] Translations into the English language have mostly been done by the authors or their colleagues, as little of the background material for this chapter is available in English.

References

Gulbrandsen, L. and Sundnes, A. (2004) *Fra best til bedre? Kvalitetssatsing i norske barnehager. Statusrapport ved kvalitetssatsingsperiodens slutt (From best to better: Quality promotion in Norwegian kindergartens. Status at the end of the period of quality improvement)* NOVA report no. 9/04, Oslo.

Norwegian Ministry of Children and Family Affairs (1998) *OECD – Background report: Thematic review of early childhood education and care policy in Norway*, www.oecd.org/dataoecd/48/53/2476185.pdf

Norwegian Ministry of Children and Family Affairs (1999) *St. meld. nr. 27 (1999–2000) Barnehage til beste for barn og foreldre (White Paper no. 27 (1999–2000) Kindergartens to the best of children and parents)*, Oslo: Norwegian Ministry of Children and Family Affairs.

Norwegian Ministry of Children and Family Affairs (2004) *Regulation no 539 of 19 March 2004 on equivalent treatment of kindergartens with regard to public subsidies*, Oslo: Norwegian Ministry of Children and Family Affairs.

Norwegian Ministry of Consumer Affairs and Government Administration (1988) *St. meld. nr. 8 (1987–88) Barnehager mot arr 2000 (Kindergartens towards the year 2000)*, White Paper, Oslo: Norwegian Ministry of Consumer Affairs and Government Administration.

Norwegian Ministry of Education and Research (2006) *Framework Plan for the Content and Tasks of Kindergartens*, www.regjeringen.no/upload/KD/Vedlegg/Barnehager/engelsk/Framework%20Plan%20for%20the%20Content%20and%20Tasks%20of%20Kindergartens.pdf

Norwegian Ministry of Education and Research (2010) *Forskrift 2010–10–29–1370 om likeverdig behandling ved tildeling av offentlige tilskudd til ikke-kommunale barnehager (Regulation No. 1370 of 29 October 2010 on equivalent treatment of kindergartens with regard to public subsidies)*, Oslo: Norwegian Ministry of Education and Research.

Norwegian Ministry of Education and Research (2011) *Framework Plan for the Content and Tasks of Kindergartens* [amended], www.regjeringen.no/upload/KD/Vedlegg/Barnehager/engelsk/Framework_Plan_for_the_Content_and_Tasks_of_Kindergartens_2011.pdf

Norwegian Ministry of Health and Care (1995) *Forskrift 1995–12–01 nr. 928 om miljoerettet helsevern i barnehage og skole* (*Regulation on environmental health care in kindergarten and school* [not available in English]), www.lovdata.no/cgi-wift/ldles?doc=/sf/sf/sf-19951201–0928.html

Norwegian Ministry of Local Government and Regional Development: The General Purpose Grant Scheme, www.regjeringen.no/en/dep/krd/Subjects/kommuneokonomi/the-general-purpose-grant-scheme.html?id=540083

Plattform for regjeringssamarbeidet mellom Arbeiderpartiet, Sosialistisk Venstreparti og Senterpartiet 2005–09 (the Soria Moria platform for governmental cooperation between the Labour Party, the Socialist Left Party and the Centre Party, 13 October 2005), www.regjeringen.no/upload/SMK/Vedlegg/2005/regjeringsplatform_SoriaMoria.pdf

Statistics Norway (2010) *Kindergartens*, Oslo, www.ssb.no/english/subjects/04/02/10/barnehager_en/

Stortinget (2000) Innst. S. nr. 207 (1999-2000) Innstilling fra familie-, kultur- og administrasjonskomiteen om Barnehager til beste for barn og foreldre (Recommendation from the standing committee on family, cultural and public administration affairs on Kindergartens to the best for children and families).

TNS Gallup (2008) *Undersoekelse om foreldres tilfredshet med barnehagetilbudet* (*Survey concerning parents' satisfaction with kindergartens*), Oslo: TNS Gallup.

Vollset, G. (2011) 'Familiepolitikkens historie – 1970 til 2000', The history of family policy 1970-2000', NOVA report no 1/11, Oslo.

EIGHT

Childcare markets in the US: supply and demand, quality and cost, and public policy

Laura Stout Sosinsky

Introduction

The dual functions of childcare, as a service to parents to support employment and as a service to children to support child development, are sometimes in conflict in the United States' market-based system (Edie, 2006; Prentice, 2009). This tension is seen in the manner in which services are structured by private for-profit providers and non-profit providers and in the public policies that intersect with childcare. Childcare provision and use is also tied to a larger debate in the US about the extent to which childrearing is a private good, benefiting families as private consumers, or a public good, benefiting society as a whole by nurturing the development of individuals who are more likely to be productive, self-sufficient citizens (Helburn, 1999). The dominant attitude in the US has been to consider the family as a private unit, to place high value on individual responsibility, and to limit government involvement in matters related to family (Meyers and Gornick, 2003; Brauner et al, 2004). Thus, there is no overall national child or family policy and no centralised federal oversight of children's services (OECD, 2004). A federal Comprehensive Child Development Act passed Congress in 1971, but was then vetoed by President Nixon, who stated in his veto message that 'the Federal Government's role wherever possible should be one of assisting parents to purchase needed daycare services in the private, open market, with Federal involvement in direct provision of such services kept to an absolute minimum' (as quoted in Zigler et al, 2009, p 37; see also Cohen, 2001). Similarly, federal quality standards failed in 1980 after 13 years of effort (Cohen, 2001; Zigler et al, 2009). Regulatory oversight and most administration of early care and education services lie instead with the individual states. State standards vary widely but are largely considered inadequate

(Zigler et al, 2009). Public funding for childcare has risen in recent years to historically high levels, but the most recent data available indicate total expenditure of US$20.4 billion on children from birth to age 5 in 2004 amounted to 0.2% of gross domestic product (GDP) compared with 3.7% of GDP on primary and secondary education in 2007 (OECD, 2004, 2007).

Most public early care and education funds are directed at children at risk due to living in poverty, such as means-tested childcare subsidies and public preschool programmes. A recent trend towards increasing public expenditure on preschool may suggest changing views towards early childhood education and care (ECEC) as a public good (Shonkoff, 2011), perhaps as a compensatory support for at-risk children's development, or even as an economic investment for all children (Prentice, 2009), though growth slowed in the current economic downturn (Barnett et al, 2010). However, despite calls for universal pre-kindergarten provision (Zigler et al, 2006), 32 programmes in the 40 states funding pre-kindergarten provision are means-tested, and many are half-day, academic-year programmes (Barnett et al, 2010), targeting some children's educational needs but falling short of supporting parents' employment. Such structural differences between childcare and preschool are manifestations of the view that care and education are separate issues, despite decades of research highlighting that quality developmentally appropriate care must include education. Childcare is often viewed as custodial care to meet basic physical care, health and safety needs while the parent works, while early education is viewed as developmentally appropriate practices fostering a child's cognitive, social and emotional development (Brauner et al, 2004).

Tensions surrounding ECEC as a public or private good and as a work or child development support contribute to a mixed bag or patchwork of childcare services (Zigler et al, 2009, p 6) which are 'expensive, fragmented, and scarce' (Prentice, 2009, p 687). This patchwork has been identified as a major issue for policy attention that leads to confusion, uneven quality and inequality of access (OECD, 2006). Despite growing demand for childcare services, and a large and growing body of evidence that childcare is a primary childrearing environment of importance 'second only to the immediate family' (Shonkoff and Phillips, 2000, p 297), the US continues to face a 'crisis' in childcare that was first identified decades ago (Keyserling, 1972; Zigler and Ennis, 1989). The lack of progress in the intervening years towards the creation of a coherent childcare system has been regarded as a 'tragedy' (Zigler et al, 2009).

This chapter will discuss the US ECEC market in terms of (1) the demand for, current usage of, and costs of centre-based childcare services; (2) the supply of, quality of, and workforce in this childcare market by for-profit or non-profit status; (3) relevant public policies, for example subsidies, tax credits, quality rating and information systems, and (4) parent choice factors in the US childcare market, for example provision of information, parent demand for specific childcare characteristics and ability to choose based on those characteristics. Although school-age childcare is also extremely important to consider, the focus in this chapter will be on early care from birth to age 5. The implications for future policy directions will be discussed.

Childcare demand and uptake

US demand for non-parental childcare is rooted in rising employment rates among mothers of children under 6 years, which began in the 1940s, reached 64% in 1999, and has remained steady. Employment rose fastest among women with children under one year, soaring from 20% in 1973 to 62% in 2000 (Goldin, 2006). At childbirth, unpaid maternity leave is the typical solution among US mothers. The 1993 passage of the Family and Medical Leave Act covered about 50% of the workforce with unpaid, job-protected 12-week leave. Three states have passed paid family leave laws in recent years (Fass, 2009). Among private-sector employees 83% receive unpaid leave and only 3% receive paid family leave (Tang and Wadsworth, 2008), and only 10% of respondents to a 2000 FMLA survey reported taking more than 60 days for maternity leave (Galtry and Callister, 2005).

Throughout the early years after childbirth, childcare challenges continue. Some mothers face work requirements if they are receiving public benefits given the reforms to welfare passed by Congress in 1996 (Robins, 2007). Many mothers feel strong financial motivation or even pressure to work, especially in single parent households, or have strong incentive to work for short- and long-term financial security, interest and preference, or all of these. Many parents want their children to have childcare experiences, seeing potential benefit of ECEC for their children, particularly preschoolers (Sosinsky, 2011), a perception supported by research (NICHD ECCRN, 2002b).

Nearly two thirds of US children under 5 – 12.7 million – were in childcare each week in 2007 (Laughlin, 2010). Statistics for rates of enrolment in various types of programme are compiled by a variety of governmental agencies and private research institutions on different schedules; here the most recent available data for each type of programme are reported. Of children in ECEC, 37% were in organised facilities (centres, nursery schools, preschools, Head Start programmes, and kindergarten for children under 5), 45% were cared for by a relative, 9% were in family childcare homes, and the rest were cared for by non-relatives; overall hours averaged 32 per week (Laughlin, 2010).

Among preschoolers, 58% of children aged 3–6 and not yet in kindergarten attended preschool or a childcare centre in 2007 (O'Donnell, 2008). About 14% of 3-year-olds and 40% of 4-year-olds were in public state funded pre-kindergarten and Head Start programmes in 2009 (Barnett et al, 2010); the rest in ECEC were in private programmes. Among infants and toddlers under age 3, about 62% were in non-parental childcare regularly each week in 2005, 18% in centre care, 35% in relative care, 10% in family childcare (FCC) homes and the rest in a variety of informal arrangements (Laughlin, 2010); 95% of this was privately funded (Meyers and Gornick, 2003).

Childcare supply and cost

The supply of childcare in the US is a complex mix of for-profit and non-profit formal centre-based settings, regulated home-based settings such as family daycare homes, and unregulated formal settings such as legally licence-exempt centres such as those run by religious organisations, unregulated informal settings, such as kith-and-kin care, informal babysitting arrangements and illegally operating unregulated family daycare homes. Market-based businesses, funded mostly by parent fees, provide a greater part of formal early care and education services in the US than do public formal arrangements for children from birth to age 5.

The first national study of childcare supply and demand in over 20 years in the US, the National Study of Early Care and Education (NSECE), will begin in 2012 (Datta et al, 2010). Until complete, estimates of childcare supply can be drawn from a variety of data sources compiled by the National Child Care Information and Technical Assistance Center and the National Association for Regulatory Administration (NCCITAC and NARA, 2008). The supply of formal registered childcare can be quantified by the number of licensed childcare facilities and places, but this is complicated by state-by-state variations in licensing policies beginning with the types of facility that each state makes subject to or exempt from licensing. Most childcare centres in all 50 states are subject to state licensing, which primarily includes health and safety regulations (Idaho was the last state to require centre licensing beginning in January 2010). Most states also license

FCC homes, although some states only license specific types of FCC, and three states do not license FCC providers at all.

There are almost 330,000 licensed facilities in the US as of 2008, the majority of which are FCC homes, providing more than 9.8 million licensed childcare places, most of which are in centres. Elements determining licence exemption can include the number of children served, hours of operation, and operation by a religious organisation, detailed more below.

There are over 107,000 licensed childcare centres in the US, with a capacity to serve over 7.4 million children. States commonly define a childcare centre as a facility serving a minimum of 13 children and operating less than 24 hours per day. About half of the states exempt facilities operating part-day or part-week which may include preschool and Head Start programmes; almost 40% of states exempt preschool programmes operated by public schools or systems, and about one quarter of the states exempt facilities operated by religious organisations from licensing regulations.

The costs of centre-based full-time care averaged USD15,900 [GBP8,163] for infants and USD11,680 [GBP5,996] for 4-year-olds per year in 2008; FCC costs can be 15–30% lower (NACCRRA, 2009). US parents pay a substantial amount for early care and education, both as a percentage of their household income and as a percentage of the total per-child cost of services. Working families spend 9% of earnings on childcare on average, but high-earning families spend about 6% of earnings while low-earning families spend about 16% on childcare (Giannarelli and Barsimantov, 2000). Among families at less than 100% of the federal poverty threshold, those who paid for childcare paid 28% of their monthly income on childcare in 2005 (US Census Bureau, 2005); the federal poverty level is intended to represent the minimum amount of income to support a family at a basic level for their family size and composition and thresholds are used to determine eligibility for public programmes including childcare subsidies and Head Start, though thresholds based on the current poverty measure are widely considered to be too low (for example, the poverty threshold was USD22,350 [GBP12,324] for a family of four in 2010).

In one analysis of the allocation of costs between private family funds and public funds, public funds covered an estimated 41% of all early care and education for 3- to 5-year-olds, with parents funding the remaining 59%. Estimating the share of costs by parents and public funds for care for infants and toddlers under 3 years is even more difficult, as rates vary by state and programme and family income (Meyers and

Gornick, 2003), but in the 1990s, fewer than 5% of infants were served in public care or receiving public subsidies for care.

Childcare quality and regulation

Examinations of the quality of care available in the US have revealed that the modal quality of care is mediocre or adequate (NICHD ECCRN, 1996; NICHD ECCRN, 2000; Coley et al, 2006). Low quality childcare has been identified by many as an urgent problem requiring immediate national attention (OECD, 2004; Zigler et al, 2009). Licensing and regulatory standards in most states have been found to be inadequate to promote optimal child development, and in many states standards are so low as to endanger child health and safety (Zigler et al, 2009).

For example, the National Association for the Education of Young Children (NAEYC, 2004) recommends infant-to-staff ratios of no more than 3 to 1, but in 2007 only three states' requirements were 3 or 3.5 to 1, whereas fourteen states had ratios of 5 or 6 to 1 (NCCITAC and NARA, 2008), hampering even basic safety procedures such as emergency fire evacuations.

For-profit and non-profit centres

About 71% of childcare centres are run as for-profit enterprises, as determined by those subject to federal income tax. Of these, 15% are multi-unit enterprises that own or operate two or more establishments (US Economic Census, 2007). About one third are run by for-profit chains, often publically traded but not always, such as KinderCare Learning Centers, the largest in North America, with 1,770 centres and a capacity of 250,000 places, Learning Care Group, Inc., Bright Horizons Family Solutions and many others, plus several national childcare franchising organisations such as Kids R Kids International and Goddard Systems, Inc. (Neugebauer, 2008). The remainder of for-profit centres is run by local independent or small chains with a handful of locations in a small geographic area.

About 29% of childcare centres are run as non-profit enterprises, as determined by those that are exempt from federal income tax. Of these, 43% are multi-unit enterprises that own or operate two or more establishments (US Economic Census, 2007). These childcare centres are run by a large mix of non-profit organisations. These include independent non-profit local small organisations, national organisations such as Easter Seals and the YMCA, public agency organisations, state pre-kindergarten services, or federally funded Head Start programmes, some of which are self-contained and some of which are other types of centres which receive a certain amount of funding from these public lines. They also include religiously affiliated centres operated by churches, synagogues or other religious organisations.

Numbers and proportions of providers have shifted over the past decade and a half since the implementation of a childcare voucher system as part of the 1996 Welfare Reform Act prompted increased supply to meet the growing demand from families moving off welfare. Between 1997 and 2002 there was a large first-response increase in the number of non-profits to represent a shift from about 30% to 35% of centres. But by 2007 the for-profit supply increased by 20% over the decade, and the percentage of non-profits shifted to about 29% of centres (Warner and Gradus, 2011).

For-profit centres are controlled by owners/shareholders who receive excess income or profit, and must pay federal and state corporate income taxes, payroll taxes, sales taxes and property taxes. They are primarily supported by parent fees, and possibly by owner/shareholder contributions. Non-profit centres are controlled by a board of directors, cannot distribute excess income to individuals but may use it only to further the mission of the centre, are exempt from federal and state corporate income tax and may be exempt from sales and property taxes, though not from payroll taxes.

Changes in public subsidy policies, described further below, and the funding structure of public ECEC programmes have blurred the line between for-profit and non-profit centres' funding sources. Most federal funds are granted to state agencies and the rest directly to local entities to provide services or tax credits. Public subsidies that go directly to parents through certificates (vouchers), can be used for any public or private provider who meets state standards, for example licensed or legally licence exempt (NCCITAC, 2010). Private providers are increasingly relying on subsidies, and non-profits are increasingly relying on parent fees. One recent partial list of the largest non-profit childcare organisations in North America found that, although a small number depended on public fees for 80–90% of their support, the majority depended on parent fees for 70–80% of their budgets (Neugebauer, 2010). Federally administered Head Start and Early Head Start grants and many states' pre-kindergarten funds can go to local non-profit and for-profit programmes (Barnett et al, 2010; NCCITAC, 2010).

In order to stay in operation, both for-profit and non-profit centres must balance the need to keep quality high with the need to keep costs low. Centres bear large labour costs owing to quality standards and regulations (minimal as they may be), and are unable to increase efficiency through technology or other productivity improvements owing to the labour-intensive nature of childcare provision (Morgan, 2005). Competition for parents as clients often cuts across sector and subsector lines, with the tightest competition among subsectors that serve mainly unsubsidised children of middle-income working families because of heavy reliance on parent fees for revenue, including for-profit chains, non-profit independents and religiously affiliated and operated centres (Helburn and Bergmann, 2002).

Centre quality by profit status

Quality in US childcare centres has been characterised as poor to mediocre (Helburn, 1995). Non-profit centres have systematically higher quality levels than for-profit centres in several studies, with one exception (Helburn, 1995), though differences are small and not found on all indicators or for care in all age groups (Morris and Helburn, 2000; Helburn and Bergmann, 2002; Sosinsky et al, 2007).

An analysis of data from the NICHD Study of Early Child Care, the most comprehensive study of early childcare to date, found higher quality on staffing characteristics (child–staff ratios and higher caregiver education levels) and more positive caregiver–child interactions in non-profit centres in classrooms serving several age groups (Sosinsky et al, 2007). Caregivers in non-profit non-religiously affiliated centres generally received the highest wages, had the lowest turnover rates, and had the highest levels of professionalism among classrooms serving 4- to 5-year-olds of all auspices. Auspice had a unique effect; controlling for family selection bias and quality variations in staff and structural characteristics, for-profit chains provided lower-quality caregiver–child interactions compared with all other subsectors. One example of an exception is Bright Horizons Family Solutions, a for-profit chain company contracting with employers to provide on- or near-site childcare, which has achieved NAEYC accreditation, to be discussed later, in over 80% of its centres (Zigler et al, 2009).

The childcare workforce

The existence, and rapid expansion, of the private childcare market in the US has been facilitated by minimal barriers to entry (for example training requirements); virtually anyone can get a job in a childcare centre or open a home-based family daycare programme. This, combined with low public support for social services, weak or nonexistent ECEC workforce unions, and large availability of low-skilled workers (mostly women), has contributed to the large supply of private market-based childcare services (Morgan, 2005). Given low barriers to entry and dependence on limited parent fees, childcare is one of the worst paying jobs in the US. The mean hourly wage for childcare workers in 2008 was USD11.32 [GBP5.81] (Bureau of Labor Statistics, 2011). Caregiver wages are typically higher in non-profit centres than in for-profit chains (Sosinsky et al, 2007). Childcare workers earn 53–66% of the average wages of all employed women (Gornick and Meyers, 2003), and most childcare workers are not offered health insurance benefits through their employer (Bureau of Labor Statistics, 2011), so the workforce is essentially subsidising the private childcare market (Morgan, 2005).

Personnel costs make up the largest portion of the budget of most centres (Morgan, 2005), and personnel are key to quality (NICHD ECCRN, 2002a). Since childcare is so labour intensive, and the private-market childcare providers are heavily dependent on parent fees, there is a 'direct relationship between the price parents pay and the wages received by childcare workers' (Morgan, 2005, p 248). This has the added effect of contributing to the unequal access to higher quality childcare. Parents who can pay more can access childcare services that pay their workers more, and caregiver wages are positively correlated with quality (Sosinsky et al, 2007).

Intersection of public policies and childcare supply and demand

Childcare policies can directly and/or indirectly influence the supply of childcare availability and quality and influence the demand for childcare by constraining or freeing parent choices (for example childcare subsidy policies can be narrow or flexible, maternity leave policies may be strict or generous). Most US public funds for childcare are targeted at the work support function of childcare and aim to increase affordability and access by lowering or subsidising per-child costs, or aim increase available places (Edie, 2006). Comparably few funds focus target the child development function of childcare, though the frame may be shifting (Prentice 2009; Shonkoff, 2011).

Childcare subsidies to help eligible low-income families pay for childcare while parents work or participate in education and training are funded largely through federal and state Child Care and Development Fund (CCDF) funds, as block grants to the states. This programme was a product of the 1996 Welfare Reform Law, which gave states greater flexibility in designing their own systems and increased federal funds for childcare subsidies from USD2.1 billion [GBP1,284,480,000] in 1997 to USD7.4 billion [GBP4,934,350,000] in 2000 (Golden, 2005). Because of inadequate funding levels, made worse in current fiscal troubles, most states ration care by setting their income eligibility levels below the federally allowed level of 85% of their state median income (Kreader, 2005), raising family co-payments, and placing more families on waiting lists (Edie, 2006).

More generous subsidy policies showed some success at supporting parental employment, increasing childcare subsidy use, lowering parent costs, reducing childcare problems that interfered with parental work, increasing use of formal care over informal care (Gennetian et al, 2002; Press et al, 2006), and helping make childcare more stable (Drentea et al, 2004). But subsidised childcare shows less success at supporting child development. Subsidised childcare quality was lower than non-subsidy-eligible childcare quality (Helburn, 1999; Jones-Branch et al, 2004; Weinraub et al, 2005), except when subsidy policies were more generous (for example more funds, higher income eligibility), especially in non-profit childcare centres (Fuller et al, 2003; Rigby et al, 2007).

Further, specific policy provisions aimed at maximising subsidy uptake, which is low (Golden, 2005), may have unintended negative effects on quality. State subsidy rates are often lower than market rates to subsidise more children, but rates are often too low to pay fees at high quality childcare settings in most communities (Helburn, 1999). Centres thus may be compelled to raise unsubsidised families' fees, lower quality levels to keep costs down, or limit or refuse vouchers because of low reimbursement rates (Washington and Reed, 2008).

Childcare tax credits through the Child and Dependent Care Tax Credit (CDCTC) are intended to lower the financial burden of families' childcare costs by issuing a tax credit to families with employed parents who pay for childcare services. The CDCTC limits the total allowable amount of the claim to USD3,000 [GBP1,824] for one child and USD6,000 [GBP355] for two or more children, which is far below the average annual childcare expenditure for full-time care in a centre or FCC, especially infant care (NACCRRA, 2009). The tax credit, intended to be progressive, is graduated on a sliding scale ranging from 20% for higher-income taxpayers to 35% for low-income taxpayers. But the CDCTC is non-refundable, so families cannot benefit from the tax credit in excess of the amount they owe in federal income taxes, and families with incomes too low to have tax liability cannot benefit from the tax credit at all. In 2006, the top fifth of income earners received 41% of CDCTC benefits, while the bottom 40% received only 4% (Rohaly, 2007).

Parent choice: at the intersection of supply and demand

The basic assumption of a market-based system of childcare is that consumers – parents – demand high quality childcare, and that this demand will increase the supply of high quality care as providers compete for consumers (Blau, 2001b). Private childcare markets, unlike public systems, are also assumed to respond to consumer demands with more flexibility, innovation and efficiency (Penn, 2009). For a childcare market to function well, parents must have adequate information to evaluate providers' quality. Without this information, parents will not be willing to pay more for higher quality care. Providers will either not be willing to provide more expensive higher quality care or will be priced out of the market by competition with lower quality centres. Inadequate quality information can therefore fill the market with low quality providers creating a market for 'lemons' (Blau, 2001b; Mocan, 2007).

In addition, elasticity becomes a concern if parent fees are the only source of revenue to cover quality-improvement cost increases. One analysis found that the cost of increasing quality from mediocre to good would be relatively modest – between 12 and 16 cents per child-hour (Mocan, 2007), or between USD392 [GBP266] and USD523 [GBP355] per child per year in 2010 dollars (US Bureau of Labor Statistics, 2011). However, centre-based providers already operate on extremely small margins of income and earnings (Whitaker, 2001; Helburn and Bergmann, 2002) and parents are already paying 6–28% of income on childcare expenses (Giannarelli and Barsimantov, 2000; US Census Bureau, 2005). Therefore, while some have proposed that elasticity in the childcare market is due to parent unwillingness or inability to pay higher prices for higher quality (Blau, 2001a), or to parents trading high quality for convenience (see Plantenga in this volume), even small price increases may drive consumers away and cause higher quality providers to exit the market (Mocan, 2007). Plus, most parents value quality, in terms of features such as trustworthiness, loving and responsible adult care, safety, or provider's qualifications and behaviour, above other childcare factors including convenience or even price (Farkas et al, 2000, p 908; Pungello and Kurtz-Costes, 1999, p 533; Sosinsky, 2011) and are willing to pay more for desirable childcare characteristics (Shlay et al, 2005).

Despite the value parents place on quality, childcare quality may be hard for parents to determine. During initial searches which can incur significant time and financial costs, many parents are first-time purchasers of childcare with little experience and immediate needs (Sosinsky, 2011). Parents are the purchasers, but not the recipients of childcare and are not in the best position to judge its quality (Helburn, 1999). The US childcare market is not well organised to inform parents of their options and provides asymmetric information to parents (Mocan, 2007). Few parents contact childcare resource and referral agencies (CCR&Rs) and those who do may find little benefit (Pungello and Kurtz-Costes, 1999; Leach et al, 2006). CCR&Rs have been historically weak though systems have grown in recent years (Zigler et al, 2009). All CCR&Rs provide information on licensing and accreditation, but only 25% provide quality indicators to parents such as child–staff ratios and caregiver training levels (Smith et al, 2003).

In the absence of better information, parents may rely on informal social networks, which may be limited and biased resources (Meyers and Jordan, 2006; Sosinsky, 2011), and may make decisions based on unsupported assumptions or on proxy indicators of childcare quality of varying accuracy (Mocan, 2007). For example, parents may consider higher-cost care, relative care, or faith-based auspice, but not consider publically owned status, as markers of high quality (Honig and Bornstein, 1995; Kuhlthau and Mason, 1996), despite evidence to the contrary (Kontos et al, 1995; Morris and Helburn, 2000; Mocan, 2007; Sosinsky et al, 2007; Dowsett et al, 2008).

Other researchers, however, report that parents can judge detailed and basic aspects of quality with reliability and validity (Shlay et al, 2005; Emlen, 2010), suggesting that parent-information initiatives might help, such as accreditation by private non-profit professional associations and quality rating and improvement systems (QRIS) by state agencies. Accreditation by NAEYC, which sets professional standards for ECEC programmes, provides national, voluntary accreditation and helps families identify high quality programmes, and has been shown to lead to improved and sustained quality (Whitebook et al, 2004), but only about 7,000 programmes, or less than 7%, are accredited.

Quality Rating and Information Systems (QRIS), in use or development in just over half of the states (26) as of writing this, employ a consumer-driven approach to quality improvement. QRIS aim to raise quality with standards, evaluations and monitoring, practitioner outreach and support, financing incentives and, finally, parent/consumer education, by means of easily recognisable rating symbols such as stars. However, parent outreach receives between less than 1% and 10% of states' QRIS budgets (Tout et al, 2010) and evaluation of effectiveness at helping parents choose higher quality care has barely begun. Parents unfamiliar with QRIS had mixed reactions to a description, with some considering it a moderately useful tool, but others not trusting state governments to carry out ratings competently or without bias (Sosinsky, 2011).

How well does the childcare market align with parents' childcare decision making? There is a positive correlation between family income and centre care quality, suggesting that parents who demand high quality and pay more actually obtain higher quality childcare, but the correlation is modest (Burchinal and Nelson, 2000). In part this may be due to a curvilinear relationship between quality and family income, as some low-income families have access to higher quality care than they otherwise would via subsidies. However, traditional financial and consumer issues are rarely the only deciding factors in a family's childcare choice. Would parents choose an arrangement that ECEC experts rate as 'high quality' if they could afford it? Possibly, but parents must make feasible childcare arrangements, which of course includes affordability but also must include central, pragmatic factors in the quality of family life. An arrangement might be poor quality for a family if it involves long or difficult commutes increasing strain and reducing opportunities to engage with each other (Emlen, 2010), is inflexible and unreliable (Gennetian et al, 2002), causes undue financial strain, or disrupts workplace effectiveness through increased worry and absenteeism (Emlen, 2010).

Beliefs and values also play a role in parental childcare decision making. Focus group and mixed-method research reveals that many parents have a deep-seated fear that their child will be unhappy or suffer in someone else's care (Farkas et al, 2000; Sosinsky, 2011). Mothers with a greater belief that maternal employment might harm their child later chose higher quality childcare (Sosinsky, 2005). Centre-based care in particular invites seemingly contradictory beliefs. Many parents, regardless of income, believe centre care provides more educational benefits, especially for preschoolers, but many lower-income families have far stronger misgivings about centre care than more affluent parents (Chaudry, 2004; Sosinsky, 2011). But for low-income families in particular, the 'heightened fear and wariness... may well reflect their experience of what is available to them in their neighbourhoods – a case of "what they see is what they are afraid they'll get"' (Farkas et al, 2000, p 22).

Conclusion

Many factors involved with choosing childcare in the US do not match well with traditional supply-and-demand assumptions. But beyond that, considering the work-support and child development functions of childcare, it may be asked, is it the best frame to consider childcare a service that can work on market principles? Childcare as support for parental employment and family self-sufficiency is certainly complicated. Childcare as support for child development, however, has importance beyond that of most other typical consumer choices especially in the early years when change is rapid and early experiences can having lasting effects (Shonkoff and Phillips, 2000) and when low quality is known to be detrimental (NICHD ECCRN, 2002b). Certainly parents and those viewing childrearing as a 'private good' see childcare in this light, but increasingly ECEC may be seen from a 'public good' perspective (Shonkoff, 2011). At the base level, as a public, there is recognition that childcare cannot be a pure free market and must be regulated (Penn, 2009). But the limited scope and minimal-to-inadequate level of regulations in the US reveal a contradiction that many developmentalists have decried (Zigler et al, 2009).

The mixed-sector childcare market in the US is likely to remain in place for the near future. There is little political will to offer new national initiatives, and political forces range widely on all sides of the debate. Some would support a federal or state role in ECEC, others would oppose it for ideological reasons, maintaining for example that any increase in public childcare dollars is discrimination against stay-at-home mothers (Cohen, 2001), and still others will avoid the issue of childcare altogether, as it is so entwined with the controversial issues of maternal employment (Morgan, 2005). Initiatives such as QRIS are aiming to take advantage of market forces to improve the supply of high quality childcare and parents' ability to demand it by incentivising high quality and by publicising professional childcare quality ratings to give parents more tools and better information to use in their choice to reduce the market for 'lemons' (Mocan, 2007). It is too early to say whether QRIS will have a positive impact on the overall US supply of high quality childcare. But childcare choices, so intertwined with maternal work decisions, are complex, dynamic, nonlinear, and interdependent, and are made more so by the complexity of the mixed market of childcare provision in the United States.

References

Barnett, W. S., Epstein, D. J., Carolan, M. E., Fitzgerald, J., Ackerman, D. J. and Friedman, A. H. (2010) *The state of preschool 2010: State preschool yearbook*, New Brunswick, NJ: The National Institute for Early Education Research, Rutgers, The State University of New Jersey.

Blau, D. M. (2001a) *The child care problem: An economic analysis*, New York: Russell Sage Foundation.

Blau, D. M. (2001b) 'Rethinking US child care policy', *Issues in Science and Technology*, vol 18, no 2, pp 66–72.

Brauner, J., Gordic, B. and Zigler, E. F. (2004) 'Putting the child back into child care: Combining care and education for children ages 3–5', *SRCD Social Policy Report*, vol 28, no 3, pp 3–15.

Burchinal, M. R. and Nelson, L. (2000) 'Family selection and child care experiences: Implications for studies of child outcomes', *Early Childhood Research Quarterly*, vol 15, no 3, pp 385–411.

Bureau of Labor Statistics (2011) *Career guide to industries, 2010–11 edition, child day care services*, Washington, DC: US Department of Labor.

Chaudry, A. (2004) *Putting children first: How low-wage working mothers manage child care*, New York: Russell Sage Foundation.

Cohen, S. S. (2001) *Championing child care*, New York: Columbia University Press.

Coley, R. L., Li-Grining, C. P. and Chase-Lansdale, P. L. (2006) 'Low-income families' child-care experiences: Meeting the needs of children and families', in N. Cabrera, R. Hutchens and H.E. Peters (eds) *From welfare to child care: What happens to young children when mothers exchange welfare for work*, Mahwah, NJ: Lawrence Erlbaum Associates Publishers, pp 149–170.

Datta, A. R., Goerge, R. and Yan, T. (2010) *Design phase of the national study of child care supply and demand (NSCCSD)*, Final Report, Chicago, IL: National Opinion Research Center at the University of Chicago.

Dowsett, C. J., Huston, A. C., Imes, A. E. and Gennetian, L. (2008) 'Structural and process features in three types of child care for children from high and low income families', *Early Childhood Research Quarterly*, vol 23, no 1, pp 69–93.

Drentea, P., Durham, S., Mwaria, M., Norman, E. and Xi, J. (2004) 'Day care hopping: Stabilizing day care options for low-income mothers through subsidies', *Child Care in Practice*, vol 10, no 4, pp 381–393.

Edie, D. (2006) 'Toward a new child care policy (Brief 2)', *Perspectives on Low-Income Working Families*, Washington, DC: The Urban Institute.

Emlen, A. C. (2010) *Solving the childcare and flexibility puzzle: How working parents make the best feasible choices and what that means for public policy*, Boca Raton, FL: Universal-Publishers.

Farkas, S., Duffet, A. and Johnson, J. (2000) *Necessary compromises: How parents, employers, and children's advocates view child care today*, Washington, DC: Public Agenda.

Fass, S. (2009) *Paid leave in the States: A critical support for low-wage workers and their families*, New York: National Center for Children in Poverty.

Fuller, B., Holloway, S. D., Bozzi, L., Burr, E., Cohen, N. and Suzuki, S. (2003) 'Explaining local variability in child care quality: State funding and regulation in California', *Early Education & Development*, vol 14, no 1, pp 47–66.

Galtry, J. and Callister, P. (2005) 'Assessing the optimal length of parental leave for child and parental wellbeing: How can research inform policy?' *Journal of Family Issues*, vol 26, no 2, pp 219–246.

Gennetian, L. A., Huston, A. C., Crosby, D. A., Chang, Y. E., Lowe, E. D. and Weisner, T. S. (2002) *Making child care choices: How welfare and work policies influence parents' decisions, the next generation project*. New York: Manpower Research Demonstration Corporation.

Giannarelli, L. and Barsimantov, J. (2000) *Child care expenses of America's families*, Washington, DC: The Urban Institute.

Golden, O. A. (2005) *Assessing the new federalism: Eight years later*, Washington, DC: The Urban Institute.

Goldin, C. (2006) 'The quiet revolution that transformed women's employment, education, and family', *American Economic Review*, vol 96, no 2, pp 1–21.

Gornick, J. C. and Meyers, M. K. (2003) *Families that work: Policies for reconciling parenthood and employment*, New York: Russell Sage Foundation.

Helburn, S. W. (1995) *Cost, quality, and child outcomes in child care centers*, technical report. Denver, CO: Department of Economics, Center for Research in Economics and Social Policy, University of Colorado at Denver.

Helburn, S. W. (1999) 'The silent crisis in U.S. childcare: Preface', *The Annals of the American Academy of Political and Social Science*, vol 563, no 1, pp 8–19.

Helburn, S. W. and Bergmann, B. R. (2002) *America's child care problem: The way out*, New York: Palgrave MacMillan.

Honig, A. S. and Bornstein, M. H. (1995) 'Choosing child care for young children', *Handbook of parenting, vol 4: Applied and practical parenting*. Hillsdale, NJ England: Lawrence Erlbaum Associates, Inc, pp 411–435.

Jones-Branch, J. A., Torquati, J. C., Raikes, H. and Edwards, C. P. (2004) 'Child care subsidy and quality', *Early Education and Development*, vol 15, no 3, pp 327–341.

Keyserling, M. D. (1972) *Windows on day care*, New York: National Council of Jewish Women.

Kontos, S., Howes, C., Shinn, M. and Galinsky, E. (1995) *Quality in family child care and relative care*, New York: Teachers College Press.

Kreader, J. L. (2005) *Introduction to child care subsidy research*, New York: National Center for Children in Poverty, Child Care & Early Education Research Connections.

Kuhlthau, K. and Mason, K. O. (1996) 'Market child care versus care by relatives: Choices made by employed and nonemployed mothers', *Journal of Family Issues*, vol 17, no 4, pp 561–578.

Laughlin, L. (2010) 'Who's minding the kids? Child care arrangements', Spring 2005 and Summer 2006, *Current Population Reports*, pp 70–121. Washington, DC: US Census Bureau.

Leach, P., Barnes, J., Nichols, M., Goldin, J., Stein, A., Sylva, K. and Malmberg, L.-E. (2006) 'Child care before 6 months of age: A qualitative study of mothers' decisions and feelings about employment and non-maternal care', *Infant and Child Development*, vol 15, no 5, pp 471–502.

Meyers, M. K. and Gornick, J. C. (2003) 'Public or private responsibility? Early childhood education and care, inequality, and the welfare state', *Journal of Comparative Family Studies*, vol 34, no 3, pp 379–411.

Meyers, M. K. and Jordan, L. P. (2006) 'Choice and accommodation in parental child care decisions', *Community Development, Journal of the Community Development Society*, vol 37, no 2, pp 53–70.

Mocan, H. N. (2007) 'Can consumers detect lemons? An empirical analysis of information asymmetry in the market for child care', *Journal of Population Economics*, vol 20, no 4, pp 743–780.

Morgan, K. J. (2005) 'The "production" of child care: How labor markets shape social policy and vice versa', *Social Politics: International Studies in Gender, State & Society*, vol 12, no 2, pp 243–263.

Morris, J. R. and Helburn, S. W. (2000) 'Child care center quality differences: the role of profit status, client preferences, and trust', *Nonprofit and Voluntary Sector Quarterly*, vol 29, no 3, pp 377–399.

National Association for the Education of Young Children. (2004) *Final Draft Accreditation Performance Criteria* [Online]. Available: www.naeyc. org/accreditation/naeyc_accred/draft_standards/ter.html

National Association of Child Care Resource and Referral Agencies (2009) *Parents and the high price of child care: 2009 update*, Washington, DC: National Association of Child Care Resource & Referral Agencies.

National Child Care Information and Technical Assistance Center. (2010) *Federal and state funding for early care and education.* Washington, DC: U.S. Department of Health and Human Services Administration for Children and Families Retrieved from http://nccic.acf.hhs.gov/poptopics/ecarefunding.html

National Child Care Information and Technical Assistance Center & National Association for Regulatory Administration (2008) *The 2008 Child Care Licensing Study*, Lexington, KY: National Association for Regulatory Administration Retrieved from www.naralicensing.org/associations/4734/files/1005_2008_Child%20Care%20Licensing%20Study_Full_Report.pdf.

Neugebauer, R. (2008) *Challenges and opportunities in early childhood: Views of the CEOs of the Big Three: twenty-first annual status report on for profit child care. Exchange* [Online], 179. Available: www.childcareexchange.com

Neugebauer, R. (2010) *Non profit leaders face new realities: Status report on non profit care. Exchange* [Online]. Available: www.childcareexchange.com.

NICHD Early Child Care Research Network (1996) 'Characteristics of infant child care: Factors contributing to positive caregiving', *Early Childhood Research Quarterly*, vol 11, no 3, pp 269–306.

NICHD Early Child Care Research Network (2000) 'Characteristics and quality of child care for toddlers and preschoolers', *Applied Developmental Science*, vol 4, no 3, pp 116–135.

NICHD Early Child Care Research Network (2002a) 'Child-care structure--process--outcome: direct and indirect effects of child-care quality on young children's development', *Psychological Science*, vol 13, no 3, pp 199–206.

NICHD Early Child Care Research Network (2002b) 'Early child care and children's development prior to school entry: Results from the NICHD Study of Early Child Care', *American Educational Research Journal*, vol 39, no 1, pp 133–164.

O'Donnell, K. (2008) *Parents' reports of the school readiness of young children from the National Household Education Surveys Program of 2007 (NCES 2008–051)*, Washington, DC: National Center for Education Statistics, Institute of Education Sciences, US Department of Education.

OECD (2004) *Early childhood education and care - Country profile: United States.* Available: www.oecd.org/dataoecd/16/14/37423831.pdf

OECD (2006) *Starting strong II: Early childhood education and care.* Paris, France: OECD

OECD (2007) *Education at a glance 2010: OECD indicators* [Online]. Paris, France. Available: www.oecd.org/document/52/0,3746, en_2649_39263231_45897844_1_1_1_1,00.html

Penn, H. (2009) 'International perspectives on quality in mixed economies of childcare', *National Institute Economic Review*, vol 207, no 1, pp 83–89.

Prentice, S. (2009) 'High stakes: The "investable" child and the economic reframing of childcare', *Signs*, vol 34, no 3, pp 687–710.

Press, J. E., Fagan, J. and Laughlin, L. (2006) 'Taking pressure off families: Child-care subsidies lessen mothers' work-hour problems', *Journal of Marriage and Family*, vol 68, no 1, pp 155–171.

Pungello, E. P. and Kurtz-Costes, B. (1999) 'Why and how working women choose child care: A review with a focus on infancy', *Developmental Review*, vol 19, no 1, pp 31–96.

Rigby, E., Ryan, R. M. and Brooks-Gunn, J. (2007) 'Child care quality in different policy contexts', *Journal of Policy Analysis and Management*, vol 26, no 4, pp 887–907.

Robins, P. K. (2007) 'Welfare reform and child care: Evidence from 10 experimental welfare-to-work programs', *Evaluation Review*, vol 31, no 5, pp 440–468.

Rohaly, J. (2007) *Reforming the child and dependent care tax credit.* Washington, DC: Tax Policy Center; Urban Institute and Brookings Institution.

Shlay, A. B., Tran, H., Weinraub, M. and Harmon, M. (2005) 'Teasing apart the child care conundrum: A factorial survey analysis of perceptions of child care quality, fair market price and willingness to pay by low-income, African American parents', *Early Childhood Research Quarterly*, vol 20, no 4, pp 393–416.

Shonkoff, J. P. (2011) Leveraging science for a new era in early childhood policy and practice, *The Edward Zigler Biennial Meeting of the Society for Research in Child Development Policy Pre-Conference*, Montreal, Canada.

Shonkoff, J. P. and Phillips, D. A. (2000) *From neurons to neighborhoods: the science of early childhood development*, Washington, DC, National Academy Press.

Smith, L., Vinci, Y. and Galvan, M. (2003) *Poised for shaping results-based early learning systems: A report on child care resource and referral in the United States*, Washington, DC: National Association of Child Care Resource and Referral Agencies

Sosinsky, L. S. (2005) 'Parental selection of child care quality: Income, demographic risk and beliefs about harm of maternal employment to children', *Dissertation Abstracts International: Section B: The Sciences and Engineering*, vol 66, no 3-B, pp 1762.

Sosinsky, L. S. (2011) 'New mothers' child care choices and the role of trust', 4th National Research Conference on Child and Family Programs and Policy, Bridgewater, MA.

Sosinsky, L. S., Lord, H. and Zigler, E. (2007) 'For-profit/nonprofit differences in center-based child care quality: Results from the National Institute of Child Health and Human Development Study of Early Child Care and Youth Development', *Journal of Applied Developmental Psychology*, vol 28, no 5, pp 390–410.

Tang, C.-Y. and Wadsworth, S. M. (2008) *2008 National study of the changing workforce: Time and workplace flexibility*, New York: Families and Work Institute.

Tout, K., Starr, R., Soli, M., Moodie, S., Kirby, G. and Boller, K. (2010) *Compendium of quality rating systems and evaluations*, Washington, DC: Child Trends and Mathematica Policy Research.

US Bureau of Labor Statistics (2011) *Consumer Price Index (CPI) Inflation Calculator* [Online].

US Census Bureau (2005) *Who's minding the kids? Child care arrangements: Spring 2005*, US Census Bureau, Housing and Household Economic Statistics Division, Fertility & Family Statistics Branch.

US Economic Census (2007), Employer and non employer data, Washington, DC: US Census Bureau, www.census.gov (accessed November 2011).

Warner, M. E. and Gradus, R. H. J. M. (2011) 'The consequences of implementing a child care voucher scheme: Evidence from Australia, the Netherlands, and the USA', *Social Policy & Administration*, vol 45, no 5, pp 569–592.

Washington, V. and Reed, M. (2008) 'A study of the Massachusetts child care voucher system: Impact on children, families, providers, and resource and referral agencies', *Families in Society*, vol 89, no 2, pp 202–207.

Weinraub, M., Shlay, A. B., Harmon, M. and Tran, H. (2005) 'Subsidizing child care: How child care subsidies affect the child care used by low-income African American families', *Early Childhood Research Quarterly*, vol 20, no 4, pp 373–392.

Whitebook, M., Sakai, L. M. and Howes, C. (2004) 'Improving and sustaining center quality: The role of NAEYC accreditation and staff stability', *Early Education & Development*, vol 15, no 3, pp 305–325.

Whitaker, B. (2001) 'Business; child care: An industry for all economic seasons', *The New York Times*, 16 December.

Zigler, E. and Ennis, P. (1989) 'The child care crisis in America', *Canadian Psychology*, vol 30, no 2, pp 116–125.

Zigler, E., Gilliam, W. S. and Jones, S. M. (2006) *A vision for universal preschool education*, Cambridge, New York: Cambridge University Press

Zigler, E., Marsland, K. W. and Lord, H. (2009) *The tragedy of child care in America*, New Haven, CT: Yale University Press.

NINE

Canadian ECEC labour shortages: big, costly and solvable

Robert Fairholm and Jerome Davis

Introduction

Canada's early childhood education and care (ECEC) sector is primarily under the jurisdiction of the provinces and territories. Each jurisdiction has its own distinct set of regulations, programmes and policies. These differences result in a diverse mix of employment settings, training requirements and availability of regulated childcare places. Despite the myriad of approaches there are a number of striking similarities in the ECEC labour market outcomes throughout Canada. The sector faces low pay, high staff turnover and persistent workforce shortages. ECEC workforce shortages are extremely costly given the short- and long-term benefits delivered by *quality* ECEC. The dynamics of Canada's ECEC labour market are unique compared with other nations. Parents are price sensitive, labour supply is extremely responsive to wage increases and governments regularly short-circuit labour market outcomes. Expansion of services in this sector often leads to a lessening of quality as more inexperienced staff are taken on. This chapter illustrates the magnitude of workforce shortages in the Canadian ECEC sector and what can be done to end Canada's recruitment and retention crisis.

The Canadian context

In Canada almost all ECEC services are under the jurisdiction of the provinces/territories. Each province/territory has a unique situation with distinct approaches to regulation, funding and policy. Provincial/territorial childcare regulations provide a baseline of health and safety standards (Doherty et al, 2003; OECD, 2004). There are differences in the types of service that are regulated and the requirements across provinces/territories, but there are a number of common features. All provinces and territories regulate childcare centres for children younger than school age and family childcare homes, though depending on the province/territory nursery schools/preschools, school-age childcare programmes and Aboriginal Head Start may or may not be regulated under the childcare legislation. Each province/territory regulates the maximum number of children that may be cared for in an unregulated family childcare home. This section relies on information provided by Doherty et al (2003) and OECD (2004). See these reports for a more thorough discussion of the Canadian situation.

There is a diverse set of regulations for childcare centres across provinces/territories according to Child Care Resource and Research Unit data (Beach et al, 2009) For example, in 2008:

- Staff–child ratios for infants in centres ranged from 1:3 in seven provinces/territories to 1:5 in Québec. The definition of infants ranged from 0–12 months in Alberta, Northwest Territories and Nunavut to 0–3 years in British Columbia (BC).
- Staff–child ratios for children of school age ranged from 1:10 in two territories and BC (if children in kindergarten or grade one were included) to 1:20 in Québec. The definition of school age ranged from 5 years and over to 7 years and over.
- Most provinces/territories specify a maximum group size for each age group, Prince Edward Island and Nova Scotia set maximum group sizes for the youngest age groups, and Québec does not stipulate the maximum group size for any age.
- Six of the provinces/territories stipulate the maximum size for centres.

Training requirements for staff vary widely. Some provinces/territories have no post-secondary training requirements for any or all staff. In contrast, Manitoba requires that at least two thirds of the staff have at least two years of post-secondary early childhood education (ECE) training. In 2005 Québec required that one third of staff have two years of ECE training, but in 2006 they announced that by 2011 two thirds of staff would be required to have two years of ECE training.

- For family childcare homes, standards address: the maximum number of children permitted in the home and the allowable mix by age category; whether the provider is required to have training; requirements for indoor and outdoor play space; record keeping; practices around substitute family childcare providers for emergency situations; back-up care arrangements; and health and safety measures (Doherty et al, 2003).

The large variation in regulations/standards for centre and family childcare means there is a large variation of outcomes across provinces/territories. In 2008, 83% of regulated ECEC places were delivered via childcare centres.

There is also a large variation in the percentage of places supplied by for-profit versus non-profit providers across the country. Most of the non-profit providers are privately operated usually by parent groups, voluntary organisations or other non-profit entities (OECD, 2004). In some provinces municipalities supply childcare places, in most they do not. In Ontario local governments have mandated roles in childcare services, which include funding, managing services and policy setting. In Québec, school boards provide school-age places where there is a demonstrated need.

Even though there is a wide degree of regulatory, policy and programme differences across Canada there are a number of similarities in the qualifications profile of staff. According to the 2006 census 'early childhood educators and assistants' in all provinces/territories have a relatively high proportion of workers with college level of education, although this varies considerably across Canada. In the Canadian economy a higher level of educational attainment is typically associated with greater economic success as manifested in lower unemployment rates, higher employment rates and higher wages. Early childhood educators and assistants (ECE&A) have distinctly lower unemployment rates and higher employment rates than other occupations throughout Canada. The 2006 census shows that for Canada as a whole, the ECE&A occupational unemployment rate was 2.6% lower than the national average.

Despite the lower unemployment rates, higher employment rates and the relatively large number of ECE&A workers who have post-secondary education than the average workers in Canada, wages for ECE&A workers are below the national average. According to the census, the average wage for full-year, full-time work for ECE&A was 41.3% of the average Canadian wage. And ECE&A with a BA earned roughly 46% of the wage earned by all workers with that level of education.

Demand for early childhood education and care

The demand for early childhood educators (ECEs) is directly linked to the demand for ECEC services and to the provincial/territorial regulations for staff–child ratios. These regulations mean that childcare centres cannot substitute technology for workers, as can happen in other industries (Warner et al, 2003). Therefore to understand the Canadian ECEC labour market it is essential to first understand the dynamics of the demand for ECEC services. The literature that examines the demand for ECEC services suggests that the Canada's demand for ECEC services has several unusual aspects.

At the most basic level all young children need care, whether parental or non-parental. There has been considerable economic research into the factors that influence the primary caregiver's decision to use non-parental care, the type of care selected and quantity used. The research has primarily focused on the decision to use services that enable the mother to be in the labour market. According to Chevalier et al (2006), the economic model underlying much of the empirical work in the ECEC literature is a *basic labour supply model*. The basic labour supply model is augmented with the childcare dimension in order to examine the joint decision regarding the mother's labour force participation and the use of childcare. The augmented model includes factors that influence the amount of non-parental childcare needed, such as:

- the availability of formal and informal childcare
- the ability to afford formal care, and
- the parents' and the children's preferences and tastes.

Factors that raise a mother's take-home pay (after work and childcare costs) will increase the probability of labour force participation and the use of childcare. This means that factors that raise the cost of childcare paid by the household will lower the probability that childcare services will be used and the mother will participate in the labour force.

Numerous studies have examined the impact of ECEC costs on mothers' labour force participation. They consistently find that higher ECEC fees are related to lower demand for ECEC services and lower labour force participation. One way to measure how much demand changes, based on a change in price, is the price elasticity of demand. This measure indicates how much demand will change in percentage terms from a 1% price increase. There is a large range of estimated outcomes for childcare services.

Relatively small price elasticities are reported by Blau and Hagy (1998) (−0.34) and Chaplin et al (1999) (−0.41) for US centre-based care, and Doiron and Kalb (2005) found for Australia that the price elasticities of demand for formal care ranged from −0.3 to −0.6 for couples, depending on the age of the child. In contrast, Connelly and Kimmel (2003), Powell (2002) and Cleveland et al (1996) all report estimates of −1.0 or larger; the latter two studies were for Canadian parents. Powell (2002) estimated the price elasticity between −1.37 and −1.99. Michalopoulos and Robins (2000) combined US and Canadian parents and reports price elasticities of −1.08 for formal childcare centres. Notably, most of the above studies that examined Canadian data showed the largest price elasticities of all the countries examined, implying that Canadian parents are more price-sensitive than parents in other countries.

Researchers find that demand for ECEC rises with women's wages and that wage elasticity (percentage change in demand relative to a 1% increase in wages) is positive for both formal and informal childcare. Choné et al (2003) estimated the wage elasticity of 0.7 to 0.77 for France, while Cleveland et al. (1996) estimated an elasticity of 0.18 for Canada and Ribar's (1995) US study found a range from 0.14 to 0.76. Blau and Hagy's (1998) US study found a wage elasticity of 0.67. These estimates put wage elasticity for Canadian mothers below that for other countries.

The literature on elasticities cited above shows that Canadian parents respond more to price changes and less to wage gains than parents in other countries. This means the demand dynamic is very different in Canada than elsewhere. For example, if both real wages and price for ECEC services rise by the same amount, demand for ECEC would rise in the US, but fall in Canada.

Notably, the literature discussed earlier tends to be focused on the *quantity* of ECEC services. However, it is essential to also examine the demand for ECEC *quality*.

A failure to communicate quality

Blau (2001) provides an extensive overview of the childcare market in the US with an emphasis on the issue of quality. Other reviews of childcare quality are by Hayes et al (1990), Lamb (1998) and Love et al (1996).

Blau and Mocan (2002) found that on average US parents of young children are unwilling to spend significantly more on formal care in order to obtain higher quality care. This result may be because parents simply do not have enough information to assess the quality of a childcare provider. The parents of young children might suffer from information asymmetry, which is exhibited when parents interpret the signals of quality incorrectly, for example equating clean reception areas with high quality ECEC. Furthermore, Mocan's (2001) US study suggests that operators of centres with clean reception areas tend to take advantage of parents' lack of knowledge by providing a lower level of quality for unobservable items. These results provide a partial explanation as to why the private market might result in low average childcare quality (Chevalier et al, 2006).

Asymmetric information in this instance can be described as a market failure. Cleveland and Krashinsky (1998) discuss various market failures in the ECEC market, including those caused by parents' lack of information on quality, educational benefits and future earnings. They also discuss the impact of market failure from credit market constraints that prevent people borrowing against future earnings. According to Cleveland and Krashinsky one of the implications of these market failures is that higher quality childcare services are underused, while lower quality services are overused. Given that quality ECEC is shown to provide both private benefits to the parents and children as well as additional positive social benefits (positive externalities), then the market will result in less quality childcare being used than that which is socially optimal. Blau (2001) for example believes that the main problem with the childcare market in the US is low quality. Market failure is a general reason for governments to intervene in the marketplace to achieve a more socially optimal level of consumption.

Most of the research that examines government policies focuses on policies that encourage an increase in the quantity of ECEC and mothers' labour force participation, and not on the implications for the quality of ECEC used. Chevalier et al's (2006) study suggests there is an inherent policy trade-off between the quantity and quality of childcare. Policies that encourage employment would allow parents flexibility in choice of quality of childcare, and policies that are most likely to encourage the use of high quality services would not impose employment requirements. Blau (2001) argues for subsidies tied to the level of quality.

Since one of the market failures in the ECEC sector is related to asymmetric information, one strategy would be for governments to make information publicly available about the quality of services offered by different providers to improve the operation of the market. In this way, parents could more easily include quality in their decision making process. At the margin, parents would shift their children to centres with higher quality ratings, centres would respond by trying to retain trained workers through higher wages, and lower quality centres would try to improve the training of their workforce. Alternatively, government policies can directly provide high quality services or influence structural quality of ECEC services through regulations for child–staff ratios, educational requirements of staff and group sizes. Other policies that affect quality include training grants and wage subsidies based on level of training.

Responsive labour supply

It is essential to understand how labour supply responds to wages and other benefits and costs of working in ECEC. There is, however, a lack of research on the elasticity of Canadian ECEC labour supply with respect to wages. The implied relative responsiveness of the Canadian ECEC labour supply can be put into context by using Canadian data with US elasticities.

From 2001 to 2008 the number of regulated places in Canada increased by 46.1% (5.6% on average per year). During this time, total employment in the 'Child Day-Care Services' industry increased by 36.8% (4.6% on average) and employment of workers paid by the hour in the childcare industry increased by 34.8% (4.4% on average) compared with an increase of 15.0% (2.0% on average) in total industrial employment. During this time, average weekly earnings (including overtime) for all employees in the ECEC sector rose by 21.4% (2.8% on average), while employees paid by the hour in the industry saw gains of 8.2% (1.1% on average). Over this period, consumer price inflation was 16.7% (2.2% on average). These data suggest that all employees in the ECEC industry saw real wage gains of 4.8% (0.6% on average) from 2001 to 2008, while workers paid by the hour saw a real decline of 8.4% (−1.1% on average).

The increase in regulated spaces from 2001 to 2008 represents a shifting out of the demand curve for ECEC employees. Normally, this should cause the real wage for ECEC workers to increase. The exact wage increase is determined by the slope of the supply curve, which reflects the wage elasticity of labour. Blau (2001) estimated an elasticity of 1.15 and Blau (1993) estimated 1.2–1.9 for the US. These figures mean that the supply curve is very elastic since they are above 1.

It should be noted that the labour supply curve will never be downward sloping because workers prefer more income to less. Even if the elasticity of labour supply is infinite, the labour supply curve would be horizontal, which implies that real wages would be constant as demand increased. Therefore, the real wage decline for hourly paid Canadian employees despite the strong increase in demand cannot be explained by the shape of the labour supply curve alone.

While imperfect competition, or discrimination (Cleveland and Hyatt, 2002), or the labour donation hypothesis (Mocan and Tekin, 2000) might explain low wages, these factors cannot explain falling real wages in the face of strong demand unless the downward pressure on wages from one or more of these sources became more intense from 2001 to 2008, which seems implausible. A more likely explanation is that the supply curve shifted out significantly and moderated or lowered real wages despite the increase in demand.

Cleveland and Hyatt (2002) suggest there might be locational monopoly power. For the ECEC services market as a whole, however, there is not, because as the price elasticity of demand rises monopoly power falls. The Lerner index, a measure of monopoly power, equals the inverse of the price elasticity of demand. Since the Canadian ECEC sector is very price elastic there would not be significant monopoly power in the overall market for which the price elasticity is measured. At most there could be locational market power, which is called monopolistic competition in the literature. The outcome for monopolistic competition depends on whether there are entry barriers and their magnitude.

Similarly, for inputs the degree of monopsonistic exploitation varies inverse with the supply elasticity of that input with respect to the price of that input. In the context of labour, if labour supply is very responsive to wages then a disproportionate number of workers would work less or not work if wages fall. Since the literature suggests the labour supply elasticity with respect to wages is very large, there is little if any monopsony power in the overall market. At most there could be monopsonistic competition because of locational market power.

The demand analysis that is presented in Appendix 9.1 suggests that the supply curve shifted out significantly and lowered the real wage rate even though demand for labour increased sharply from 2001 to 2008. Such a shift in supply might occur if, for example, a large influx of lower qualified people sought employment in the ECEC sector. Chevalier et al (2006) suggested that employers hire less qualified staff when faced with a rise in demand, which moderates the rise in wages. This phenomenon appears to be at work in Canada.

In Canada there have been instances when childcare centres have sought exemptions to the training regulations. For example, in Manitoba in 2001, 39% of childcare centres had an exemption from staff education restrictions owing to problems with recruiting enough qualified staff

(Mayer, 2001). And interviews with stakeholders in the sector suggest that the number of educational exemptions given by governments rise during periods of rapid demand increases. This means that governments are short-circuiting the labour market outcome, which should be for higher demand to lead to higher wages for trained workers. Instead there is downward pressure on wages as less qualified workers enter the workforce. This dynamic will remain as long as the primary focus of governments is on the quantity of ECEC services as opposed to the quality of ECEC services.

Staff turnover

Low wages discourage qualified workers to stay in the ECEC sector because college trained workers can earn higher wages elsewhere. An analysis of the labour force survey and census data by Fairholm (2009b) suggests there is a much higher turnover rate in this occupation than for all occupations. Also he found that the ECEC sector's recruitment challenges are primarily caused by staff turnover, with close to nine of every ten new recruits being required to replace existing staff.

Moreover, the 2006 census data show that most of the people who are trained to work in the ECEC sector have either left the sector or never entered. These data illustrate that the most common qualification of those employed in the ECEC sector is a college diploma with a specialisation in ECE (Classification of Instructional Programs, 19.0709 Child Care Provider/Assistant). Of those people with this qualification, only 35.7% worked in the ECEC sector, 41.2% were employed in other sectors of the economy, 19.4% had dropped out of the labour force altogether and 3.8% were unemployed.

Quit rates are influenced by both monetary and non-monetary benefits. One way to increase non-monetary benefits of a job is to improve job satisfaction. Improvements in job satisfaction can be more cost effective than changes in monetary benefits. Changing the job satisfaction rate from completely dissatisfied to completely satisfied would lower the quit rate dramatically and be the equivalent to a huge increase in pay. For women, monetary factors matter less than for men, but working conditions and a higher degree of flexibility carry a larger weight in their job preferences. The literature on job satisfaction indicates that human resource management (HRM) practices can influence workers' overall job satisfaction and their satisfaction with pay. Therefore changes in and improvements of HRM could provide fairly low cost improvements in recruitment and retention challenges faced by the ECEC sector (Fairholm, 2009b).

Public policy has a direct impact on the recruitment and retention of ECEC workers. To date the primary focus by governments have been on expanding places and increasing the quantity of workers available. The best choice for governments would be to encourage an increase in the number of trained ECE workers working in the sector, which would improve the general quality of ECEC services. And Fairholm (2009b) indicates that the retention of more qualified workers could lead to a virtuous cycle whereby the retention of more qualified workers would improve working conditions, which would reduce quit rates and help to retain other qualified workers.

Turnover and the resulting workforce shortages are the bane of this sector. Without concerted action ECEC workforce shortages are likely to occur more often in this sector than in other sectors and to persist for longer (Fairholm, 2009b). To understand the size of the problem the authors estimated the magnitude of workforce shortages.

Workforce shortage estimates

A detailed discussion of the methods used to estimate workforce shortages in ECEC in Canada is given in Appendix 9.2.

To estimate workforce shortages, vacancies and structural unemployment are subtracted from the unemployment rate to give a workforce surplus rate. Multiplying the workforce surplus rate by potential employment (the employment that would be created if all vacancies were filled) gives the number of surplus workers. Worker surpluses or shortages for Canada and each province during the period 1998–2007 are listed in Table 9.1. Positive values indicate a surplus of workers and negative values indicate a shortage of workers.

Table 9.1: Worker surplus (number of ECEC workers)

	1998	1999	2000	2001	2002	2003	2004	2005	2006	2007
Canada	2,726	1,446	469	−664	−1,868	−2,949	−3,853	−4,865	−5,775	−4,802
Newfoundland and Labrador	98	88	46	47	28	23	−1	−23	−39	−88
Prince Edward Island	35	37	38	42	41	33	28	28	17	26
Nova Scotia	166	114	79	60	32	11	−17	−39	−81	−84
New Brunswick	170	93	87	75	75	54	60	50	32	73
Quebec	599	331	72	−290	−555	−994	−1,240	−1,498	−2,030	−1,429
Ontario	1,780	1,160	783	346	−87	−414	−687	−1,130	−1,405	−1,035
Manitoba	−7	−52	−104	−150	−189	−225	−274	−310	398	−325
Saskatchewan	35	11	−6	−19	−33	−57	−70	−91	−89	−142
Alberta	80	−28	−192	−271	−338	−505	−559	−599	−728	624
British Columbia	569	350	258	111	23	−101	−248	−371	−520	−429

Source: Fairholm (2009c)

Nationwide there has been a workforce shortage since 2001, which has steadily increased each year. In 2007, there was a workforce shortage of around 5,000 ECEC workers. The largest shortages were in Québec and Ontario with roughly 1,400 and 1,000 respectively. The Atlantic Provinces are least affected by workforce shortages, but these estimates might be influenced by data quality issues with respect to the rounding of the data to the nearest 100 people in the Labour Force Survey. For example, an examination of census data shows that provinces without an overall workforce shortage have shortages of qualified workers. And workforce shortages, particularly for qualified staff, matter because they have short- and long-term implications for the economy and society at large.

Socioeconomic benefits of ECEC

To understand the implications of workforce shortages for the economy it is essential to first determine the net benefits of ECEC. Economic benefits and costs of ECEC programmes can be examined in the long term or short term. The literature that estimates long-term benefits and costs of quality ECEC programmes consistently shows that benefits outweigh costs (Cleveland and Krashinsky, 1998; Belfield, 2005; Karoly and Bigelow, 2005; Chevalier et al, 2006; Temple and Reynolds, 2007; Kilburn and Karoly, 2008; Fairholm, 2009d; Fairholm and Davis, 2010). The magnitude of the benefits and costs as well as the benefit–cost ratio depends on the characteristics of the children. Disadvantaged children benefit the most from quality ECEC. For example, for the US, the Carolina Abecedarian and High Scope/Perry Programs show costs being repaid several times over, with the calculated benefit–cost ratio being 3.8:1 (Masse and Barnett, 2002).

Other types of ECEC programs show positive – albeit generally smaller – net benefits to society per dollar spent. Kilburn and Karoly (2008) cite an average of 48 preschool programmes that have a benefit–cost ratio of 2.4. Karoly and Bigelow (2005) estimate that a universal ECEC programme in California would yield a benefit-cost ratio of 2–4:1 (depending on the assumptions). Belfield (2005) estimates future benefits exceed costs by a ratio of 2.3:1 for the Louisiana ECEC system. Chevalier et al (2006) estimate that a universal programme in Ireland will yield an astonishing benefit-cost ratio of 4.6–7.1:1 (depending on the assumptions).

For Canada, Cleveland and Krashinsky (1998) estimate that a universal high quality ECEC programme will return a benefit-cost ratio of more than 2:1. Fairholm (2009d) found that the net present value of benefits exceed costs by a factor of 2.5:1. And Fairholm and Davis (2010) found that for Ontario the introduction of the proposals recommended by Pascal (2009) would provide a benefit–cost ratio of 2.0:1 for ongoing operations. Notably, these latter recommendations included an increase in labour income for qualified early childhood educators by 83% to a level above the provincial average.

There are a number of studies that examine the short-term economic effect of an increase in activity (called output in the economic literature) in the ECEC sector. For Canada as a whole the multiplier that includes direct, indirect and induced effects is 2.3 dollars of increased economic activity per initial dollar of spending (Fairholm, 2009d).

Conclusion

The Canadian ECEC sector faces several market failures that make workforce shortages worse and therefore cause short- and long-term losses to the economy. Market failures are a reason why governments can intervene in the market to ensure a more socially optimal outcome. Since the full long-term gains of ECEC require the provision of quality services, which require trained staff, the overarching objective should be to expand quality ECEC services.

To help alleviate the problems in the ECEC sector governments have several options ranging from the market oriented to public oriented solutions. A market oriented solution would be to make the ECEC product and labour markets work better. This can be done by addressing market failures. For example, they can provide information on the quality of ECEC services. A public oriented solution would be to directly provide quality ECEC services to all who need these services, similar to the provision of primary school education.

Another option for governments would be to change regulations to ensure that only qualified ECEs provide these services, and stop issuing educational exemptions, so that the full benefits of early childhood education are obtained. A further option for governments would be to subsidise the consumption or production of quality ECEC services. Finally employers in the sector can help themselves by addressing their recruitment and retention challenges by improving human resource management practices, which will improve job satisfaction and reduce quit rates and have the potential to kick start a virtuous cycle of gains.

References

Beach, J., Friendly, M., Ferns, C., Prabhu, N. and Forer, B. (2009) *Early childhood education and care in Canada 2008*, Toronto, Ca: Childcare Resource and Research Unit, 8th edition.

Belfield, C. R. (2005) 'An economic analysis of Pre-K in Louisiana', Pre-K Now, June, pp 1–16.

Blau, D. (1993) 'The supply of child care labor', *Journal of Labor Economics*, vol 1, no 2, pp 324–347.

Blau, D. (2001) *The child care problem: An economic analysis*, New York: Russell Sage Foundation.

Blau, D. and A. Hagy (1998) 'The demand for quality in child care', *Journal of Political Economy*, vol 106, no 1, pp 104–46.

Blau, D. and H. Mocan (2002) 'The supply of quality in child care centers', *Review of Economics and Statistics*, vol 84, no 3, pp 483–496.

Chaplin, D., Robins, P., Hofferth, S., Wissoker, D. and Fronstin, P. (1999) *The price sensitivity of child care demand: A sensitivity analysis*, unpublished manuscript.

Chevalier, A., Finn, C., Harmon, C. and Viitanen, T. (2006) 'The economics of early childhood care and education', Technical Research Paper for the National Economic and Social Forum.

Choné, P., Le Blanc, D. and Robert-Bobee, I. (2003) 'Female labor supply and child care in France', Working Paper, CESifo GmbH, pp 1–34.

Cleveland, G. and Krashinsky, M. (1998) *The benefits and costs of good child care: The economic rationale for public investment in young children*, Toronto, Ca: University of Toronto Centre for Urban and Community Studies, Child Care Resource and Research Unit.

Cleveland, G., Gunderson, M. and Hyatt, D. (1996) 'Child care costs and the employment decision of women: Canadian evidence', *Canadian Journal of Economics*, vol 29, no 1, pp 132–51.

Cleveland, G. and Hyatt, D. (2002) 'Child care workers' wages: New evidence on returns to education, experience, job tenure and auspice', *Journal of Population Economics*, vol 15, no 3, pp 575-597.

Connelly, R. and Kimmel, J. (2003) 'Marital status and full-time/part-time work status in child care choices', *Applied Economics*, vol 35, no 7, pp 761–777.

Doherty, G., Lero, D., Goelman, H., LaGrange, A. and Tougas, J. (2000) *You bet I care - A Canada-wide study on: Wages, working conditions, and practices in child care centres*, Guelph, Ca: Centre for Families, Work, and Well-Being, University of Guelph.

Doherty, G., Friendly, M. and Beach, J. (2003) *OECD thematic review of early childhood education and care – Canadian background report*, Paris: OECD.

Doiron, D. and Kalb, G. (2005) 'Demands for child care and household labour supply in Australia' *The Economic Record*, vol 81, no 254, pp 215–236.

Fairholm, R. (2009a) *Literature review of ECEC labour market – Understanding and addressing workforce shortages in early childhood education and care (ECEC) Project*, Ottawa, Ca: Child Care Human Resource Sector Council.

Fairholm, R. (2009b) *Recruitment and retention challenges and strategies– Understanding and addressing workforce shortages in early childhood education and care (ECEC) Project*, Ottawa, Ca: Child Care Human Resource Sector Council.

Fairholm, R. (2009c) *Estimates of workforce shortages – Understanding and addressing workforce shortages in early childhood education and care (ECEC) Project*, Ottawa, Ca: Child Care Human Resource Sector Council.

Fairholm, R. (2009d) *Literature review of socioeconomic effects and net benefits – Understanding and addressing workforce shortages in early childhood education and care (ECEC) Project*, Ottawa, Ca: Child Care Human Resource Sector Council.

Fairholm, R. and Davis, J. (2010) *Early learning and care impact analysis*, for the Atkinson Charitable Foundation. www.atkinsonfoundation.ca/updates

Hayes, C., Palmer, J. and Zaslow, M. (1990) *Who cares for America's children? Child care policy for the 1990s*, Washington, D.C.: The National Academy of Sciences Press.

Karoly, L.A. and Bigelow, J.H. (2005) *The economics of investing in universal preschool education in California*, Arlington, VA: Rand Corporation.

Kilburn M. R. and Karoly, L.A. (2008) 'The economics of early childhood policy: What the dismal science has to say about investing in children', Arlington, VA: RAND Occasional Paper.

Lamb, M. (1998) 'Non-parental childcare: Context, quality, correlates and consequences', in W. Damon (ed) *Child psychology in practice: Handbook of child psychology*, New York: Wiley, (5th edition).

Love, J., Schochet, P. and Meckstroth, A. (1996) *Are they in any real danger? What research does - and doesn't tell us about child care quality and children's well-being*, Princeton, NJ: Mathematica Policy Research.

Masse, L. and Barnett, W.S. (2002) *A benefit-cost analysis of the Abecedarian early childhood intervention*, New Brunswick, NJ: National Institute for Early Education Research

Mayer, D. (2001) *Building the career corridor: Manitoba's early childhood labour market strategy project report*, Winnipeg, MB: Manitoba Child Care Association.

Michalopoulos, C. and Robins, P. (2000) 'Employment and child care choices in Canada and the United States', *The Canadian Journal of Economics*, vol 33, no 2, pp 435–470.

Mocan, H. (2001) *Can consumers detect lemons? Information asymmetry in the market for child care.* Working Paper, no. 8291, NBER.

Mocan, H. and Tekin, E. (2000) 'Nonprofit sector and part-time work: An analysis of employer-employee matched data on child care workers', Working Paper, no. 7977, NBER.

Morissette, R. and Zhang, X. (2001) 'Which firms have high job vacancy rates in Canada', *Business and Labour Market Analysis*, no 176, Statistics Canada, pp 1–36.

OECD (2004) Early childhood education and care policy: Canada country Note, Paris: OECD.

Osberg, L. and Lin, Z. (2000) 'How much of Canada's unemployment is structural?' *Business and Labour Market Analysis*, no. 145, Statistics Canada, pp 1–31.

Pascal, C.E. (2009) *With our best future in mind: Implementing early learning in Ontario*, Report to the premier by the special advisor on early learning, Ontario: Ministry of Education.

Powell, L. (2002) 'Joint labor supply and childcare choice decisions of married mothers', *Journal of Human Resources*, vol 37, no 1, pp 106–128.

Ribar, D. (1995) 'A structural model of child care and the labor supply of married women', *Journal of Labor Economics*, vol 13, no 3, pp 558–97.

Roy, R., Henson, H. and Lavoie, C. (1996) 'A primer on skill shortages in Canada', R-96–8E, Applied Research Branch, Strategic Policy, Human Resources Development Canada, pp 1–68.

Temple, J. and Reynolds, A. (2007) 'Benefits and costs of investments in preschool education: Evidence from the Child–Parent Centers and related programs', *Economics of Education Review*, vol 26, no 1, pp 126–144.

Warner, M., Ribeiro, R., and Smith, A. (2003) 'Addressing the affordability gap: Framing child care as economic development', *Journal of Affordable Housing and Community Development Law*, vol 12, no 3, pp 294–313.

Appendix 9.1

The dynamic in the ECEC labour market can be examined using the demand analysis approach employed by Blau (2001) and Fairholm

(2009a). This method of analysis estimates what the increase in real wages should have been based on the rise in demand for ECEC workers combined with an assumed ECEC labour supply elasticity. If the actual change in the real wage is smaller than what the supply curve suggests, then we can infer that the supply curve has shifted out for some reason. Blau used a price elasticity of demand for ECEC of −0.34 and a labour cost share estimate of 0.70 in childcare centres, which implies an elasticity of demand for ECEC labour of −0.238 (−0.34*0.70). Given the supply elasticity of 1.15, a 46.2% increase in demand for ECEC would cause the real ECEC wage rate to rise by 33.2%.

As indicated by Blau (2001), the basis for the calculation is simple supply–demand analysis.

$Log(Qs)=\alpha Log(W)+Log(X),$

$Log(Qd)=\beta Log(W)+log(Y),$

Where:

Qs is the quantity of childcare labour supplied,

Qd is the quantity of childcare demanded,

α is the supply elasticity,

β is the demand elasticity,

W is the childcare wage,

X is a factor that causes supply to shift, and

Y is a factor that causes demand to shift.

In equilibrium, Qs=Qd, and we can solve for the percentage effect on ECEC wages of a given percentage demand shift as

$\Delta Log(W)=[1/(\alpha-\beta)]*\Delta Log(Y).$

In our calculations for the ECEC sector over 2001–08,

$\Delta Log(W)=[1/(1.15-(-0.238))]*\Delta Log(Y) =0.72*\Delta Log(Y).$

The observed demand shift of 46.1% means the predicted increase in real wages is 0.72*46.2%=33.2%.

Canadian demand for ECEC services is more price sensitive than in the US and labour costs represent a larger share of total costs. For example, Doherty et al (2000) found that 84.2% of total costs were labour costs (wages plus benefits). A higher price elasticity or labour cost share means the implied real wage increase is less. If we use a labour cost share of 84.2%, the highest elasticity of supply with respect to wages discussed above of 1.9, and a price elasticity of demand of $-1, -1.37$ or -1.99 then the implied real wage increase is 14.8%, 13.3% or 11.3% respectively. Notably, these implied real wage gains are larger than the 4.8% increase for all employees, and stand in complete contrast to the 8.4% drop for employees paid by the hour.

Appendix 9.2

A variety of approaches can be used to estimate the size of workforce shortages in ECEC. Fairholm (2009c) uses the UV technique, since Roy et al (1996) state that this is the simplest and most common approach used by analysts to assess the presence of a shortage or a surplus in a given occupation. Consistency in definitions of unemployment and vacancies is a must. Based on Morissette and Zhang's (2001) unemployment and vacancy definitions, the UV technique for this analysis is defined as: 'A workforce shortage exists if the number of vacancies is larger than the number of unemployed who are qualified to work in the occupation.'

For the UV technique to be successfully applied, data are needed for the number of vacancies, number of unemployed and number of unemployed who are qualified to work. Creating consistent data for these components is discussed in the following section.

Estimates of workforce shortage components

Estimating the unemployed

The national and provincial unemployment data series is given by the labour force survey. The data are quite variable, particularly for smaller provinces. To counteract this variability a Hodrick-Prescott (HP) filter is used to smooth out the data.

Estimating the unqualified unemployed

Two methods are used to give a maximum and minimum range to bracket number of unqualified unemployed. To be conservative, the lower range of 1.2% is used (these numbers would vary according to province).

For the maximum range, Osberg and Lin (2000) find that: 'less than one-eighth of the national unemployment rate could be due to structural mismatch between the skills demanded in available jobs and the skills possessed by the unemployed.' This would correspond to a maximum structural mismatch unemployment rate of 1.04% in 1998 (national unemployment was 8.3% in 1998). Adjusting for higher vacancy rates in the ECEC sector, the maximum structural mismatch unemployment rate for the ECEC sector would be 1.36%.

For the minimum range, one can look at the workers dismissed from their ECEC jobs as a percentage of all workers leaving their current ECEC job. Assuming that the currently unemployed ECEC workers are no better qualified than those leaving their jobs, the number of unqualified unemployed workers can be estimated. Doherty et al (2000) analysed the reasons for ECEC workers leaving their job and found that 21.1% are unqualified to work in the field. Multiplying this number by the unemployment rate in 1998 of 5.7% gives a mismatch unemployment rate of 1.20%.

Estimating vacancies

Vacancy rates for childcare centres nationally and by province were estimated in Doherty et al (2000). These data were generated through a survey which asks heads of childcare centres how many vacancies they currently have. However, Morissette and Zhang (2001) define vacancies as those being available to applicants outside the firm. Examining the industries most similar to ECEC from The Workplace and Employee Survey (WES) it is found that around 80% of vacancies are available to outside applicants.

Extrapolating vacancy rates

There is no times series data for vacancy rates in ECEC. However, there is an almost perfect negative correlation between The Help Wanted Index (HWI) and the unemployment rate. Therefore the ECEC specific unemployment rate can be used to extrapolate vacancies from 1998 onwards. Morissette and Zhang (2001) give two ways to estimate the vacancy–unemployment relationship. One way is to summarise the WES data where vacancy rates are listed for several levels of unemployment. The other is to regress the WES vacancy data on unemployment rates and use the estimates to generate expected vacancy rates for each level of unemployment. This report uses the summarised vacancy rates rather than the expected vacancy rates, since the summarised vacancy rates are a direct measurement rather than a proxy measurement. The vacancy rates from Morissette and Zhang (2001) are then adjusted to measure the percentage of vacancies available to outside applicants.

Morissette and Zhang (2001) indicate that there is a linear unemployment–vacancy relationship for low unemployment values. In 1998 the childcare centre unemployment rate was 5.7% and the vacancy rate was 2.9% (adjusted). At a smoothed or trend unemployment rate of 5.7% the overall industry vacancy rate was 2.3%. Therefore, to convert the general unemployment–vacancy relationship to the childcare unemployment–vacancy relationship, the results are multiplied by the ratio (2.9–2.3).

Assuming the vacancy–unemployment relationship stays constant over the period 1998–2007, the above estimates allow the extrapolation of the vacancy rates over the same time period. There seem to be large structural differences in the vacancy rates for each province, most vividly illustrated by Newfoundland and Labrador, which combines high vacancies with high unemployment.

TEN

Raw and emerging childcare markets

Helen Penn

Introduction

Childcare markets in high income countries are subject to some kind of external intervention, in the form of regulation, tax credits, subsidies, data collection and monitoring. The chapters in this book describe many such interventions, from weak demand-led interventions to very strong regulatory controls and high supply-led public subsidies. But some childcare markets are 'raw' markets, a term that I have coined to describe a situation where there is minimal or no government intervention of any kind. Examples of raw markets are commonly found in low-income countries where there are no curbs or controls on childcare entrepreneurial activities (ADEA, 2004). In raw childcare markets there is no routine information collected, no regulation and no subsidy. These circumstances exist for a variety of interconnected reasons: lack of government finance for early education and care; low prioritisation and lack of expertise within government; or more disabling still, weak or dysfunctional government or a history of national conflict. In the case of post-socialist countries it may be because the government, having once provided an entirely state-led system of ECEC, has found it difficult to consider how markets might operate and what legislation or regulation might be necessary, and entrepreneurs themselves are unsure of their rights and powers (Mandel and Humphrey, 2002). In this case I use the expression 'emerging markets' to describe the process of transition from state services to a mixed economy of childcare.

In this chapter I consider examples of childcare markets, both in low income countries, and in post-socialist countries, where there is little or no government intervention. I explore the consequences of these raw or emerging markets, for parents and for entrepreneurs themselves. First I discuss the example of Namibia, as an example of an African childcare market where there is no intervention. Then I discuss some examples of childcare markets in post-socialist countries. These examples are of interest because one of the claims for early childhood education and care is that such services can promote equity. They are supposed to enhance children's long-term chances of becoming productive adults as well as improve their more short-term opportunities in achieving good school outcomes (UNESCO, 2007). Data, admittedly much of it problematic, suggest that there has been a considerable increase in ECEC in most countries and this increase is generally held to be a sign of progress (UNESCO, 2007). But overall figures may blur considerable inequities, between rural and urban provision, between government and for-profit and non-profit provision, and between the provision accessible to educated and better off parents and provision available only to poor parents.

These trends (towards an increase in provision) risk perpetuating intergenerational poverty and inequalities and are the very opposite of internationally agreed policy priorities (Woodhead et al, 2009: p viii).

The argument of this chapter is that some structuring of the childcare market by government is necessary to achieve, or at least work towards, equity. Raw childcare markets exacerbate inequality, and are unlikely to contribute to educational goals. In emerging markets, there are some, albeit problematic, controls, but there are still considerable issues over equity.

An example of a raw market: the childcare market in Namibia

There are very few confirmatory data from African – and other low income countries – of the nature and extent of the childcare market. Reliable information, where it exists, is likely to be secondary – from household surveys and other investigations of family circumstances. On this basis, Woodhead et al (2009) suggest for example that 25% of Ethiopian children attend preschool, but they do so in an entirely private market. Other countries may have a limited amount of government provision, but it is likely that childcare provision is overwhelmingly provided by small entrepreneurs.

Nor is there much information about the entrepreneurs themselves. Entrepreneurs are lumped together with other providers as part of the spectrum of provision, by NGOs, and in rare examples, state provision, in a given country. There is rarely any consideration that their use might present particular and separate issues from other providers. For instance the recent World Bank report on policies for early child development in low income countries mentions only that governments should adopt structures and strategies which include private providers but does not discuss how or why encouraging such providers might be appropriate or inappropriate, or what controls might need to be in place (Naudau et al, 2010). Recent work by the World Bank tries to rate all countries according to the early childhood education and care (ECEC) or early child development (ECD) systems in place in their countries. This rating scale, known as SABER (System Assessment and Benchmarking Educational Results) also ignores the for-profit private sector as a category of provider. It does not include equitable access to ECEC services as an issue which must be addressed by governments seeking to develop their systems (Garcia, 2011).

This study about Namibia is therefore unusual. It arose from a sector-wide education programme funded by the EU, which was intended to develop policies to promote more equitable access to education and to reduce drop-out and improve school performance. The overall education programme, as part of its remit, proposed to invest in private entrepreneurs as a major avenue for increasing access to early childhood education and care provision, on the assumption that, as the provision already existed, it could be utilised for policy development. The data used here come from an investigation on the costs and benefits of childcare in Namibia, commissioned by the Ministry of Community and Gender Equality (MGECW) in order to inform this wider education programme. This work is reported in more detail elsewhere (Penn, 2008).

Namibia has the dubious distinction of being the world's most unequal country. Its Gini measure of inequality ratio is .74 (UNDP, 2010), that is almost twice as unequal as the US (Gini ratio .40), which itself has one of the highest ratings of any high income country. This extreme inequality in Namibia is a legacy of unequal land distribution, whereby the poorest black communities were given the poorest land, and mineral rights were given to multinational mining industries under apartheid. But nothing that has been done since independence in 1990 has been able to lessen inequality; it has only served to increase it (Penn, 2008). Promoting more equitable access to education was seen as an important attempt to reduce inequality, in the absence of economic restructuring.

Namibia is sparsely populated, and has a small and widely dispersed population administered from 13 regional centres. The capital, Windhoek, and its major township Katutura, appear to have many nurseries. The regional centres and small towns have a few nurseries of varying sophistication. In the poor, mainly rural North of Namibia, there is very little provision of any kind.

MGECW has in principle a remit to oversee childcare, to collect data about local childcare provision, disburse a small amount of capital grants to support childcare entrepreneurs, and to offer training. However in practice, this remit was largely inoperable. The agents for collecting and recording data and allocating funds were local community development officers, based at regional offices. Most of these community development officers were relocated agricultural development officers who not only had little knowledge about the childcare sector, but who also had little or no access to transport in order to visit entrepreneurs. Communication was mainly by fax, so if a centre did not have a fax it was uncontactable. Most centres did not have telephones, let alone faxes.

The only standardised data about take-up of childcare provision came from a household survey six years out of date at the time the research was carried out. A more recent piece of commissioned research from the University of Namibia covering three Northern regions suggested most of the information about centres held in the regional offices was so inaccurate as to be worthless, partly because of very high turnover (Haihambo et al, 2004). In effect there was no systematic data collection about the number of centres, the numbers, ages or circumstances of children attending, or any other information concerning the centres, and no foreseeable means of obtaining it.

There was a limited capital fund notionally available to childcare entrepreneurs to help them develop or extend their centres, but mostly this budget was unspent, partly because of the difficulty of carrying out visits or doing any kind of monitoring. There were a number of aid agencies who had contributed to childcare centres (the American embassy, Swedish SCF, the Icelandic embassy, German church organisations) but my observation was that their money went to larger and more established centres, where they could track impact, at least minimally. These charitable interventions were carried out independently of the regional officers, who may or may not have been informed about them.

Small local charities had set up various small-scale training schemes, which were very basic and not systematised or transferable. There were two childcare training officers within MEGWC, but they had few resources, and no transport budget. They were sometimes able to work with the charities, but without resources were unable to coordinate activities.

There was some talk of regulation within MGECW, but the basic problem of where to pitch standards was irresolvable. If the Ministry adopted standards from the global North, regarding health and safety, curricula, record keeping, or any other matter, most centres could not meet the minimum requirements. But to lower standards to a level where most centres could meet them made the regulation exercise largely pointless, from any professional point of view, especially since there were no personnel to oversee the implementation of regulations or support centres seeking to improve.

The centres

I went on several field trips across Namibia. I visited 20 centres in the regions, and a further ten in Katutura, the main township outside the capital, Windhoek. Some of these contacts were given to me by the MGECW. Others I found by asking a variety of local NGOs, or simply by walking or driving by. The childcare I saw varied in location from spacious well-equipped ex-nursery schools in two town centres to shacks and huts in the townships. At the top end in the two ex-nursery schools, the standards were those of the global North. Before independence there were a number of nursery schools, and nursery teacher training under the Ministry of Education. As these schools were seen as a symbol of the white elites, after independence all nursery schools were sold or disbanded, and all nursery teacher training was discontinued. The facilities of the ex-nursery schools I visited were excellent, the classrooms well resourced, the playgrounds were secure and well equipped, the teachers were trained, the class sizes were regulated and the record keeping and accounting were immaculate, and the hours were relatively short from 8.30–9 am to 5 pm. At the bottom end of the scale none of these things pertained. The facilities were typically a corrugated roofed shack without running water and at best a pit latrine; the classroom resources were minimal, the playground was unfenced, the children were packed into the small space, the teachers untrained, and there were no records or visible accounts.

In each centre I visited I asked about the hours open, the numbers and ages of children attending and their backgrounds, the price of a place per child per week, the outgoings of the centre (rent, upkeep, and so on) and staff wages. I also visited regional offices and collected whatever local documentation that existed.

In each place the main or only reason for children to attend centres appeared to be that their mothers were at work. Many women are employed as domestics in private households or in the tourist industry, or as market traders, and they work long hours with tenuous job protection. Most centres tended to be open long hours too, from 6.30 or 7.00 am to 6 pm at night. The income of the centre, unless it had some external charitable support, in each case was solely from parent fees.

My rule of thumb calculations clearly illustrated the difficulties of self-funding and entrepreneurial viability. In order to set up an ECD centre there needs to be some kind of capital outlay; some kind of shelter, some kind of designated outside space, preferably fenced, and some kind of equipment. The site may be very basic indeed, no more than a tree, unusable in the rainy season. Any kind of capital outlay is problematic in poor communities. There are also questions of scale. The bigger the centre, the more it is likely to be financially viable, although the bigger the centre, the more capital outlay is required.

With these caveats in mind, standard monthly costs for a small centre employing one person would be roughly as shown in Table 10.1.

Table 10.1: Standard monthly costs for a small childcare centre

Expenditure	Per month @ 2006 prices	Income
Caregiver salary	£45	Parental fees @ £5 per month per child
Equipment and consumables	£5	
Rent and rates (depending on site)	£10	
Total	£60	

In order to make ends meet (and with no margins for capital repayments, transport to attend training or registration or any form of contingency) there would have to be a minimum of 20 children, all parents paying £5 per child per month without fail, with no food provided. Most women's work is in the informal sector and incomes are irregular, so there are no reliable figures on average incomes or percentage of people living below the absolute poverty line; but poverty rates are high, and an estimated 40% live in poverty (UNDP, 2010). This fee expenditure simply cannot be met by poor parents under present conditions in Namibia. The poorest centres usually have fewer than 20 children. If they charge no more than £2 per month, they *still* face considerable problems of non-payment. The caregiver receives little or no money for herself, and cannot afford to purchase or replace equipment or meet any other costs. She is likely to be dealing with hungry children, some of whom may be orphans or children living in difficult circumstances. The turnover indicated by the Haihambo study was so high that centres were characterised as 'here today, gone tomorrow' (Haihambo et al, 2004: p 34).

Even where parents were in regular work, and could pay more, margins for the centres were very tight and staff salaries were extremely low. Some entrepreneurs in the townships were able to make a profit, by having very large classes (50+) and poorly qualified staff. At the top end, where facilities were good and staff were trained, the cost of a place, around GBP35 per month per child, could only be afforded by those on relatively high incomes such as senior civil servants or white ex-pats.

In a raw market, where entrepreneurs are the majority, if not the only, provider quality is directly related to ability to pay. In a very unequal society like that in Namibia, this situation exacerbates the inequality that exists. Since all childcare is entirely self-funding, the richer the parent and the more she can pay, the better the service. Poor children receive inadequate care or no care and their education is impoverished; rich children receive good care which enhances their educational prospects.

The education plan for Namibia originally intended to support the 'best' private nurseries, and enable them to improve their resources and to skill their teachers. Poorer children were to be encouraged to attend such nurseries by means of a grant or subsidy scheme – highly problematic in poorer communities, partly because of the practical costs of identifying recipients and administering such grants, partly because it would require young children to travel out of the townships or villages. All attempts at identifying vulnerable children have been highly problematic because of poor data and the absence of tracking. To encourage private entrepreneurship as a means of broadening equitable access to education is highly unlikely to succeed under these conditions.

Other examples of raw markets

Namibia provides a clear-cut example of the inequalities which are perpetuated in a raw market. However it is by no means unique. In neighbouring South Africa there has been a concerted effort to formulate a coherent integrated policy, to provide accurate data, to subsidise the poorest children in non-profit centres, to extend nursery classes within schools, to introduce regulation for all providers, and to coordinate a national training programme. In addition, the government has given per capita subsidies directly to non-profit childcare which provides nursery education; and has launched a cash transfer scheme for the poorest children (a kind of child benefit), which has mitigated extreme poverty (Dawes et al, 2009). But such an ambitious interventionist scheme has nonetheless failed to significantly reduce educational inequality. Again there are a variety of reasons, not least the difficulties of government coordination – horizontally across departments, and vertically across states and districts. But the main reason is because of the substantial size of the private sector and the failure to address it. The levels of inequality in the country undermine attempts to achieve equality of opportunity for children. Rich parents buy into the best provision, and the poorest provision in the poorest areas caters for the poorest parents, and again inequality is exacerbated (Penn and Maynard, 2010; Dawes, 2010).

On a recent field trip to Orange Free State, in South Africa, organised by the University of the Free State, I visited a range of centres from good, ex-nursery school centres to the poorest shacks in remote townships. The cost of a 'good' nursery was 1,000 rand (GBP90) per month; the cheapest was 40 rand (under GBP3.60) per month. The differences in resources were so great that it made little sense to regard the services as comparable or in any way as equitable. Ironically, the better nurseries were registered as charities and were eligible for education grants; but the poorest nurseries were not able to complete the complicated registration process, and were therefore not eligible for any state grants (Penn, 2011b).

Woodhead et al (2009) in their large-scale project 'Children's Lives' documenting 6,000 children's experiences in India, Peru and Ethiopia, also suggest that 'the impact of a growing private sector is to reinforce rather than reduce inequities of access to quality education' (Woodhead et al, 2009: p ix). They conclude that a large private sector is 'incompatible with achieving social equity' and that there are:

> significant shortcomings in the realization of scientifically grounded claims made for the power of early childhood services to support greater social equity, and as a cost-effective investment in human capital with potential to bring high rates of return. (Woodhead et al, 2009, p 78)

The most recent report from the UN General Assembly on the status of the Rights of the Child states that:

> The combination of growth in private provision and weaknesses in public programmes means that, overall, the early childhood care and education sector is rarely pro-poor. Large discrepancies in early childhood care and education enrolment between children from the poorest versus the

most affluent 20 per cent of households are reported for countries such as Ghana (23 per cent versus 87 per cent) and Georgia (17 per cent versus 70 per cent). (UN General Assembly, 2010, p 9)

Much more scrutiny then, is necessary, of the operation of the private market and the position of childcare entrepreneurs in low income countries.

Emerging markets

In post-socialist countries, where the markets are commonly described as 'emerging' rather than as raw, there are also substantial issues of equity and access. Most post-socialist countries had wide-reaching and comprehensive kindergarten services, often of a standard much higher than in Western Europe in that they offered all-round healthcare as well as education (Bronfenbrenner, 1972). Much of this provision was workplace based, and when the state farms and factories closed so did their kindergartens. The remaining kindergartens were forced to introduce charges, usually for food, which were beyond the means of many parents. In Kazakhstan for example, after transition, the percentage of kindergartens fell from 55% to 11%, and those that remained introduced charges which had the effect of excluding the poorest families (Penn, 2005). Rural families were particularly hard hit by closures of the facilities at collective farms.

The changing situation for women and children in transitional economies was monitored from 1990 for a 15 year period by UNICEF-IRC. All in all 27 countries were monitored. The countries differed considerably in outcomes, and the experiences of women and children varied – their situation was much worse in the seven countries experiencing ethnic conflict. But overall the pattern is similar. The number of children living in absolute poverty rose to about a quarter of all children; the birth rate fell by over a third, well below the level of replacement in some countries. Inequality has increased in most countries, especially the energy rich countries. The position of women has also substantially changed. Before transition women were expected to work – indeed the requirement for women to work was compulsory in some countries such as Hungary, albeit with generous maternity leave (Korintus, 2009). After transition women's work was seen as expendable, although in some countries benefits were introduced to encourage and enable them to stay at home, often set at a very low level (UNICEF, 2006). A number of reports have illustrated how women have experienced a substantial worsening of their status and conditions, and were literally left 'holding the baby' in the absence of family support services (Gal and Kligman, 2000).

But in addition the UNICEF (2006) report comments on the considerable time it has taken to reorganise government administration. In almost all countries this reorganisation is 'unfinished'. After complete state control, the procedures are simply not in place to deal with a more entrepreneurial society, and in some few countries, crime, tax evasion and fraud have been widespread as a consequence.

Post-socialist countries have tried to sponsor market entrepreneurship, but with varying approaches and results. Users have relatively little experience of markets of any kind, and are resentful or uncomfortable at paying for goods or services which were once free. Entrepreneurs themselves may be uncomfortable and unsure about what they are doing and what their scope for action may be (Mandel and Humphrey, 2002). Governments are being encouraged to decentralise all services to local authorities, and are confused about their powers of regulation and appropriate administrative formats in relation to a spectrum of services, not only childcare.

In accession countries (post-socialist countries now members of the European Union) services for children under 3 have been considerably cut back, as women have left the labour market. The few services which remain are mainly private, although there has been relatively little development of private services for older children and state services remain the norm. A recent survey of regulatory conditions in accession countries suggest that most do not have any specific regulatory requirements for the private sector, and they provide very few data about the extent of the sector. They have not addressed the question of regulatory conditions for the private childcare market or how they might be enforced (Penn, 2013). There is still some pride in state provision. In Moscow, a rich city thanks to gas and oil, there has been a substantial new *state* kindergarten building programme, reviving previous grand traditions where kindergartens were equipped with swimming pools, dance halls and medical suites (UNESCO, 2010).

Emerging markets face the same problem in one sense as raw markets. What kind of regulatory and cost controls have to be introduced to make sure that the poorest children can access good childcare? Can or should entrepreneurial childcare in any way be used to compensate for wider inequalities?

Government intervention in markets

Human capital arguments for investing in early childhood do not usually take account of the mode of delivery of services, nor of the difficulties in providing services in very unequal societies. But not everyone agrees with the diagnosis that heavy reliance on private entrepreneurs in education leads to increased inequalities. Tooley and his colleagues argue that in low income countries private education is widespread – if officially unrecorded – in poor areas, and that it is frequently preferred by parents to low quality poorly functioning state schools. Moreover it produces better results than state schooling and poor parents make financial sacrifices in order to use it (Tooley, 2008). Tooley has a vested interest – as well as being an academic, his website proclaims that he is education director of a global fund that promotes private education – but few other people have investigated the scope of the private market in such depth. However his argument has not been about inequality per se, but about the contribution that private entrepreneurs can and do make in supplementing and augmenting the state education system.

The arguments for early childhood services are somewhat different as it is a less established service. There is widespread international support for developing early childhood services. The UNESCO Education for All (EFA) initiative has as its first goal: 'expanding and improving comprehensive early childhood care and education, especially for the most vulnerable and disadvantaged children (UNESCO, 2007).

Addressing inequality is a specific target in this reckoning. The simplistic or default solution is that it can be provided by (someone? somehow?) offering especially targeted programmes without addressing the issues presented by raw and emerging childcare markets.

What kind of policies and financial strategies might work to lessen the inherent stratification within raw childcare markets, and protect the poorest children? It is possible to create a government-led service for young children which benefits all children equally, poor and rich, urban and rural, and there are a very few notable examples from low- and middle-income countries (although more from high-income countries) where this has happened, Cuba being the most well known (Carnoy, 2007; Tinajero, 2010). But for most low- and middle-income countries entrepreneurial activity is the default position. In this situation, what practical steps are possible to move towards a more equitable system? Woodhead et al (2009) suggest that, as for high-income countries, the solutions are better coordinated systems of care and education, better links to schooling, focusing on the most vulnerable and disadvantaged children, and more effective governance of the private sector. INGOs and charities seeking to advocate for ECEC fall back on standard precepts about what they think children *ought* to have in the way of developmentally appropriate interventions rather than exploring demand and supply more critically (Penn, 2011a).

The entrepreneurial childcare cited in the example of Namibia was almost all set up in order to provide childcare for working mothers. Only for the most well-to-do was it explicitly a nursery education service. Heymann (2006) argues one of the most significant demographic changes in the south is migration-urbanisation, where men and women from the countryside migrate to towns and cities. Existing family support networks are badly disrupted, and there are high percentages of single parents. Women in the townships or favelas are likely to be working long hours in the informal economy in jobs such as hawkers and traders or as domestic servants, and are desperately in need of childcare. Without it many young children are left alone or inadequately cared for by siblings – amongst others; Heymann cites the figure of 29% of children of working mothers in Botswana left alone during the day, with high accident rates as a result. Having some grasp of numbers of working women with young children, the money they earn, and the kind of arrangements they are forced to make in order to work, would seem to be an essential policy component.

Developmental interventions supported by the World Bank (WB) and other major funders, and international non-governmental organisations (INGO) such as UNICEF, tend to prefer 'family motivator' interventions, whereby women, usually volunteers, are trained to work with 'families' to teach them rudiments of psychosocial development and nutrition. An example is the extensively researched World Bank Early Childhood Development Programme in the Philippines (Armecin et al, 2006). A particular irony of focusing on supporting mothers at home in the Philippines is the very high level of migrant women workers – mothers who leave their families in the care of relatives in order to work as childcarers, nurses and sex workers in high income countries, and send remittances home (Ehrenreich and Hothschild, 2003).

The WB project says nothing about family expenditure, or the preferences of the women involved, or the experiences of the children, or delivery mechanisms for childcare. Instead it provides analyses about the effectiveness of the intervention on child outcomes depending on the length of time of programme exposure. Similar projects have been reported in many countries, most notably in Jamaica (Grantham-McGregor et al, 2007). To be poor is in a sense to forfeit choice and what is deemed best for families and children is determined by others.

Yet in these countries there is also a thriving private market, which is barely recorded or regulated.

These two examples, Heymann's studies in documenting women's work and child outcomes in Botswana and the Philippine's intervention study, illustrate the difficulties, but also the necessity, of having a clearer, broader yet also localised view of demand and supply in order to understand how local childcare markets operate.

Summary

The problem about access to early childhood education and care services delivered in a raw market is poverty. Poor families cannot afford to pay enough to cover the costs of a reasonable standard of early education and childcare; and the early education and childcare settings they use cannot function well on the income they receive. Those who work in the sector mostly do so in extremely trying conditions for very little money. It is unrealistic at present to expect governments in low income countries – short of a revolution – to fund universal ECEC services, or to tightly control markets. But it is the norm in most European countries, and there is no a priori reason to rule it out as a long-term and important goal.

In emerging markets, the for-profit sector is most likely to be aimed at the well-to-do, but this is speculation, since there are so few data. Basic regulatory controls of adult–child ratios, staff training, curricula, health and safety and so on can only be implemented if other systems are in place. Regulation also implies monitoring, support and sanctions if conditions are not met; the personnel to do this need to be in place and they need to be able to get about. There are no short cuts or easy remedies to supporting and working with entrepreneurs in raw or emerging markets. For it to be done successfully, it has to be done within a well-thought-out and evolving government framework. It requires considerable expenditure as well as legislation. Entrepreneurs working in raw or emerging markets offer a variable service. At bottom is the question of whether it is acceptable that young children from rich backgrounds should have good early experiences, with trained staff in well-resourced conditions, while young children from poor backgrounds only have access, if at all, to meagre experiences in bleak settings. Working for childhood equity within an entrepreneurial framework requires both expenditure and vigilance.

References

ADEA (2008) Working group on ECD www.adeanet.org/workgroups/en_wgecd.html

Armecin, G., Behrman, J., Duazo., Ghuman, S., Gultiano, S., King, E and Lee, N. (2006) *Early childhood development through an integrated program: Evidence from the Philippines*, Impact Evaluation Series no. 2. WPS3922-IE. Washington: World Bank.

Bronfenbrenner, U. (1972) *Two worlds of childhood*, London: Penguin.

Carnoy, M. (2007) *Cuba's academic advantage: Why students do better in schools*, Stanford California: Stanford University Press.

Dawes, A., Bray, R., and van der Merwe, A. (2009) *Monitoring child well-being: A South African based rights approach*, Cape Town: HSRC Press.

Dawes, A. (2010) Personal communication, December.

Ehrenreich, B. and Hothschild, A. (2003) *Global woman: Nannies, maids, and sex workers in the new economy*, New York: Metropolitan Books.

Gal, S. and Kligman, G. (2000) *The politics of gender after socialism*, New Jersey: Princeton University Press.

Garcia, M. (2011) *SABER: Recent developments in World Bank policies on early childhood development*, Seminar given at Open Society Foundation, London: November 2012

Grantham-McGregor, S., Cheung, Y.B., Cueto, S., Glewwe, P., Richter, L., Strupp, B. and the International Child Development Steering Group (2007) 'Child development in developing countries: 1. Developmental potential in the first 5 years for children in developing countries', *Lancet*, 369: pp 60–70.

Haihambo, C., Mushaandja, J. and Hengari, J. (2004) *Situation analysis on IECD provision in Karas, Kavango, and Omusati Regions of Namibia*, Draft for Consultative Workshop, December, Windhoek: MGECW.

Heymann J. (2006) *Forgotten families: Ending the growing crisis confronting children and working parents in the global economy*, Oxford: Oxford University Press.

Korintus, M. (2009) 'Hungary and Slovenia: Long leave or short?' in S. Kamerman and P. Moss (eds) *The politics of parental leave policies: Children, parenting, gender and the labour market*, Bristol: The Policy Press, pp 135–157.

Mandel, R. and Humphrey, C. (eds) (2002) *Markets and moralities: Ethnographies of post-socialism*, Oxford: Berg.

Naudeau, S., Kataoka, N., Valerio, A., Neuman, M. and Elder, L. (2010) *Investing in young children: An early childhood development guide for policy dialogue and project preparation*, Washington: World Bank.

Penn, H. (2005) *Unequal childhoods*, London. Routledge.

Penn, H. (2008) 'Working on the impossible: Early childhood policies in Namibia', *Childhood*, vol 15, no 3, pp 378- 398.

Penn, H. and Maynard, T. (2010) *Siyabonana: Building better childhoods in South Africa*, Edinburgh: Children in Scotland.

Penn, H. (2011a) 'Travelling policies and global buzzwords: How INGOs and charities spread the word about early childhood', *Childhood*, vol 18, no 1, pp 94–113.

Penn, H. (2011b) *Is it possible to have a relevant curriculum in an unequal society?*, Shaping Strong Foundations for Young Children, Seminar, University of the Free State, 30 September.

Penn, H. (2013; forthcoming) 'The business of childcare in Europe'.

Tinajero, A. (2010) *Scaling up early childhood development in Cuba: Cuba's EducateYour Child Program: Strategies and lessons from the expansion process*, Working Paper 16. Washington: World Bank/Wolfenson Centre for Development.

Tooley, J. (2008) *E. G. West: Economic liberalism and the role of government in education* (Continuum Library of Educational Thought), New York and London: Continuum.

UNESCO (2007) *EFA Global monitoring report: Early childhood care and education, 2007*, Paris: UNESCO.

UNESCO (2010) *Proceedings of the World Conference on early childhood care and education*, Paris: UNESCO.

United Nations Development Programme (UNDP) (2010) *Human development index 2010 rankings. http://hdr.undp.org/en/statistics.*

UNICEF IRC (2006) *Innocenti social monitor 2006: Understanding child poverty in SE Europe and the Commonwealth of independent states*, Florence: UNICEF Innocenti Centre.

United Nations General Assembly 65th Session (2010) *Status of the convention of the rights of the child: Report of the Secretary General.* A/65 /206. New York: UNICEF.

Woodhead, M., Ames, P., Vennam, U., Abebe W. and Streuli, N. (2009) *Equity and quality? Challenges for early childhood and primary education in Ethiopia, India and Peru*, Working paper no 55, Studies in Early Childhood Transitions. The Hague, the Netherlands: Bernard van Leer Foundation.

Part Three

Ethics and principles

ELEVEN

Need markets be the only show in town?

Peter Moss

Introduction

This chapter is about what happens when democracy becomes sclerotic and a society falls prey to fundamentalist dogma that claims to have the right answer for everything: in short, when neoliberal capitalism becomes a hegemonic system of thought and practice, with its unswerving belief in the virtues of markets and the private, of competition and inequality, and of calculation and individual choice. But it is not a general account of this phenomenon, rather a study of how it plays out in one small part of the neoliberal world – early childhood education and care (ECEC) in England.

Nor is this chapter solely critique. It is also about the possibility of thinking differently and an exercise in putting the neoliberal approach to ECEC where it belongs: in perspective, as but one of a number of alternatives, a possibility rather than a necessity. In particular, the chapter explores just one of these alternatives, an ECEC inscribed with democracy as a fundamental value. But first, by way of introduction, a short account is needed of how ECEC in England came to take its current form, what might be termed an ECEC of regulated markets.

ECEC in England: a case study in regulated markets

England presents a distinctive system of early childhood education and care. It is a split system: despite administrative unification within the education ministry, the country continues to have two quite distinct sectors – 'childcare' and 'early education' – each with different access, funding, workforces and, to a large extent, types of provision. Nothing strange there, most countries have such systems (Kaga et al, 2010). But then add in other ingredients: marketisation of both sectors, with providers competing for the business of parent-consumers; a mixed bag of public and private providers, including a large number of 'childcare' services run as businesses for profit; and last but not least, a centralised system of regulation by a powerful nation state. All this adds up to a regime that might be typified as a centrally regulated market.

Why did England come to adopt this approach to ECEC? Like many English-speaking countries, ECEC was low on the policy agenda in England for decades after the Second World War (Tizard et al 1976; Randall, 2002; Penn, 2009). In a typical male breadwinner society, only a minority of women with preschool age children were employed, most part time; 'childcare' was mainly a matter of informal arrangements, such as grandparents or fathers caring for children while mothers worked evenings or weekends. Formal services – officially termed 'day care' – were largely private, predominantly 'childminders' (family day carers), with a few nurseries. Many public nurseries were closed soon after the war, and those that remained became increasingly 'social welfare' services for children deemed to be at risk or in need of additional support.

Alongside 'day care', some services existed primarily to provide 'nursery education' to 3- and 4-year-olds. Playgroups, set up to fill the gap left by patchy public provision, were mainly run by non-profit 'voluntary' organisations, often local parent-led groups. Nursery classes were provided in some primary schools, while the first class of primary education – 'reception class' – took increasing numbers of 4-year-olds, starting before the compulsory school age of 5 years. School-based provision was completed by a small number of separate schools dedicated to 3- and 4-year-olds – 'nursery schools'. Provision in school varied from place to place, nursery education being widespread in left-wing local authorities, but less common elsewhere. Both playgroups and nursery classes offered predominantly part-time attendance, ranging from a daily morning or afternoon session to just two or three sessions a week.

Things began to change in the second half of the 1980s. The number of employed women with young children, and the number working full time, began to rise, reflecting a new group of well-educated women who resumed employment after maternity leave (Brannen and Moss, 1998). In response, day nursery provision began to rapidly increase, nearly doubling in England between 1989 and 1994 from 75,400 to 147,600 places. Moreover, these new nursery places were provided by a particular sector: private for-profit providers. During these five years, places in public nurseries fell from 28,800 to 22,300, while private (mainly for-profit) places nearly trebled, from 46,600 to 125,300 (The

Stationery Office, 1999:Table 2).'Childcare' was becoming big business, based on the market.

The trend has continued since. The 'market report' on United Kingdom nurseries for 2009–10 (Laing & Buisson, 2010), estimated there to be 662,835 places in nurseries providing full daycare, more than three quarters provided by the for-profit sector; put another way, for-profit providers accounted for 81% of the estimated £3.9 billion value of the UK 'childcare market'. Most of these providers are small, 'one nursery' businesses, though the share of nursery chains is increasing. The link between 'childcare' and business extends beyond the provision of nurseries for profit. Increasingly, business is funding these nurseries through subsidising employees' childcare costs: 'While the market is primarily funded by fee-paying parents – to the tune of £2.3 billion in 2009–10 – corporate spending through childcare vouchers has increased dramatically from 6.4% in 2004 to more than a quarter last year' (Evans, 2010).

The initial growth in 'childcare', driven by increasing parental demand, was followed by increased government attention given to early education. In 1996, towards the end of the last Conservative administration (1979–97), a commitment was made not only to increase education provision for 3- and 4-year-olds but also to stimulate a market in such provision. A voucher system was proposed, which parents would use to purchase nursery education from a mix of public and private providers; this was taken as far as piloting in four local authorities.

The Labour government, returned in 1997, took forward the belated policy interest in early childhood by introducing a universal entitlement to free part-time early education for all 3 and 4-year-olds, 12.5 hours per week initially, extended to 15 hours in 2010. It scrapped the voucher proposal, but retained the Conservatives' faith in markets and a mixed economy. A range of providers – public, voluntary and private; schools, nurseries, playgroups and childminders – were encouraged to offer free education for 3- and 4-year-olds, receiving a 'nursery education grant' if meeting certain conditions, for example working with a 'foundation stage' of the National Curriculum. Today, attendance is almost universal for 3- and 4-year-olds at 95%. Though most provision for 4-year-olds is in maintained schools, most 3-year-olds receive their early education in the private sector, in nurseries, playgroups or schools (Department for Education, 2010).

'Childcare' and 'nursery education' differ in some key respects. The former is dominated by private for-profit nurseries and childminders, relies on 'childcare workers' with low levels of qualification and poor pay, and is treated as primarily a private responsibility of parents.

'Nursery education', by contrast, is more evenly divided between maintained schools (60%) and private providers (40%), includes a substantial proportion of graduate teachers with relatively good pay, and is considered a public responsibility, with direct funding of services. What both share is a market approach emphasising competition by providers and individual choice by parents.

How did this market domination of ECEC come about? While the post-1997 Labour government undoubtedly gave much greater attention to ECEC, compared with previous governments, many policies had much in common with its Conservative predecessors. In education, the 1986 Education Act, at the height of Margaret Thatcher's premiership, is widely seen as starting a major process of reform, including an emphasis on diversity of provision, school autonomy and parental choice. Whitty et al (1998) have described the result as 'quasi-markets', seeking to make public services behave like the private sector, in particular through state funded schools competing with each other. In nursery education, not only were these schools to compete with each other, but successive governments, Conservative and Labour, actively enabled private sector services to enter the fray, turning a quasi-market of public and private providers into an actual though, as we shall see, regulated market.

While the development of market approaches in early education policy can be documented and dated, as part of a wider educational reform project, the process is less clear in 'childcare'. Post-war governments, of left and right, viewed mothers' employment either with hostility or indifference; either way, 'childcare' was deemed a purely private matter, except for basic regulation of all 'day care' services to ensure minimum standards. There was a small market, mainly among childminders, and this was never questioned as the means to provide what was variously termed 'day care' or 'child care'. It was, one might say, a market by default. This remained the case in the late 1980s and early 1990s as growing maternal employment drove private nursery expansion. The first glimmer of more active policy was the introduction in 1994 of the 'childcare disregard', a modest system of demand subsidy for some parents, significant as a form of funding linked to market approaches; its rationale was to enable low income consumers to enter the market from which they might otherwise be priced out.

The Labour administration, 1997–2010, broke with the past by adopting wholehearted support for maternal employment and prioritising policies to increase such employment (Cohen et al, 2004). 'Childcare', a term and concept to which the government remained attached despite transferring responsibility for daycare services from health to education, was boosted as part of a 'Childcare Strategy', to be achieved through encouraging yet more private providers into the market and by active state stimulation of the market. This stimulation took three main forms. First, developing an extensive tax credit scheme, a demand subsidy approach to funding that went beyond the earlier 'disregard' to enable more lower income parents to pay nursery and childminding fees. Second, providing start-up support for private providers in poor areas where markets might struggle to get established. Third, facilitating the functioning of markets: in 2006 the government stated that 'there is already a diverse market in childcare, in which the private, voluntary and community sectors play a major part. However, gaps remain and we need to develop in every area a thriving childcare market which will respond to parents' needs' (Sure Start, 2006, p 3). To plug the gaps, the 2006 Childcare Act defined the primary job of local authorities to be childcare market management of provision supplied by the private sector, both for-profit and not-for-profit providers. Local authority provision, though, should be a last resort: a 'mixed market' meant in practice a market limited to private providers.

But why this allure of the market? In studies of the welfare state, England, like other English-speaking countries, is usually allocated to the category 'liberal welfare regime', with three core elements:

> It is, firstly, residual in the sense that social guarantees are typically limited to 'bad risks'.... [It] is, secondly, residual in the sense that it adheres to a narrow conception of what risks should be considered 'social' ... The third characteristic of liberalism is its encouragement of the market. (Esping-Andersen, 1999, p 75)

In the 1980s, Thatcherite Britain, along with Reaganite America, went into a period of hyper- or neoliberalism: there was a 'dramatic consolidation of neo-liberalism as a new economic orthodoxy regulating public policy at the state level' (Harvey, 2005, p 22). Neoliberalism placed even higher value than liberalism on targeting, on reducing the scope of social risk and on markets, while emphasising the importance of individual choice, competition, and private provision of services. The citizen-subject of neoliberalism was the autonomous consumer, able and willing to assume personal responsibility for a wide range of risks and able to flourish in the market by using information and rational calculation to find best value for money, to keep providers on their toes and to drive down costs.

Post-Thatcher governments have retained a strong attachment to neoliberalism. True, the Labour government invested more public money in ECEC, increased subsidies to parents for 'childcare' and developed an extensive network of Children's Centres, that is multifunctional services for young children and their families, with 3,500 set up by 2010, one for each community in the country. But behind these reforms, the strong lines of neoliberal thinking remain visible: the importance of the 'childcare market' was acknowledged and its development supported; public provision was discouraged; there were strong elements of targeting in the Children's Centre policy. Also these new services were introduced alongside, not in place of, a massive and expanding privatised nursery sector, with ECEC provision within Centres to be 'self-sustaining and run on business lines' (DCSF, 2007, p 16).

But while markets, operating with a mixed economy of providers, have been a driving principle of English ECEC policy since the 1990s, and especially under the Labour administration, they have assumed a particular form: centralised regulation by a powerful nation state. The state has argued the virtues of choice and diversity on the one hand. But on the other hand it has introduced an array of agencies and mechanisms that have given it substantial control over childcare and nursery education.

First, it developed prescriptive regulations, combining standards and curriculum and covering the whole of early years: the Early Years Foundation Stage (EYFS). In two volumes – a statutory framework and practice guidance – running to 160 pages, the EYFS set out 69 early learning goals, educational programmes for each of 'six areas of learning and development' and assessment arrangements, culminating in the Early Years Foundation Stage Profile. The Profile assessed children on 13 scales, each divided into nine 'points', with the procedure specified in detail in a handbook running to 90 pages. This dense and detailed network of norms and criteria left little scope for interpretation or supplementation, being very much in the tradition of what OCED's *Starting Strong* report refers to as the 'pre-primary approach to early education' (OECD, 2006, p61). This contrasts with a 'guiding framework' curriculum, which 'allow local interpretation, identify general quality goals and indicate how they might be obtained' (p 209).

Second, the implementation of this curriculum, and overall government monitoring and regulation of individual services, was to be assured by a state agency, the Office for Standards in Education, Children's Services and Skills (Ofsted), through regular inspection of all ECEC services. Ofsted was not only a key means of central regulation.

It also had a key role in the market system. Its reports on individual services, made publicly available, were intended to provide parents acting as calculating consumers with information on which to base their purchasing decisions.

Third, a training system for 'childcare workers' was based on a detailed set of 'national occupational standards' broken down into elements, which in turn contained detailed criteria against which the performance of workers can be assessed. The work, in short, was conceptualised as a set of task-defined competencies and prescribed behavioural standards, and the qualified worker as someone who has demonstrated an ability to conform to these standards. Workforce development included the goal of what was termed 'a graduate-led early years workforce', with nurseries and non-school settings to be headed by a graduate, the Early Years Professional, qualification for which required meeting 39 defined standards (Children's Workforce Development Council, 2011).

Making sense of regulated markets under New Labour

What emerged under the Labour government was explicit advocacy of markets in childcare and nursery education combined with a comprehensive and complex system of standardisation, surveillance and control. This required an immense exercise in detailed policy making and direction by central government, expressed, communicated and directed through a mass of documentation. How and why did this happen? How did the English state espouse both neoliberalism and central regulation?

At a somewhat superficial level, one explanation is that the state has done this because it could. England has long been one of the most centralised states in Europe (Colley, 2003). The Thatcher government, 1979–90, reduced still further alternative centres of power to national government, such as local government and trades unions. With its centralising traditions and weak counterbalances, the English state was able by the 1990s to exert detailed control over a burgeoning but fragmented ECEC sector.

But we must seek deeper levels of explanation if we are to answer the question: why did a state committed to resurgent market liberalism choose to exercise its powers? I will pursue two of several lines of explanation. One concerns the relationship between neoliberalism and conservatism. Michael Apple, writing about the mixture of markets and management apparent in the US compulsory education sector, but redolent of both this sector and ECEC in England, has described an alliance – a 'new hegemonic bloc' – of neoliberals and neoconservatives. This is 'tense and filled with contradictory tendencies', but still capable of exerting leadership in educational policy and reform: the former emphasising the relationship between education and the market, the latter agreeing with the neoliberal emphasis on the market economy, but seeking stronger control over knowledge, morals and values through curricula, testing and other means (Apple, 2004, p 174). More generally, Harvey (2005, p 82) has pointed to 'the increasing authoritarianism evident in neo-liberal states such as the US and Britain', equating this authoritarianism with a strain of neo-conservatism which, while concurring with the neoliberal agenda of elite governance, mistrust of democracy and the maintenance of market freedoms

> ... veers away from the principles of pure neo-liberalism and has reshaped neo-liberal practices in two fundamental respects: first, in its concern for order as an answer to the chaos of individual interests, and second, in its concern for an overweening morality as the necessary social glue to keep the body politic secure in the face of external and internal dangers. (Harvey, 2005, p 82)

The tensions between neoliberalism and neo-conservatism are particularly acute within Conservative politics, and indeed reflect two different conservative constituencies, one eager to engage with the demands and opportunities of globalisation and to prepare cosmopolitan citizens, the other more traditional and local in perspective.

But England's new-found policy interest in ECEC mainly took place during a Labour administration, within which the political dynamic was somewhat different. 'New Labour' – following a Third Way politics – adopted the market with enthusiasm and confidence. Across a wide range of policy areas and services, New Labour espoused the values of neoliberalism: individual choice, competition and entrepreneurship, and the ideal of the self-regulating and autonomous subject managing his or her own risk through informed and calculating engagement with the market.

At the same time, this strong espousal of neoliberalism did not preclude an active state. The goal was, in the words of Giddens (1998, p 99), 'a new mixed economy', with a 'social investment state' replacing the welfare state, concerned less with redistribution 'after the event' and more with a 'redistribution of possibilities' through 'a cultivation of human potential', in particular through investment in education, also desirable to ensure national survival in an increasingly competitive global economy. In the new mixed economy, the market would no longer be subordinate to the state. It would instead be harnessed, its dynamism acting in the public interest, with a new synergy between public and private sectors.

The use of the market and private entrepreneurial flair in the provision of services is one of three main methods deployed by the 'social investment state'. The second is a strong technical role for research, research understood and deployed as 'a producer of means, strategies, and techniques to achieve given ends' (Biesta, 2007, p 18). Such technical research provides clear 'evidence' of 'what works', to ensure effective investment in the best performing technologies and to calculate the returns made from that investment. The third is new public management, inscribed with the ethos of business, the rationality of markets and the image of the citizen as customer, and providing the social investment state with an array of new technologies for more effective governing.

With the use of markets, technical research and new public management, government sought to act like a modern business organisation, managing a wide array of production units at a distance, through setting objectives, allocating resources, and endlessly auditing their attainment. Providers of services – production units – have greater day-to-day autonomy and freedom to compete with each other, freed as they are from direct bureaucratic management. Yet they do so within a highly prescribed framework of national standards and targets. Providers compete with one another, but as part of an internal market subsumed within a national corporate entity – England plc, which is engaged in competing with other similar national corporations.

At the time of writing, the future of the regulated market in ECEC in England is unclear. Not the market part. The current Conservative-led Coalition government shows a desire and a will to extend marketisation (and privatisation) deeper into public services. Announcing a 'public sector revolution' in a newspaper article titled 'How we will release the grip of state control', the Prime Minister, David Cameron, stated that all 'public services should be open to a range of providers competing to offer better service' (Cameron, 2011). While marketisation does not necessarily entail more privatisation of provision, for example, there can be markets between public providers such as schools, Cameron here makes it clear that he sees privatisation of supply as a driver of marketisation.

At the same time, the government is talking about reducing the degree of central control of markets in public services, within a discourse of localism in which responsibility is handed down to local stakeholders and communities. A recent review of the EYFS envisages less central prescription, including 69 early learning goals cut to 17 (Tickell, 2011). How far this will actually happen, how far the centre will let go the reins of government, and how this will impact on ECEC, remains to be seen. What seems likely, though, is more markets and less regulation.

Escaping the dictatorship of no alternative

ECEC in England has, to a large degree, been handed over to the market and to competition between a mixed group of providers, including a high proportion of for-profit businesses. The market is, for sure, regulated by the state. But the state has little doubt that the market, with all its attendant values and assumptions, is the way to deliver services and that these services should be viewed, treated and encouraged as competing businesses.

There are causes for concern about how the market in ECEC works (Vincent and Ball, 2006; Moss, 2009) as discussed in the chapters by Penn and Plantenga in this volume. But a deeper cause for concern, at least to the author of this chapter, is the absence of contestation in England about marketisation, a symptom of the sclerotic state of democracy, no longer able to envisage and articulate alternatives or to deliberate the claims of conflicting ideas. Instead, the nation gradually absorbed and came to speak a new hegemonic early childhood discourse, market-thinking becoming taken for granted as the only way to go. So, there was no moment when government explicitly argued the case for a market approach to 'childcare' and 'nursery education'; no policy document where different options were considered and the market option justified; no parliamentary or public debate on the subject; no national evaluation of the experiment in marketisation and privatisation. Yet by 2008, a senior civil servant could state in a public presentation that a 'diverse market (is) the only game in town' (Archer, 2008).

We find ourselves, in England, in what Roberto Unger terms 'the dictatorship of no alternative', a dictatorship of marketised, privatised and economistic thinking. But it need not be and should not be like this. In the last book he wrote before his untimely death, Toby Judt gave a warning and a challenge:

> The materialistic and selfish quality of contemporary life
> is not inherent in the human condition. Much of what
> appears 'natural' today dates from the 1980s: the obsession

with wealth creation, the cult of privatization and the private sector, the growing disparities of rich and poor. And above all, the rhetoric which accompanies these: uncritical admiration for unfettered markets, the disdain for the public sector, the delusion of endless growth ... (Judt, 2010, p 2)

We cannot go on living like this ... And yet we seem unable to conceive of alternatives. This too is something new ... Our disability is discursive: we simply do not know how to talk about these things any more. (Judt, 2010, p 34)

In response to his challenge, I (for no longer can I hide behind the presumed objectivity and neutrality of the academic third person) want to sketch one alternative in ECEC, as a provocation intended to make the familiar strange and as an attempt to overcome discursive disability and renew a democratic discourse of conflicting ideas. For there are, of course, alternatives, and a truly democratic society should envisage, discuss and argue about them, not treating one – marketisation – as if it was the only possibility, so reducing politics to the minor role of management and regulation.

Opening up resistance to the dictatorship of no alternative and, therefore, opening up to alternatives means going back to asking and seeking answers to what have been termed 'critical' or 'political' questions. Chantal Mouffe, to take one example, argues that 'contrary to what neoliberal ideologists would like us to believe, political questions are not mere technical issues to be solved by experts ... [they] always involve decisions which require us to make a choice between conflicting alternatives' (Mouffe, 2007). The mere act of asking political questions helps pull politics free from its collapse into economics and re-asserts education as, first and foremost, a political (and also ethical) practice.

Political questions in ECEC, or indeed any form of education include:

- What is the purpose of ECEC?
- What are the fundamental values of ECEC?
- What are the ethics for ECEC?
- What is the concept of education and of care?
- What do we mean by 'learning' and 'knowledge'?
- What is our image of the child, the educator, the early childhood centre?
- What do we want for our children?

Space precludes offering full answers to all these questions; for a fuller response, see Fielding and Moss (2010). To give an indication of how such questioning opens up to the richness of conflicting alternatives, consider two of these questions. First, what are the fundamental values of ECEC? Current English policy on ECEC embodies values that are central to the neoliberal project, such as competition, individual choice, contractual relations, based on the commodification of everything, inequality, private enterprise. The reverse side is deep suspicion of democratic politics and anything public. An alternative to marketisation might be based on quite different values: cooperation, equality, solidarity, the public good – and democracy, understood as a multidimensional concept covering not only governance at all levels but also relationships and everyday living; or in the words of John Dewey, democracy as 'a mode of associated living embedded in the culture and social relationships of everyday life' and as 'a way of life controlled by a working faith in the possibilities of human nature…[and] faith in the capacity of human beings for intelligent judgement and action if proper conditions are furnished' (Dewey, 1939, pp 229–30).

Second, what is our image of the early childhood centre? Under the current regulated market regime of English ECEC, two images come to mind: the centre as a factory producing predetermined and normative outcomes from children by applying effective 'human technologies' (Rose, 1999) and the centre as a private business selling a commodity – 'childcare' and/or 'education' – in the market to a parent-consumer. An alternative image, which connects with the alternative values outlined above, is the early childhood centre as a public institution, responsibility and space, a place of encounter for citizens (of all ages), and a collaborative workshop where, from such encounter, many purposes and projects are collectively realised – educational, political, ethical, social, cultural, aesthetic, economic, including democratic practice. This is the centre as a place of possibility and a public good, open to all as a matter of citizen entitlement.

From these and other alternative answers to critical questions, we can build another policy for ECEC. The direction – 'where to?' – would be the development of an ECEC system characterised by collaborative working, within and between centres; democratic practice, in governance, learning, evaluation, experimentation and all facets of everyday life; universal access, as an entitlement for children as citizens; and a strong public ethos, emphasising responsibility for and benefit to all children, all parents and the wider community. With such parameters defined, policy could then define the means to pursue this direction of travel and to turn away from the current marketised and privatised system. To this end, government has many resources and tools at its disposal, for example policy frameworks defining values and goals, a wide array of regulation, for example, placing duties on local authorities and individual services to promote democratic practice in the governance and everyday practice of services, funding, both money itself and the way it is allocated, support for experimentation, with an emphasis on what Unger (2005) calls 'democratic experimentalism', commissioning research and evaluation, and so on.

Such broad-brush thinking is important. As Unger reminds us, 'although ideas all by themselves are powerless, to overcome this dictatorship [of no alternative] we cannot overthrow it without ideas' (Unger, 2005, p 1). But ideas need combining with detailed work on how they might be put into practice to achieve transformation. There are, as Erik Olin Wright (2009) discusses, at least three stages in the process of transformation. *Desirability*, which is about laying out values, ethics and goals; *viability*, which is about designing new policies and institutions based on desirable principles; and *achievability*, which is about the process of transformation and the practical political work of strategies for social change, asking of 'proposals for social change that have passed the test of desirability and viability, what it would take to actually implement them' (Wright, 2009, p 16).

At this stage, my own thinking has moved from desirability to the next stage of viability, with its two kinds of analysis: 'systematic theoretical models of how particular social structures and institutions would work, and empirical studies of cases, both historical and contemporary, where at least some aspects of the proposal have been tried' (Wright, 2007, p 27). On viability, I am drawn to cases such as the pioneer Children's Centres set up in the 1970s (Tizard et al, 1976) and the municipal schools that have provided early childhood education and care in Reggio Emilia and other Italian cities for more than 40 years (Rinaldi, 2006). However, viability clearly calls for more research, especially research in its cultural role that provides 'a different way of understanding and imagining social reality' (Biesta, 2007, p19), working with critical case studies of innovative provision and practice to understand better the conditions and processes that might stimulate and sustain alternatives.

With these limitations in mind, it is still possible to envisage a demarketised system based on Children's Centres, each serving all families in a local catchment area; each generating a wide range of projects in response to local encounters; each working in a collaborative network with other Centres; many willing to experiment with new pedagogical ideas and practices, supported by the kind of innovative roles, such as *pedagogistas* and *atelieristas*, so important to the longevity and dynamism of Reggio Emilia; each provided either publicly or by a non-profit private organisation, but all accountable to and supported by a democratically elected local authority; each funded through general taxation. Some might have their origins as private-for-profit nurseries, whose owners were prepared to convert their business into a democratically accountable and non-profit organisation. Those private providers unwilling or unable to make that change could continue in business, but with public funding gradually withdrawn, similar to existing private schools.

For those who find the prospect desirable, even perhaps viable, but doubt its achievability, I end with a short story that may give some hope or, at least, pause for thought. Susan George observes that '(i)n 1945 or 1950, if you had seriously proposed any of the ideas and policies in today's standard neo-liberal toolkit, you would have been laughed off the stage or sent off to the insane asylum' (George, 1999, p 1). Yet such threats did not stop some from thinking and planning alternatives, waiting for the times to change, encouraged by a sense of historical perspective:

> Only a crisis – actual or perceived – produces real change. When that crisis occurs the actions that are taken depend on the ideas that are lying around. That, I believe, is our basic function: to develop alternatives to existing policies, to keep them alive and available until the politically impossible becomes politically inevitable.

The author of these words? Milton Friedman writing in the early 1960s, a central figure in the neoliberal resurgence that gained momentum from the 1970s to become today's hegemonic regime (Friedman, 1962, p ix). There are crises enough facing us today. Time to develop alternatives!

References

Apple, M. (2004) *Ideology and curriculum*, 3rd edn, London: Routledge Falmer.

Archer, M. (2008) 'Childcare and early years provision in a diverse market – The government's approach', paper presented at a seminar organised by the International Centre for the Study of the Mixed Economy of Childcare, 12 May, www.uel.ac.uk/icmec/seminar/index.htm

Biesta, G. (2007) 'Why "what works" won't work: Evidence-based practice and the democratic deficit in educational research', *Educational Theory*, vol 57, no 1, pp 1–22.

Brannen, J. and Moss, P. (1998) 'The polarisation and intensification of parental employment in Britain: Consequences for children, families and the community', *Community, Work and Family*, vol 1, no 3, pp 229–247.

Cameron, D. (2011) 'How we will release the grip of state control', *The Daily Telegraph*, 20 February, ww.telegraph.co.uk/comment/8337239/How-we-will-release-the-grip-of-state-control.html.

Children's Workforce Development Council (2011) *The 39 Standards*, www.cwdcouncil.org.uk/eyps/standards.

Cohen, B., Moss, P., Petrie, P. and Wallace, J. (2004) *A new deal for children? Re-forming education and care in England, Scotland and Sweden*, Bristol: The Policy Press.

Colley, L. (2003) *Captives: Britain, empire and the world 1600–1850*, London: Pimlico.

Department for Children, Schools and Families (2007) *Sure Start children's centres: Phase 3 planning and delivery*. London: DCSF, www.education.gov.uk/publications/eOrderingDownload/DCSF-00665-2007.pdf.

Department for Education (2010) *Provision for children under five years of age in England: January 2010 (SFR 16/2010)*, www.education.gov.uk/rsgateway/DB/SFR/s000935/sfr16–2010.pdf.

Dewey, J. (1939)) 'Creative democracy – The task before us', address given at a dinner in honour of John Dewey, New York, 20 October, www.faculty.fairfield.edu/faculty/hodgson/Courses/progress/Dewey.pdf.

Esping-Andersen, G. (1999) *Social foundations of post-industrial economics*, Oxford: Oxford University Press.

Evans, M. (2010) 'Analysis: Providers wait for mists to clear on early years landscape', Nursery World 2 June, www.nurseryworld.co.uk/news/1006925/Analysis-Providers-wait-mists-clear-early-years-landscape/.

Fielding, M. and Moss, P. (2010) *Radical education and the common school: A democratic alternative*, London: Routledge.

Friedman, M. (1962) *Capitalism and freedom*, Chicago: University of Chicago Press.

George, S. (1999) 'A short history of neoliberalism: Twenty years of elite economics and emerging opportunities for change', paper given at conference *Economic Sovereignty in a Globalising World*, Bangkok, Thailand, 24–26 March 1999, www.globalexchange.org/campaigns/econ101/neoliberalism.html.

Giddens, A. (1998) *The third way: The renewal of social democracy*, Cambridge: Polity Press.

Harvey, D. (2005) *A brief history of Neoliberalism*, Oxford: Oxford University Press.

Judt, T. (2010) *Ill fares the land*, London: Allen Lane.

Kaga, J., Bennett, J. and Moss, P. (2010) *Caring and learning together – A cross-national study on the integration of early childhood education within education*, Paris: UNESCO.

Laing & Buisson (2010) *Children's nurseries UK market report*, London: Laing & Buisson Ltd.

Moss, P. (2009) *There are alternatives! Markets and democratic experimentalism in early childhood education and care*, The Hague: Bernard van leer Foundation, www.bernardvanleer.org/publications_results?SearchableText=B-WOP-053.

Mouffe, C. (2007) 'Artistic activism and agonistic spaces', *Art and Research*, vol 1, no 2, www.artandresearch.org.uk/v1n2/mouffe.html

OECD (2006) *Starting strong II*, Paris: OECD.

Penn, H. (2009) 'Public and private: The history of early education and care institutions in the United Kingdom' in K. Schweiwe and H. Willekens (eds) *Child care and preschool development in Europe – Institutional perspectives*, Basingstoke: Palgrave Macmillan.

Randall, V. (2002) 'Child care in Britain, or how do you restructure nothing?' In: S. Michel and R. Mahon (eds) *Child care policy at the crossroads: Gender and welfare state restructuring*, London: Routledge, pp 219 – 238.

Rinaldi, C. (2006) *In dialogue with Reggio Emilia: Listening, researching and learning*, London: Routledge.

Rose, N. (1999) *Powers of freedom: Reframing political thought*, Cambridge: Cambridge University Press.

Sure Start (2006) *Capital guidance: Sure Start children's centres, extended schools and childcare*, London: Sure Start, www.childrens-centres.net/SupportDocuments/Sure%20Start%20Capital%20Guidance%20Dec%2006.pdf.

The Stationery Office (1999) *Children's day care facilities at 31 March 1999 England*, www.archive.official-documents.co.uk/document/dfee/daycare/cdc-03.htm.

Tickell, C. (2011) *The early years: Foundations for life, health and learning*, London: Department for Education.

Tizard, B., Moss, P. and Perry, J. (1976) *All our children: Pre-school services in a changing society*, London: Maurice Temple Smith.

Unger, R.M. (2005) *What should the left propose?*, London: Verso.

Vincent, C. and Ball, S. (2006) *Childcare, choice and class practices*, London: Routledge.

Whitty, G., Power, S. and Halpin, D. (1998) *Devolution and choice in schools*, Buckingham: Open University Press.

Wright, E.O. (2007) 'Guidelines for envisioning real utopias', *Soundings*, no 36 (Summer), pp 26–39.

Wright, E.O. (2009) 'The tasks of emancipatory social science', Chapter Two of final pre-publication draft of *Envisioning Real Utopias*, www.ssc.wisc.edu/~wright/ERU_files/ERU-CHAPTER-2-final.pdf

ABC Learning and Australian early education and care: a retrospective ethical audit of a radical experiment

Jennifer Sumsion

Introduction

This chapter unfolds in three parts. It commences with the cautionary narrative of ABC Learning, an Australian childcare corporation that became the world's largest for-profit childcare provider within a few years of its listing on the Australian Stock Exchange. It then revisits findings of an ethical audit (Sumsion, 2006) of ABC Learning's operations from 2001–05 in light of subsequent developments. The chapter concludes with reflections on some of the many questions prompted by the rise and fall of ABC Learning.

Some familiarity with the Australian early childhood education and care (ECEC) context is needed to fully comprehend the enormity of the ABC Learning epic. In brief, as Brennan and Newberry (2010) outline, the Whitlam Labor Government, 1972–75, introduced supply-side funding for not-for-profit long-day care, that is full daycare and education for children aged from 6 weeks to 5 years of age. This initiative positioned childcare provision primarily as a public responsibility and led to a significant expansion of the not-for-profit community-based sector. In 1991, the Hawke–Keating Labor Government, 1983–96, extended government subsidies to private for-profit providers, thus legitimating childcare provision as a profit making undertaking. A market approach became entrenched under the Howard Liberal-National Coalition (Conservative) Government, 1996–2007. Supply-side funding was dismantled when operational subsidies for not-for-profit services were removed in 1997. In 2000, the Child Care Benefit, a demand-side subsidy to parents that flowed directly to the centre attended by their child was introduced. These policy levers increasingly positioned childcare as a private responsibility best provided through market forces. The attractions of a business model underpinned by a secure government-funded revenue stream led to the rapid expansion of for-profit provision and created market conditions conducive to the entry of corporate operators such as ABC Learning (Brennan and Newberry, 2010; Brennan, this volume).

ABC Learning: an epic narrative

The rise and fall of ABC Learning began, uneventfully enough, in 1988 in the Australian state of Queensland when the 22-year-old entrepreneur Eddy Groves and his wife, Le Neve, bought a licence to operate a childcare centre in suburban Brisbane. They expected that Queensland's rapidly growing population, fuelled in part by an influx of young, two-income families from other states who had little extended family support, would make childcare a 'recession proof' growth industry (Fraser, 2004). Assisted by increased government subsidies for for-profit childcare operators, they gradually expanded their childcare business. Twelve years later, in 2000, their company, ABC Learning, owned 31 centres in Queensland and Victoria (Wisenthal, 2005).

In 2001, to gain access to significant capital to fund further expansion, ABC Learning was floated on the Australian Stock Exchange. It rapidly became one of the best performing stocks with net profits rising 1,100% in the period from June 2002 to June 2006 (Brennan and Newberry, 2010) and its share price increasing sevenfold from 2002 to 2004 (Alberici, 2004). Its performance attracted admiring commentary in the financial pages of the press and large numbers of shareholders wanting to ride the first wave of corporate investment in childcare.

ABC Learning's rapid growth also generated heated opposition from small, for-profit providers, not-for-profit providers and their advocates, social-democratic-leaning media commentators, and academics – not least because the Child Care Benefit accounted for approximately 50% of ABC Learning's revenue (ABC Radio National, 2004). Moreover, allegations abounded concerning reductions in the employment of qualified staff and in food, equipment and cleaning budgets following its takeover of existing centres, along with anecdotal reports of centres gaining accreditation despite not meeting required standards (Sumsion, 2006). Suspicion and anger was further fuelled by Eddy Groves's widely perceived confrontational style and his status, in 2006, as the wealthiest man in Australia under 40 years of age, according to the *Business Review Weekly*'s Young Rich List (*The Age*, 2006). Nevertheless, ABC Learning seemed unstoppable. Less than four years after floating on the stock exchange it owned or operated approximately 20% of Australian long-day care centres. It had also bought a major toy supplier, established a staff training college, and planned to move into out-of-school provision and to establish fee-paying primary schools (Sumsion, 2006).

In November 2005, ABC Learning became the world's largest listed childcare provider following its acquisition of the Learning Care Group, the third largest childcare company in the US, with 460 centres attended by approximately 69,000 children (Rochfort, 2005) and franchises in Indonesia, the Philippines and Hong Kong (Brennan, 2007). Groves immediately announced plans for further US expansion, followed by expansion into the UK, New Zealand and China. Canadian not-for-profit activists mounted an extensive and ultimately successful national campaign to thwart Groves's plans for expansion into Canada (*Canada Newswire*, 2007). By late 2007, ABC Learning owned or operated more than 2,300 centres across at least five countries and was by far Australia's largest childcare provider (Brennan and Newberry, 2010).

In February 2008, on the cusp of the global financial crisis, came the shock announcement that ABC Learning's profit for the first half of the financial year had slumped more than 40% in comparison with the previous year. Within a month, its share price had dropped by more than 65%, triggering a series of margin loan calls on its directors (Carson, 2008b). To meet the margin calls, Le Neve Groves sold all her ABC Learning shares, while Eddy Groves retained only a token shareholding from a portfolio worth AUD295m [GBP124m] at its peak in May 2007 (Korporaal and Meade, 2008).

ABC Learning's rapidly deteriorating financial situation led to a sudden forced sale of 60% of the company's US holdings (Carson, 2008a). Its share price continued to plunge. In August 2008, it was suspended from trading. In September 2008, Eddy and Le Neve Groves resigned from their positions at ABC Learning after a series of continued delays to the release of its full-year financial results (Walsh, 2008). In November 2008, ABC Learning went into voluntary receivership and its highly questionable accounting practices that grossly overinflated its value were exposed (Brennan and Newberry, 2010). To keep the remaining centres open until a buyer could be found, the Australian Government poured in AUD56m [GBP24m] to cover operating costs. It also announced a Senate Inquiry into the provision of ECEC, including the impact of ABC Learning's collapse (The Senate Education Employment and Workplace Relations References Committee, 2009). Eventually, the centres were sold to a consortium of not-for-profit charities, bringing to an end a radical experiment in corporate childcare provision (Brennan, 2007).

Challenging ABC Learning's ascendancy

ABC Learning's ascendancy exemplified the Howard Government's [1996–2007] market-based ECEC policy agenda outlined earlier in the chapter. Endeavours to challenge the policy wisdom of allowing the unfettered expansion of ABC Learning failed to gain traction, with opposition to its growing market domination apparently ignored by government or dismissed as ideologically driven (Horin, 2008). The difficulties were compounded by the seemingly almost insurmountable challenges of obtaining 'hard' empirical evidence to support growing anecdotal evidence and analytical and philosophical arguments about the dangers posed by ABC Learning's increasing market concentration.

Disaggregated data enabling comparison between not-for-profit centres, privately owned for-profit centres and corporate childcare chains were not publicly available (Sumsion, 2006). Moreover, in effect, ABC Learning was 'off limits' to researchers, despite claims to the contrary by CEO Eddy Groves. Difficulties in obtaining funding for what could seem a politically motivated project, nervousness about ABC Learning's history of initiating legal proceedings against critics and the complexity and lack of transparency of its business structures further hindered research into the nature, effects and implications of ABC Learning's operations, particularly in the first few years of its rapid expansion (Horin, 2008).

An ethical audit

To contribute to efforts to force a policy debate about whether the corporatisation of ECEC, that is a growing concentration of ECEC provision by listed companies with legal responsibilities to maximise shareholder profits, was in the public interest, and employing a framework proposed by Cribb and Ball (2005), I undertook an 'ethical audit' of what was then known about ABC Learning (Sumsion, 2006). The audit covered the period from floating of the company in 2001 through to late 2005 and the beginning of its international expansion. A secondary aim was to identify evidence gaps and to propose a research agenda that could address those gaps. This chapter revisits and extends that earlier audit by drawing on information that has since come to light and on developments in the period from 2006–10.

Central to the notion of an ethical audit is the premise that considerations of the public interest should be viewed through an ethical lens that tries to find a way of balancing often competing interests, perspectives and goals, rather than simply focusing on primarily economic considerations (Cribb and Ball, 2005). Drawing on Cribb and Ball's notion of clusters of goals, obligations and dispositions, taken respectively from theories of consequentialism, deontology and virtue theory (see Cribb and Ball, 2005 for elaboration), the 2006 audit endeavoured to provide a balanced discussion of concerns that had been raised about corporatisation, and particularly ABC Learning. Using ABC Learning as a case study, it focused specifically on the interrelated issues of opportunity costs, market concentration, quality, workforce and 'corporate citizenship'. This chapter picks up those threads.

Through the ethical lens of goals

Theories of consequentialism suggest that goals can be seen as reflections of intent, emanating from weighing up potentially positive and negative consequences of possible courses of action (Cribb and Ball, 2005). Following Cribb and Ball, the 2006 audit was based on assumptions that even if shared goals are desirable, the strategies used to achieve them should be subject to careful scrutiny, including consideration of opportunity costs, that is costs involved in following one particular course of action rather than another. The 2006 audit pointed to what, at face value, seemed congruent goals of the Australian Government and ABC Learning: providing good quality ECEC services and enabling parents a choice of services (Patterson, 2004). A particular focus of the audit was the opportunity costs of hastening the policy shift away from not-for-profit centres with their tradition of contributing to the social fabric of their local communities (Press, 1999), to for-profit, specifically corporate, provision. The effects of market concentration, in terms of long-term financial viability, political influence and homogeneity were a further focus (Sumsion, 2006).

The 2006 audit anticipated two quite different scenarios. The first involved possible effects should ABC Learning's plans for ongoing domestic and international expansion prove successful. For example, what was the likelihood that, if it continued to expand, ABC Learning might outgrow the capacity of government to regulate it (Crouch, 2000), or pursue its vested interests at the expense of broader social and economic interests, for instance, by opposing the introduction of paid parental leave (Brennan, 2009)? Would it intensify its already widely perceived undue political influence (Jokovich, 2005), or through its emphasis on standardisation, homogenise ECEC provision (Press and Woodrow, 2005)? Conversely, the second scenario concerned the potentially far reaching implications should ABC Learning's plans for ongoing domestic and international expansion be thwarted. The risks associated with expansion were considerable. They ranged from the possibility of demographic or other social changes causing a decline in demand for ECEC, increased competitive pressures and/or market saturation, to poor financial decisions, and lack of funding or adequate staff to support further expansion, through to reputational damage, and regulatory change unfavourable to ABC Learning's interests (Wilson HTM, 2003). Ultimately, both scenarios eventuated – unparalleled expansion and market concentration through to mid-2007, followed by complete corporate collapse by late 2008 – resulting in enormous opportunity costs.

ABC Learning reached its Australian peak of 1,084 centres in July 2007 (The Senate Education Employment and Workplace Relations References Committee, 2009), an increase of 64% on the 660 Australian centres held in June 2005 (ABC Learning, 2005) as reported in the earlier audit. Estimates of its market share varied from at least 20% (Australian Government Department of Education Employment and Workplace Relations, nd) to 30% (Groves, 2006, cited by Brennan and Newberry, 2010) to possibly even 50% in Victoria and Queensland (Gittens, 2008). Yet tellingly, increasing market concentration did not translate to a substantial overall growth in the number of childcare places (Brennan, 2007). Moreover, given the aggressively anti-competitive strategies used by ABC Learning to consolidate its market position (Hills, 2006; Press and Woodrow, 2009), there seemed little basis for assertions that the net effect was a greater choice for parents of high quality services.

Nuanced analyses are needed, however, as parents' experiences of the childcare market and the choices available to them vary according to context (Harrison et al, 2011). An important consideration is whether the market is 'thick', offering many services and with consumer capacity to pay a premium for quality, or 'thin', offering a small number of services and with little capacity to pay more for higher quality (Cleveland and Krashinsky, 2009). Nuanced analyses about the effect of ABC Learning's expansion on parents' choice of services are constrained by scant systematic, fine-grained quantitative and qualitative evidence – but the limited evidence available gives little cause for confidence.

Harris (2008), for example, interviewed 20 mothers about their experiences of choosing childcare in Townsville, a large regional town in north Queensland. Congruent with high internal migration to the town, two thirds of the participants had no extended family in Townsville, leaving them especially reliant on the childcare market. With a population of approximately 154,000, average income levels slightly above the national average, and 66 early childhood centres

(Harris, 2008), Townsville could be considered a 'thick' market, theoretically with sufficient services, competition and income levels to enable consumer choice to drive up quality (Cleveland and Krashinsky, 2009).That was not the experience of the participants in Harris's study. They sought centres that were embedded in the community to build their community connections and reduce their social isolation.Yet of the 66 centres, only 12 were not-for-profit and community-based. Of the 44 for-profit centres, almost 70% were owned by corporate chains, primarily ABC Learning. Many participants who had used or approached corporate centres found a 'one size fits all' model that was 'unresponsive to the needs of their regional community' (Harris, 2008, p 48).

Although the findings of Harris's study are not generalisable, Press and Woodrow's (2009) analysis of ABC's market concentration in large regional towns in New South Wales (NSW) highlighted the potential for similar experiences to be replayed many times over. Several much smaller NSW country towns, quintessentially 'thin' markets, lost their only childcare centre after ABC Learning sold the centres to Child Care Providers Pty Ltd, a little-known but closely connected company, prompting allegations that ABC Learning was attempting to 'bury' unprofitable services while deflecting criticism of its operations (Horin, 2007). Although the centres were a vital part of the social and educational infrastructure of these small communities, local organisations were allegedly refused opportunities to discuss taking over their operation (Horin, 2007). Parent and community concerns about ABC Learning's market concentration were also reported in 'thick' metropolitan markets (AAP, 2006).

In the hundreds of documents reviewed for the 2006 ethical audit and for this chapter, other than statements by Groves himself (for example Groves, 2006), there is barely, if any, mention of ABC Learning contributing to local communities beyond providing a childcare service. On the contrary, its business model focused heavily on exclusive global supply agreements (Press and Woodrow, 2009) that did relatively little to support local suppliers. This lost opportunity to strengthen local economies was yet another facet of ABC's poor track record of contributions to strengthening communities, thus constituting further significant opportunity costs.

ABC Learning's subsequent collapse brought further heavy financial and opportunity costs.When forced into receivership by insolvency in November 2008, it provided for over 100,000 children and employed approximately 16,000 staff (DEEWR, 2009). The risks of substantial adverse economic and social impact were therefore considerable.

Consequently, as noted previously a package up to AUD56m [GBP24m], in addition to receivership costs, was made available to keep the 400 loss-making ABC Learning centres open until the end of 2008, and subsequently to keep 262 centres still considered unviable by the receivers open until March 2009 (DEEWR, 2009). This 'rescue package' was in addition to AUD300m [GBP144m] paid to ABC Learning in 2008 alone as taxpayer funded subsidies (Bita and Fraser, 2008). Eddy Groves argued that ABC Learning's massive investment in physical infrastructure of close to AUD100m [GBP48m] up to 2006 (ABC Learning Centres Ltd, 2006) and an undisclosed amount since, had left a substantial legacy. Yet, as not-for-profit advocates argued, government funding poured into ABC Learning could have achieved 'a much better outcome... a high quality community owned service in every community around the nation' (Romeril, 2006).

Proponents of market forces claim that competition generates robustness, and implicitly sustainability, along with consumer choice and quality (Crouch, 2000). This proved not the case with ABC Learning. Its corporate model was clearly not sustainable; nor did it appear to give parents a greater choice. Questions arose, as well, about whether ABC Learning met its obligations to provide good quality services.

Through the ethical lens of obligations

From theories of deontological reasoning, Cribb and Ball (2005) take the notion of obligation as encompassing a sense of one's ethical duty. Obligations, therefore, extend beyond instrumental considerations concerning how to achieve goals to issues of ethical consequences. The Howard Government appeared sanguine about Eddy Groves's assurance that ABC Learning could fulfil its obligations to provide high quality ECEC, while meeting its legal requirements to maximise shareholder benefits (Patterson, 2004). Yet the 2006 audit revealed widespread scepticism about Groves's assurances that quality and profits could be achieved through economies of scale, by spreading costs over a large number of centres, given that the costs of employing staff account for a high percentage of operating costs (IBISWorld, 2003). Allegations concerning cost-cutting measures that inevitably undermine quality – such as severe reductions in the employment of qualified staff and in food and equipment budgets – were widely reported (ABC Radio National, 2004; Alberici, 2004; *Business Review Weekly*, 2003), including under parliamentary privilege (Hills, 2006). Critics contended that ABC Learning might have found ways of circumventing regulatory requirements (Sumsion, 2006).

Similar doubts about ABC Learning's capacity to meet its obligations to provide good quality services were raised by academics and other commentators who pointed to international evidence indicating that, on balance, for-profit centres generally provide lower quality ECEC than their not-for-profit counterparts, and that for-profit chains, on average, provide lower quality than privately owned, for-profit centres (Harrison et al, 2011; Sosinsky, this volume). As Harrison et al (2011) caution, however, Australia's long-standing commitment to means-tested fee support for families using childcare and regulatory frameworks may mean that trends elsewhere are not borne out in Australia.

Only two studies (Rush, 2006; Rush and Downie, 2006) appear to have endeavoured, albeit indirectly, to ascertain the quality of ABC Learning centres. Both were undertaken by an independent research institute seemingly not bound by constraints typically imposed by university ethics committees, including employer permission to approach staff. The first study (Rush, 2006) involved a stratified random sample of childcare staff from 462 centres (approximately 10% of all centres). Analysable responses were received from 578 staff (slightly less than approximately 1% of childcare centre staff Australia-wide) from 217 centres (approximately 5.5% of all centres). The highest response rate was from not-for-profit centres (66%), followed by private for-profit (43%) and corporate chains (30%).

Survey respondents were asked about time available for staff to develop individual relationships with children, the centre's programme and equipment, the nature and amount of food provided to children, staff turnover and staff–child ratios, as well as open-ended questions to ascertain their perceptions of the quality of the centre at which they worked (Rush, 2006). Staff at corporate centres consistently rated their workplaces lower on these dimensions than did staff from not-for-profit centres. The differences were statistically significantly different, in contrast to the small, non-significant differences between the responses of staff from not-for-profit and privately owned, for-profit centres. The study attracted considerable media attention, especially the finding that 21% of respondents from corporate centres would not send their own child aged under 2 years to a centre of equivalent quality to their workplace because of quality concerns, compared to approximately 5% of respondents from not-for-profit and private for-profit centres, (Rush, 2006). Telephone interviews were subsequently undertaken with 20 survey respondents from ABC Learning centres (Rush and Downie, 2006) to tease out concerns identified by the survey, but these yielded mixed and inconclusive findings.

The respective limitations of these studies, such as reliance on self-reported perceptions, small sample size, no comparison sample, mean that the findings must be interpreted with caution. Nevertheless, they suggest sufficient grounds to warrant more substantive investigations into possible differences in quality between centres of different auspice types, even taking into account the likely unevenness of quality amongst centres of the same auspice type (Cleveland and Krashinsky, 2009). Robust studies that have enabled comparisons of quality in not-for-profit and for-profit centres have been undertaken in several countries, but notably not in Australia (Harrison et al, 2011). As noted previously, nor have existing data collected for regulatory purposes been made publicly available in ways that facilitate comparison between auspice types, including corporate chains.

So far, this chapter has focused on ABC Learning's relatively poor track record of serving the public interest, when considered through the lenses of goals and obligations. The discussion now moves to dispositions, the third lens of Cribb and Ball's (2005) ethical audit framework.

Through the ethical lens of dispositions

Obligations encompass a spectrum from strictly obligatory to high ideals (Beauchamp and Childress, 2001). Dispositions can be thought of as inclinations, or otherwise, to go beyond the strictly obligatory, and to contribute to the 'flourishing' of individuals and society (Cribb and Ball, 2005, p 117). Following Cribb and Ball, it is pertinent to ask what dispositions ABC Learning should have been required to demonstrate, given its high level of taxpayer support. The 2006 audit raised questions about its disposition to provide higher than a minimally acceptable quality of ECEC, and to enhance pay, conditions, status and overall professionalism of the ECEC workforce in excess of minimum legal obligations.

ABC Learning's highest concentrations of centres were in Queensland and Victoria, which had amongst the lowest standards for staff qualifications in Australia. This distribution suggests that ABC Learning preferred to operate primarily in a low pay environment. This impression was reinforced by its attempt to challenge Queensland regulations concerning the maintenance of staff–child ratios during meal breaks (Horin, 2003) and its unsuccessful application for exemption from paying increased wages on the basis of financial hardship (Peacock, 2004) at a time when it reportedly anticipated making an AUD100,000 [GBP38,000] annual profit from each centre (*The Age*, 2004). Its unprecedented defamation action against the Liquor, Hospitality and Miscellaneous Union (LHMU), Australia's largest childcare union, for attempting to disseminate information to ABC Learning staff concerning their legal entitlements to certain working conditions further fuelled allegations about the company's motives (*Business Review Weekly*, 2003). On the other hand, ABC Learning claimed that it offered staff access to profit sharing arrangements, a benefit that contributed to a supposedly much lower staff turnover (7.5%) than the industry average (ABC Radio National, 2004), estimated to be as high as 40% (CSMAC, 2006). If this figure is correct, and not based solely on its relatively small proportion of permanent staff, ABC Learning's seemingly impressive retention rate suggested a much higher degree of staff satisfaction than claimed by its critics.

ABC Learning's mixed report card in its treatment of its workforce continued through to its collapse. In early 2006, its unsuccessful appeal to the Victoria Supreme Court over an AUD200 [GBP42] fine for a breach of regulations, in an attempt to shift blame from the corporation to individual employees (Faroque, 2006), attracted much derisory press coverage. Perhaps recognising its vulnerability to criticism that it was not meeting its obligations concerning quality, and possibly concerned about the tight labour market, in December 2006, ABC Learning signed a formal national workplace agreement, negotiated by the LHMU to substantially improve pay and conditions (Summers, 2007). Given ABC Learning's history of hostility to unions (Brown, 2009), the 'landmark' agreement would have been inconceivable at the time of the earlier, 2006, audit. As Summers (2007, p 31) noted at the time, '… it will be worth tracking whether this agreement marks a turnaround in conditions – and perceptions. If so, getting into bed with the union might turn out to have been a smart business move.' Ironically, a month before Summers's observation, ABC Learning and the LHMU were 'still at a stand off' about 'how to interpret' the agreement, following protests by ABC Learning staff about underpayment, with the LHMU reportedly accusing ABC Learning of 'outrageous' behaviour (*Mandurah Coastal Times*, 2007, p 5). The relationship between ABC Learning and the LHMU continued to deteriorate and in October 2008 the LHMU initiated formal action against ABC Learning, alleging that it had breached the national workplace agreement (Press, 2008). It is difficult, therefore, to conclude that ABC Learning demonstrated a disposition to enhance, in any substantial way, the pay, conditions and professional status of the ECEC workforce.

Reflections

The rise and fall of ABC Learning poses many questions concerning market-based ECEC provision. Why, for example, was ABC Learning, as a single corporation, allowed to assume such a dominant position in the Australian ECEC market? Could a similar scenario happen elsewhere? Might ethical audits assist in monitoring market operations and their consequences?

ABC Learning clearly constituted a vast, unprecedented and unsuccessful experiment in Australian ECEC provision (Brennan, 2007, p 13). Traces of damning evidence had emerged by the time of the 2006 audit. Probing questions were asked publicly of ABC Learning and government by ECEC experts from industry and academia for several years (Horin, 2008). A small number of academics eventually managed painstakingly to piece together damning forensic evidence about ABC Learning's legally and ethically dubious operations – see especially Brennan and Newberry (2010), Press (2008), Press and Woodrow (2009). Why, then, did it take ABC Learning's collapse and a parliamentary motion from the Australian Greens to pressure the Rudd government into eventually holding a Senate inquiry (Brennan and Newberry, 2010)? The endemic lack of transparency surrounding ABC Learning suggests that answers to many of the questions arising from the ABC Learning experiment and the full extent of the real and opportunity costs incurred, will probably never be fully known. Explanations for why there was, seemingly, so little political and policy attention to ABC Learning throughout its ascendancy conceivably lie in a combination of factors, including ideological blindness about market operations (Crouch, 2000), inertia arising from a sense of inevitability concerning ABC Learning's increasing market concentration, a reluctance to take political risks associated with disrupting the status quo (Althaus, 2008) and the Australian Public Service's reported weakness in producing 'informed and forward looking advice' (Rudd, 2010, p 3).

Presumably, such factors are not specific to Australia. It is interesting to speculate, therefore, about whether similar events might have happened in other countries in which ABC Learning had established a presence, had its trajectory not been curtailed by the global financial crisis or its ultimately unsustainable business model. Likewise, could an equivalent corporation emerge from mixed market ECEC provision in other national contexts, including those discussed in this volume? Moreover, in positioning parents as ECEC consumers and sources of government-guaranteed income streams, does demand-side funding inevitably invite opportunistic corporate behaviour of the kind that characterised ABC Learning? What checks and balances are needed, in Australia and elsewhere, to safeguard against the 'costly and dysfunctional outcomes' (Brennan and Newberry, 2010, p 5) of the ABC Learning experiment? Collectively, the chapters in this volume generate insights into questions such as these.

A stark lesson from the ABC Learning epic is the need for policy accountability beyond calculating and managing political risk. Cribb and Ball's (2005) ethical audit framework, used in this chapter and in the 2006 audit, is inevitably somewhat reductionist, for endeavouring to tease out goals, obligations and dispositions, and their consequent effects artificially separates complex interrelations, as evident in the case of ABC Learning. Nevertheless, the framework provides a useful analytical tool for closely monitoring market-based ECEC provision. It focuses attention, for example, on the interplay between social, political and economic issues and tensions in ECEC provision and the ethical demands inherent in negotiating them. It also reinforces the importance of building a sound evidence base from which to evaluate the benefits and costs of approaches to ECEC provision. Moreover, it provides a scaffold for considering how one might develop a rich mosaic of evidence types and sources of the kind advocated by Luke (2005). To be effective, the nature and focus of ethical audits would need to be adapted to suit the context, and every effort made to ensure they were used in non-trivialised ways. Within these caveats, the potential of ethical audits to inform policy development, analysis and evaluation appears to warrant further exploration.

A postscript

In 2010, DEEWR commissioned an analysis of gaps in research evidence concerning Australian ECEC, including the effects of market operations. Whether it will act on the recommendations – which included the need for transparency and the development of an Australian evidence base (Harrison et al, 2011) – is yet to be seen. More transparency, responsiveness to sector concerns and commitment to a drawing on a rich array of evidence would, indeed, be a welcome outcome of the ABC Learning debacle.

Acknowledgement
I would like to thank Dr Frances Press for her insightful feedback on a draft of this chapter.

References

AAP (2006) 'Parents fight bid by childcare giant', News.com.au, 4 April.

ABC Learning (2005) 'So much more than childcare!', www.childcare.com.au.

ABC Learning Centres Ltd (2006) *Annual report 2006*, www.cpaaustralia.com.au/cps/rde/xbcr/cpa-site/ABC-learning-annual-report-2006.pdf.

ABC Radio National (2004) *Childcare profits. Background briefing.* www.abc.net.au/rn/talks/bbing/stories/s1214400.htm.

Alberici, E. (2004) 'Childcare companies in the spotlight: The 7.30 Report', 29 March, *Australian Broadcasting Corporation.* www.abc.net.au/7.30/content/2004/21076521.htm

Althaus, C. (2008) *Calculating political risk*, Sydney: UNSW Press.

Beauchamp, T. and Childress, J. F. (2001) *Principles of biomedical ethics*, Oxford: Oxford University Press.

Bita, N. and Fraser, A. (2008) 'Imploding as easy as ABC', *The Australian*, 15–16 November.

Brennan, D. (2007) 'The ABC of child care politics', *Australian Journal of Social Issues*, vol 42, no 2, pp 213–226.

Brennan, D. (2009) 'Child care and Australian social policy', in J. Bowes and R. Grace (eds) *Children, families and communities: Contexts and consequences* (3rd edn), South Melbourne: Oxford University Press, pp 205–18.

Brennan, D. and Newberry, S. (2010) 'Indirect policy tools: Demand-side funding and lessons to be learned: Early childhood education and care', Paper presented at the 6th Asia Pacific Interdisciplinary Research In Accounting Conference, Sydney, July.

Brown, T. (2009) 'As easy as ABC?', *Labor Studies Journal*, vol 34, no 2, pp 235–51.

Business Review Weekly (2003) 'Playgrounds of profit', *Business Review Weekly*, 13–19 November.

Canada Newswire (2007) 'Advocates mark International Day of the Child with proclamations against the spread of 'big box' child care', *Canada Newswire*, 21 November.

Carson, V. (2008a) 'ABC's top guns jump ship', *The Age*, 23 April.

Carson, V. (2008b) 'Child-care giant in debt crisis', *The Sydney Morning Herald*, 27 February.

Cleveland, G. and Krashinsky, M. (2009) 'The nonprofit advantage: Producing quality in thick and thin child care markets', *Journal of Policy Analysis and Management*, vol 28, no 3, pp 440–462.

Community Services Ministers' Advisory Council (CSMAC) (2006) *National children's services workforce study*, Melbourne: Victorian Department of Human Services.

Cribb, A. and Ball, S. (2005) 'Towards an ethical audit of the privatisation of education', *British Journal of Educational Studies*, vol 53, no 2, pp 115–128.

Crouch, C. (2000) *Coping with post-democracy*, London: Fabian Society.

DEEWR (Australian Government Department of Education Employment and Workplace Relations) (2009) *Inquiry into the provision of childcare: Submission to the Senate Education, Employment and Workplace Relations Committee.*

Faroque, F. (2006) 'It's not fair says company founder', *The Age*, 27 April, www.theage.com.au/news/national/its-not-fair-says-company;founder/2006/04/

Fraser, A. (2004) 'Child's play', *Weekend Australian*, 11–12 September.

Gittens, R. (2008) 'Child-care rebate bad for kids', *The Sydney Morning Herald*, 19 March.

Groves, E. (2006) 'Human services in 2020: A view from for profit providers', Paper presented at the NCOSS Council of Social Services of New South Wales.

Harris, N. (2008) 'Women's reflections on choosing quality long day care in a regional community', *Australian Journal of Early Childhood*, vol 33, no 3, pp 42–49.

Harrison, L., Sumsion, J., Press, F., Wong, S., Fordham, L. and Goodfellow, J. (2011) *A shared early childhood development research agenda: Key research gaps 2010–2015*, Report commissioned by the Australian Research Alliance for Children and Youth on behalf of the Australian Government Department of Education, Employment and Workplace Relations, www.deewr.gov.au/Earlychildhood/Resources/Documents/ASharedECDResearchAgenda.pdf.

Hills, B. (2006) 'Cradle snatcher', *The Sydney Morning Herald*, 11–12 March.

Horin, A. (2003) 'When making money is child's play', *Sydney Morning Herald*, 4 October.

Horin, A. (2007) 'Nowhere to go for hundreds of children as child-care centres close', The Sydney Morning Herald, 17 November.

Horin, A. (2008) 'Women tolled warning bells but no one wanted to listen', *The Sydney Morning Herald*, 8–9 November.

IBISWorld (2003) *Childcare services in Australia*, Report 08710. Melbourne: IBISWorld Pty Ltd.

Jokovich, E. (2005) 'Family payment: About face muddies the waters', *Rattler*, vol 73, pp 6–7.

Korporaal, G. and Meade, K. (2008) 'Flash suit, but Eddy's been stripped', *The Australian*, 8 March.

Luke, A. (2005) 'Evidence-based state literacy policy: A critical alternative', in N. Bascia, A. Cumming, A. Datnow, K. Leithwood and D. Livingstone (eds) *International Handbook of Educational Policy*, Dordrecht, the Netherlands: Springer, pp 661–675.

Mandurah Coastal Times (2007) 'Workers protest', *Mandurah Coastal Times*, 13 June.

Patterson, K. (2004) *Senate Official Hansard*, 6 December, no 3, 2.21pm Commonwealth of Australia Parliamentary Debates, p 25, Available at www.aph.gov.au/hansard/senate/dailys/ds061204.pdf.

Peacock, S. (2004) 'Main game child's play for young king of kids', *The West Australian*, 11 September

Press, F. (1999) 'The demise of the community-owned long-day care centres and the rise of the mythical consumer', *Australian Journal of Early Childhood*, vol 24, no 1, pp 20–26.

Press, F. (2008) 'ABC Learning: The downfall of the corporate childcare giant and the ramifications for the childcare sector', *Rattler*, vol 88, pp 20–25.

Press, F. and Woodrow, C. (2005) 'Commodification, corporatisation and children's spaces', *Australian Journal of Education*, vol 49, no 5, pp 278–291.

Press, F. and Woodrow, C. (2009) 'The giant in the playground: Investigating the reach and implications of the corporatisation of child care provision', in D. King and G. Meagher (eds) *Paid care in Australia: Politics, profits, practices*, Sydney: Sydney University Press, pp 231–248.

Rochfort, S. (2005) 'ABC Learning big on US littlies', *The Sydney Morning Herald*, 17 November.

Romeril, B. (2006, 14 March), in N. Woolrich, *Concerns over ABC Learning's dominance of childcare*, Radio National, PM.

Rudd, K. (2010) 'Equipping the Australian public service for Australia's future challenges', *The Australian Journal of Public Administration*, vol 69, no 1, pp 1–8.

Rush, E. (2006) *Child care quality in Australia*, Discussion Paper Number 84, Canberra: The Australia Institute.

Rush, E., and Downie, C. (2006) *ABC Learning centres: A case study of Australia's largest child care corporation*, Discussion Paper Number 87: The Australia Institute.

Summers, A. (2007) 'Child-care agreement gets back to valuing workers', *The Sydney Morning Herald*, 14–15 July.

Sumsion, J. (2006) 'The corporatization of Australian childcare: Towards an ethical audit and research agenda', *Journal of Early Childhood Research*, vol 4, no 2, pp 99–120.

The Age (2004) 'ABC childcare empire looks to grow', *The Age*, 13 September, www.theage.com.au/articles/2004/0913/1094927463432.html? oneclick=true.

The Age (2006) 'Childcare king Groves tops BRW Young Rich', *The Age*, 13 September, www.theage.com.au/news/business/childcare-king-groves-tops-brw-young-rich/2006/09/13/1157827004561.html#.

The Senate Education Employment and Workplace Relations References Committee. (2009) Provision of childcare, www.aph.gov.au/senate/committee/eet_ctte/child_care/report/index.htm

Walsh, L. (2008) 'Groves quit embattled ABC group', *The Courier Mail*, 2 October.

Wilson HTM Ltd (2003).

Wisenthal, S. (2005) 'Oh baby, Eddy's just done it again', *The Weekend Australian Financial Review*, 19–20 November.

THIRTEEN

Childcare markets and government intervention

Gillian Paull

Introduction

Childcare is different from other goods and services traded in markets. Its unique set of characteristics raises issues and choices which have been addressed with great diversity across the world. Indeed, the range of issues that has been explored in this book reflects both the multitude of concerns and social objectives as well as the breadth of academic disciplines that have contributed to the discussions presented here.

To summarise this diversity into a single comparative framework is simply not feasible. Instead, this chapter draws together the economic elements to assess the role of the market in childcare provision and the case for government intervention. It begins by describing the advantages of a private market and then summarises the evidence presented above on the problems in the operation of this market, the social objectives that have driven government intervention and the policy solutions that have been used around the world.

The advantages of a market

One of the more unusual features of childcare is that it can have a dual purpose for parents: to allow parents (primarily mothers) to undertake formal employment and to provide developmental or educational benefits to the child which are not available from parental care. Although it is often argued that parents value both benefits, it is the facilitation of maternal care which appears the dominating factor (for example, as suggested by Blackburn in his discussion of the UK and as reported by Penn in the case of Namibia and Sosinsky in the case of the US).

As highlighted in several of the chapters (for example, Plantenga, Mitchell), the provision of childcare through a market mechanism, like other goods and services, has a number of advantages. First, a flexible price which reflects both consumers' preferences and suppliers' costs of production results in a selection of goods being produced which best meets consumers' preferences given the constraint of available resources. In a childcare market, this means that the bundle of childcare type and quality that is provided and used by parents is the best possible mixture given the amount that parents can spend on childcare. Second, competition between providers ensures that the good is produced at minimum cost and that the price paid by the consumer is set equal to this minimum cost. In a childcare market, this means that parents pay the lowest possible cost for their childcare. Finally, the profit motive and competition from new competitors generates incentives for providers to innovate or adopt new methods to produce a better service or to reduce costs.

Private producers also have access to commercial funding to make investments to improve or expand production. In a childcare market, this means that childcare options for parents should improve and/ or costs and prices decline whenever technologically is possible. For example, Blackburn reports that the growth in the nursery market in the UK has been largely facilitated by private investment.

Hence, a freely functioning market should give parents their best possible choice of childcare at the least cost in order to meet the dual objectives of providing educational and developmental benefits to the child and of facilitating maternal employment.

Problems in childcare provision: market failures

Childcare is not a typical good or service. Its inherent nature contains a number of characteristics which creates problems in the functioning of the market and means that the market outcomes may not meet parents' preferences at minimum cost and prices. Although these problems may be termed as 'market failures' they are actually problems which could arise in any method of childcare provision. These problems fall into five main categories.

First, parents may not make the best choices. As suggested by Fairholm and Davis, some of the benefits from using childcare are long term but parents may not take into account these longer-term benefits in making their decisions because they lack information or understanding of long-term benefits; they are myopic in making decisions, they are risk averse in investing in the uncertain longer-term returns or they are credit constrained and cannot afford to pay for current childcare on the basis of future financial returns. In addition, care quality is a multidimensional concept with no consensus that one particular element or package is best for a particular child or, indeed, better than parental care. Hence, parents may rely on instinct and impression to make choices about care quality or may have different valuations from 'expert opinion'. Plantenga cites a number of examples of this in the Dutch childcare market, while Sosinsky highlights how parents in the US may be poor judges of quality or give greater weight to pragmatic factors than experts do. Blackburn reports that a significant proportion of parents in the UK prefer informal to formal childcare because they believe it offers the most secure environment. Finally, some elements of childcare choice affect the child directly and some have direct impacts only on the parent (for example, Blackburn notes that important demand factors for informal care in the UK are its flexibility and convenience). However, the parent makes the care decisions and may place 'too much' weight on those elements affecting themselves rather than the child. Yuen, in the context of Hong Kong, argues that the market approach privileges the interests of the adults or institutions over those of children.

Second, there is considerable variation in the quality of care (highlighted by Mitchell in the New Zealand case and by Penn in the Namibian case), but quality is difficult to observe. Given that parents value quality, it is in the providers' interests to advertise the levels of quality offered, for example, as staff qualification levels or turnover levels. Indeed, nursery groups may aim to build a high quality brand identity, for example, as reported by Blackburn for the UK. However, many elements of quality are hard to capture and convey to potential parents or even for parents to perceive from usage and parents may remain uncertain about care quality. For-profit providers have incentives to minimise their costs by minimising quality to an acceptable standard or standard which cannot be easily differentiated from higher quality levels. Not-for-profit providers have an incentive to minimise quality in the same way if it generates savings in effort (such as shorter working hours) or in financial terms that can be channelled back to the providers (such as higher salaries). As argued by Sosinsky, if information on quality is not adequate, parents will not pay more than is necessary for the observable level of quality of care, and if parents are not prepared to pay for higher quality care, providers have no incentive (or even financial ability) to provide it. Indeed, Sosinsky reports that quality of childcare has been characterised as poor to mediocre in the US where provision is dominated by a virtually free market.

Third, competitive pressures to provide what parents want may be reduced by parental reluctance to express dissatisfaction or to switch between providers for several reasons. The buyer–seller relationship is complicated by the need for a good relationship and communication between parents and the provider which may place parents in a weak position to complain or to threaten to change provider, particularly as parents tend to have limited experience in this type of relationship. Children also need continuity in care for the child, which creates a substantial switching cost to changing providers. Even if quality can be observed once care is used, it may not be observable a priori and there may be a large degree of risk aversion to trying out untested options. Parents have a shorter time horizon to benefit from provision quality or lower prices (owing to the finite duration that the child will be in the childcare) than providers have to benefit from resisting parental pressures, so that providers may have stronger incentives than parents to set conditions and prices favourable to them. Plantenga provides evidence of the reluctance of parents to switch provider in the Dutch market and argues that efficiency of the market is almost impossible because the buyer does not act as a mobile, detached consumer. On the other hand, the purchase of childcare is time limited by the ageing of the child and providers need to constantly compete for the next generation of business which can enhance competitive pressures.

Fourth, competitive pressures may also be reduced by high entrance costs for new providers, again for several possible reasons. It may be difficult for new childcare providers to enter the market owing to the reluctance of parents to switch from existing providers and the reluctance of parents looking for first-time childcare to risk an untested provider without a proven reputation. Government regulation may raise the costs of entry for new providers, such as needing to pay the costs of registration or of meeting health and safety standards. Some types of childcare (such as centre-based care) derive significant benefits from large-scale operations (such as lower per-child costs, a greater range of facilities and greater scope for interaction with other children), which means that new providers must take large risks to open on a competitively large scale. Smaller scale childcare (individual home providers) is less likely to present such potential barriers to entry. The long waiting lists cited by Plantenga in the Dutch childcare market are indicative of barriers to entry.

In addition, as shown by Sumsion in the case of ABC Learning in Australia, high entrance costs are conducive to anti-competitive behaviour. Providers with large financial resources (such as chains) may be able to undercut competitors and obtain a market dominance or local monopoly. In addition, the need for proximity in childcare provision means that local monopolies are particularly likely in smaller, geographically isolated communities. The Australian case highlights that such domination of an important service like childcare can lead to political influence on government regulation, little parental choice and poor quality and, ultimately, financial failure requiring government assistance to maintain a service essential to the economy. On the other hand, Blackburn suggests that market domination is unlikely in the UK case because childcare is not an easy service to brand and corporatise owing to the regularity framework which makes it difficult to differentiate from other competitors, while the staff-based nature of the service makes it difficult to homogenise standards within a group. Blackburn also suggests that the benefits of scale efficiencies from large groups may be outweighed by the operating costs of a centralised management.

Fifth, it may be difficult for providers to obtain a highly qualified workforce. A prerequisite for being able to use good quality staff is a system of experience or training recognition (such as regulated qualifications) for employers to be able to identify the quality of potential employees. There are incentives for this to be provided by the market (such as through private training colleges), but issues of maintaining training standards may require government regulation. However, potential care workers will only undertake training if the future returns in terms of earnings (and other work conditions) justify the financial, time and opportunity costs of training. As highlighted by Fairholm and Davis in the Canadian case, the level of training and the retention of trained workers within the childcare sector will be limited by the amount that parents will pay for higher quality care through childcare fees. Sosinsky argues that minimal training requirements and the large availability of low-skilled workers in the US have made childcare one of the worst paying jobs, reducing the quality of the workforce and childcare provision. Relatedly, there may not be the infrastructure required to support a competitive childcare market. Penn highlights the lack of structural support for the development of a childcare market in Namibia in terms of a lack of basic skills in the workforce, start-up capital and a sufficiently large reliable customer base.

The first two problems affect the ability of parents to make the best choices or express their preferences over childcare options, while the last three reduce competitive pressures for providers to produce the best mixture of type and quality, to produce at minimum cost, and to set prices equal to cost. Hence, there are many 'market failure' reasons which can justify government intervention in the childcare market.

Social objectives

Even if a perfectly functioning childcare market precisely delivered parents' ideal childcare choices, social interests can present additional objectives for childcare outcomes:

* to encourage (discourage) the use of childcare beyond (below) that chosen by parents because the social net benefits are greater (less) than the private net benefits to parents;
* to alter childcare opportunities and choices either to prevent childcare outcomes creating greater inequity within society or in order to counterbalance other inequities.

In addition, childcare policies may be used to reduce gender inequities in the labour market, but this issue has received less attention as a justification for government intervention in childcare provision and is not discussed in any further depth here.

Private parental choices about childcare may not match the best ones from a social perspective if there are developmental and educational social benefits such as enhancing the employment productivity of future generations, some of the benefits of which accrue to employers (or investors) and other workers. Developmental benefits could also have social externalities in other areas, for example better health for the child, improved social behaviour in adult life or better adult relationships. However, the evidence suggests that whether non-parental care has better outcomes for a particular child may depend upon the quality and type of non-parental care, the background of parents and the age of child.

The social returns from maternal employment may also be greater than the private returns. Mothers' employment may enhance the productivity of other factors in the economy (both capital and workforce), but the returns accrue either to employers (or investors) or other workers. These effects can operate both in immediate terms and in the longer term through greater work experience and incentives to train created for women. Mothers' employment may also reduce dependency on state funded welfare benefits, but the savings from these are dispersed across all taxpayers. On the other hand, it could be argued that the social returns to mothers' employment is lower than the private ones if there are social benefits from the contributions made by non-working mothers to their community and wider society.

Government intervention in childcare in different countries has been driven by a mixture of these objectives, although they broadly divide into those aimed at improving the standard and equality of education and those aimed at enhancing maternal employment for poorer families. In the case of Hong Kong, the focus is on the developmental and educational benefits for all children, which has translated into little support for non-parental childcare for the under-2s (who are seen as best looked after by parents at home) and support for part-time care for those aged 3–6. Educational benefits were also the focus in New Zealand, with '20 hours free ECE' for 3- and 4-year-olds, and Mitchell reports that the government's vision in introducing childcare reform was for all children to participate in quality early childhood education no matter what their circumstances. In Norway, the learning and development of children has been the main objective, with priority given to short-time attendance rather than full-day.

On the other hand, the emphasis on the benefits to employment means that the focus has been on increasing the female employment rate with contributions from employers in the Dutch case. In the US case, Sosinsky recognises that most US funds for childcare are targeted at the work support function and that most public early care and education funds directed to children living in poverty through means-tested childcare subsidies and public preschool programmes.

For the UK, Moss documents how government policies have focused on both objectives, with enhanced means-tested childcare support for working parents introduced alongside free part-time early education for all 3- and 4-year-olds aimed at 'redistributing possibilities through investment in education'. On the other hand, Blackburn suggests that policy in the UK may be shifting towards the equity objective with recent cuts in the childcare support for working parents and government support for early years provision likely to focus on targeted interventions for the poorest families in the future.

Social decisions

How well government intervention may achieve social objectives and address the problems inherent in childcare provision depends critically on the incentives and abilities of the individuals making decisions about childcare provision. These decisions may take different forms. They may be indirect choices about the structure of subsidies or direct regulation or about information delivery, or competition legislation made at the national level. Or they may involve local-level direct provision or commissioning of childcare services. The distinctive feature of these 'social decisions' about childcare is that they are made by a collective group which is likely to include individuals other than the parents who use the childcare. This section considers how and why these decisions, in general, may differ from those made by individual parents in a market.

Government involvement in childcare provision may be expected to give greater weight than the private market to the social benefits and equality objectives. However, there are two reasons why there is no guarantee that social decisions will generate a coherent set of objectives or that the consequent outcomes are better than those in a childcare market.

First, the achievement of some social objectives may not be consistent with others and could mean less equality or fewer social benefits than the market outcome. For example, the childcare voucher scheme in Hong Kong described by Yuen focuses on educational benefits, but the part-time element is less favourable to poorer families who have both parents working. Or Sosinsky reports that low childcare subsidy rates in the US aim to maximise uptake, but can have adverse effects on quality. Hence, there may be no simple 'socially best' outcome in terms of objectives and there may be some trade-off between objectives.

Second, achieving social objectives generally involves costs for a broad band of society including those with no direct private benefit. The willingness of society to pay will depend upon the size of the social benefits relative to the cost and on the degree of support for any implicit redistribution. In the case of childcare, the perceived or actual social benefits may seem very small relative to the substantial costs potentially involved. In addition, the implicit redistribution from non-parents to parents may not command widespread support, particularly if other means of redistribution are seen as more effective and raising children is viewed as a private rather than a social responsibility. For example, in the case of New Zealand, Mitchell emphasises that substantial funding accompanied each stage of the strategic action plan for early childhood education. In contrast, Sosinsky reports that the dominant attitude in the US has been to consider the family as a private unit and to limit government involvement in family matters. In low-income countries, such as the Namibian case described by Penn, there are simply not enough resources to cover the costs of a reasonable standard of early education and childcare.

A greater role for the state in childcare choices may help to overcome deficiencies in parental choices. The larger scale and longer time-frame of decision making at the community or national level is likely to involve better collection and use of information and is likely to be less myopic or credit-constrained in acting in the longer-term interest. However, this may not always be the case if public decision makers are focused on short-term outcomes (for example, to meet targets or electoral expectations) or are credit-constrained by short-term funding considerations. Non-parental input to decision making may also give greater weight to the child's interests as well as those of the parent. In addition, the coordination of state intervention may provide better monitoring of providers and greater power to ensure providers deliver the desired levels of care. On the other hand, parental choice places decisions with those most closely informed about outcomes within their local childcare settings and with the specific needs of their children. It could also be argued that parents have the greatest incentives to take the time and effort to make the best decisions and monitor outcomes, while those involved in state interventions may be less motivated. In addition, the lack of consensus on what constitutes best quality in some areas may mean that state-determined choices in the types of care may give little weight to some dimensions of 'quality'. For example, Mitchell reports that in New Zealand it has largely been the private sector that has filled the need for all-day provision from working parents. On the other hand, Jacobsen and Vollset report that the state-supported kindergarten system in Norway caters for a wide range of care needs.

A major concern with state involvement in the provision of childcare (and, indeed, most other types of service) is the potential lack of competitive pressures to create incentives to produce the service in an efficient manner and minimise cost to those ultimately paying for the childcare. It should be noted that providing the desired type and quality of childcare in the most efficient manner possible is not simply a market-driven concern: making the best use of limited resources allows greater benefits whatever the delivery method. Indeed, the capacity of a country to offer universal minimum standards of childcare may depend upon the ability to use limited resources in the most cost efficient manner. Higher costs may take the form of excessive profits for providers in a profit-making context, but could also take other forms in a non-profit context including non-profit returns to providers (such as unusually high wages or shorter shift hours) or simple inefficiencies (such as not obtaining the lowest cost for material inputs).

In a market context, lower cost offers from new suppliers benchmark the costs of current providers and the threat of loss of business creates powerful incentives for current providers to operate in an efficient manner. Government intervention may reduce this threat of loss of business. Public funding of childcare could reduce the incentives for parents to choose the lowest cost option as they bear little or only part of the cost directly, while the incentives for government bodies commissioning or directly providing services to seek or use the least-cost alternatives will depend upon the budget constraints imposed by the funding. The degree of competitive pressure in publicly provided or commissioned childcare depends upon the ability of the decision makers to be aware of alternative providers and to be willing to make switches, but they may suffer from the same inhibitions as parents in changing providers to uncertain alternatives. This would particularly be the case if they were commissioning or supporting alternatives which might not yet be in operation and could affect a sizable number of children. On the other hand, social decision makers may have better information about costs and be better placed to monitor and enforce the containment of costs than individual parents and they may also be less compromised than individual parents by wishing to maintain a good relationship with those directly providing care. Moreover, because of the scale of operation, social provision or commissioning could reduce barriers to entry for new providers by offering immediate business of a sufficiently viable scale.

A related concern about state intervention is the effect on the incentives for innovation and development to better meet the needs of parents and children. Within the market, the risks of change are borne by providers who will suffer losses if their innovations are unsuccessful but obtain unusually high profits (at least in the short term) if successful. In the non-market context, the risks would be borne by those choosing providers or selecting managers (or even approving specific changes themselves), for whom the costs of unsuccessful change may be considerable while the rewards for success more limited. Hence, the incentives to take risks with innovative change may be greater for market providers than for social decision making. On the other hand, as Penn mentions in chapter two, market providers may be secretive about sharing information with competitors, while non-market mechanisms may encourage the sharing of experience and actively promote the spread of new successful methods. For example, the Centres of Innovation programme in New Zealand was developed to facilitate the building of innovative approaches to teaching and learning and to share the models of practice with other providers.

One of the major reasons for government intervention is to address the inequities in childcare which may arise from income inequalities. However, income-related variation in childcare outcomes may not be directly driven by income per se but reflect other underlying differences across families. For example, higher-income families may seek out better childcare options because they are more active and better consumers; lower-income families may have greater access to family and other sources of informal childcare because they are less mobile and less likely to have moved away from established social networks; higher-income families may have a preference for more formal childcare arrangements because they are familiar with operating within more formal and professionalised occupations, while lower-income families may be more comfortable with less formal and ad hoc arrangements; and higher-income families may place more value on intimacy and emotional development in their childcare arrangements, while lower-income families may be more concerned about safety or the risk of physical neglect or harm (see for example, Vincent et al, 2008).

Although these relationships may not always occur, policy design should be careful not to impose the preferences of the richer families on poorer ones. For example, reducing the cost of care options for lower-income families may not lead to the same choices as those currently made by higher-income families. Indeed, Sosinsky reports that many low-income families in the US have far stronger misgivings about centre-based care than more affluent families. Or universal direct provision may lead to even better care outcomes for higher-income families if they are more able to seek out the better options. Yuen suggests that families of high socioeconomic status have been more positive about the voucher scheme in Hong Kong because they know how to act autonomously as informed consumers. Or support for particular types of care may be more beneficial to families who prefer that type of care and who may not necessarily be lower income families. Monitoring of the usage and beneficiaries of government childcare provision and subsidisation is therefore required to ensure that policies do actually enhance intended equity objectives.

Policy options

The discussion above has highlighted three key reasons for governments to be involved in the childcare market: to address the inherent problems in childcare provision (market failures); to influence parental childcare choices to incorporate social benefits and costs and to reduce inequities in childcare outcomes; or to use childcare to mitigate other inequities. This section considers the advantages and drawbacks of a number of specific policy options in meeting these aims. In practice, a mixture of these policies may be employed, particularly when the introduction of one policy requires another to counterbalance some impacts. For example, the introduction of childcare subsidies might be accompanied by price regulation. In addition, the distinction between market and non-market is not always well defined. For example, there may be strong competition between not-for-profit providers and parental cooperatives bidding to be commissioned by government bodies.

Subsidisation of childcare

Childcare subsidies have been used to incorporate social benefits into childcare choices and to overcome some of the market failures in parental decision making by encouraging greater use of childcare (or of a particular type of childcare) and by enhancing incentives for maternal employment, especially when tied to work requirements. Subsidies have also been used for equity reasons through means testing, being targeted towards specific vulnerable groups such as lone parent families or by subsidising higher quality care options which are underutilised by lower-income families.

A key concern in the use of childcare subsidies is that they may cost a substantial amount without changing behaviour in the desired manner. For example, Blackburn reports in chapter three that although the childcare tax credit in the UK has a large number of recipients, its actual impact on childcare use is not well known. Subsidies may simply raise suppliers' prices and profits if providers have sufficient market power, although such strong market power is extremely rare, especially if the subsidies are large and offer considerable returns to potential new entrants. Or subsidies may simply lower childcare costs for families without any effect on childcare or employment choices. In this case, they would be a simple payment to families using childcare, but this is unlikely to be the best means of providing financial support to poorer families. Or a basic subsidy could increase expenditure on childcare, but would offer no control on whether it raised the hours of care or the quality of care or had any effect on maternal employment, although the subsidy could be designed to better achieve any one of these objectives (for example, see Paull, 2003).

The equity effects of subsidies are not unambiguous. For example, subsidies that can only be used for lower quality options may increase the quality divide between those using them and those who have sufficiently high income not to require the subsidy. Alternatively, a universal subsidy without restrictions on use may benefit higher-income families more if they make better use of the funding through choosing better facilities.

Plantenga reports that the introduction of a demand-side subsidy in the Dutch childcare market led to lower prices and greater use of childcare, although the effect on quality was less favourable. In the case of the introduction of the '20 hours free ECE' in New Zealand, Mitchell states that costs to parents fell substantially and there was a considerable effect on attendance. Sosinsky reports that more generous subsidy programmes in the US showed some success at supporting parental employment, lowering parent costs, and increasing use of formal over informal care, but also notes that subsidised childcare quality has been found to be lower than non-subsidised childcare quality. Sosinsky also points out that while the childcare tax credits are intended to be progressive, the credit is non-refundable so that families with low or no tax liabilities receive little or no benefit. Finally, Sumsion notes that the expansion of ABC Learning in Australia was assisted by the increase in government subsidies for for-profit childcare operators.

Support for staff training

The subsidisation of staff training or financial support for the operation of a system of staff training can be used to incorporate the social benefits of higher-quality care or to address failings in the market for qualifications. If there are shortages of qualified staff prior to subsidisation because the earnings-return to being qualified does not cover the costs of training for a sufficient number of people, the subsidisation will raise the incentives to train and reduce the shortages. If shortages are not an initial problem, the subsidisation may reduce the cost of hiring qualified staff which, depending upon the competitiveness of the childcare market, should be passed on in lower prices for higher-quality childcare and greater incentives to use higher-quality care. Hence, subsidisation of training creates incentives for a reduction in childcare costs and/or an improvement in quality of care.

One drawback of policies supporting staff training is that because the earnings-return to being qualified remains unchanged (or may even decline), there is no incentive for existing qualified individuals who are not currently working in childcare to enter or re-enter childcare employment. Mitchell reports that the qualification incentives in New Zealand had a striking impact on improving the quality of provision of childcare provision for those services that took up the opportunities, but take-up, which was voluntary, only occurred where management was sufficiently supportive.

Government involvement in the provision of childcare may alone improve the supply of highly qualified childcare workers if it enhances the certainty that investment in training will generate sufficient employment and earnings returns. A longer-term interest and broader social perspective on the part of those funding childcare provision may also create preferences for providers who invest in workforce training.

However, the supply of qualified workers will still ultimately be limited by the level of training that childcare funding can pay for, whether the source is parents directly or the collective choice of taxpayers.

Provision of childcare quality information

A direct response to the difficulty of observing childcare quality is for the government to provide better information to parents on the quality offered by each provider such as the variety of measures suggested by Plantenga. However, there are some strong caveats on how well publicly provided information can reveal quality, including how well periodic inspections can identify quality and the difficulty of deriving measures suited to all views about what constitutes quality. In addition, Sosinsky reports that the Quality Rating and Information Systems developed in some states in the US had limited usefulness, partly because of a mistrust of the reliability or impartiality of the government-provided report, highlighting the importance that such information would need to be provided by independent reliable sources.

Regulation of childcare quality, prices or provider–parent relations

Direct regulation of the provision of childcare can be a means of addressing the problems of poor information or lack of consumer/parental power in the childcare market. It could also be applied if poor parental decision making or social benefits made it desirable to raise the level of quality above that chosen by parents or could be used for equity objectives by raising standards at the lower end.

The need for regulation of basic health and safety conditions to protect children in childcare generally receives broad acceptance. As Penn observes in chapter two, almost all high-income countries have introduced regulations on quality. However, the setting of regulatory minimum standards for 'quality' over and above very basic levels can have significant implications. Standards set 'too low' may prove ineffective in achieving the minimum guarantee required by some parents and could reduce usage among those reluctant to use care without greater regulation. In the case of the US, Sosinsky argues that state-set standards of regulation of early care and education services are largely considered inadequate, while Fairholm and Davis report a diverse set of regulations for childcare centres across provinces/territories in Canada with some notable gaps in coverage. On the other hand, standards set 'too high' may raise the cost of care above the level that many parents are willing or able to pay or may run into supply constraints in the availability of staff with sufficient qualifications. For example, Penn highlights how adopting standards from the global north is simply not feasible in Namibia. When other checks on standards are weak, finding the correct level of quality regulation can be critical to the functioning of the childcare market. In the case of Norway, Jacobsen and Vollset report that strong regulation means that there are few systematic differences between publicly and privately owned kindergartens, suggesting a case where regulation has found the correct level. On the other hand, the accounts of poor quality in ABC Learning facilities highlighted by Sumsion emphasise how difficult it can be to ensure quality through regulation, particularly when large providers may be influential in its enforcement.

Price regulation may be justified when a lack of competitive forces mean that providers have a high degree of market power and can raise prices above the competitive level. Price regulation may be particularly warranted when childcare is subsidised and there is a risk that taxpayer money may simply be transferred to providers' profits. For example, Yuen reports that maximum fee levels were introduced with the voucher subsidy scheme in Hong Kong. There are also fixed parents' fees for the publicly funded kindergartens in Norway. Regulated prices ideally would be set at the levels that would prevail within a competitive market and just meet costs (with an appropriate return to the use of capital), but this may be difficult for regulators to identify. A final type of regulation could enhance parental consumer power through requirements on providers to facilitate parental coordination in raising concerns or complaints about the service such as the mandatory parent committees in the Netherlands described by Plantenga. These types of measure could enhance both the 'voice' of parents in expressing issues of concern and the power of the threat of a coordinated mass switch in provider if these concerns are not addressed. Such measures may also improve parental power by allowing concerns to be passed from one generation of childcare users to the next.

Encouraging not-for-profit provision or parental cooperatives

Provider-targeted subsidisation or start-up support for not-for-profit and parental cooperatives childcare providers would support suppliers without a profit motive to raise prices, although, as discussed above, inefficient production may still occur in forms other than profits. In addition, parental cooperatives may allow a greater voice for parents either directly through specific management decisions or indirectly through the threat of management replacement. In the case of the UK, Blackburn suggests that the third (not-for-profit) sector offers the greatest scope for childcare growth, with new legislation making it easier for non-profit groups to become service providers and with the promotion of the 'Big Society' encouraging parents, in partnership with third sector organisations, to take over childcare currently provided by local government.

Competition regulation and incentives to enhance competition

Direct measures can be used to enhance competition and to reduce anti-competitive behaviour. These may take the form of traditional methods of competition regulation to control the market share of any single provider through merger and acquisition regulation, planning controls, and legislation against anti-competitive behaviour such as price undercutting. The enforcement of these types of measure could have been used to prevent the negative consequences of the expansion of ABC Learning in Australia.

Other incentives to enhance competition would include financial and regulatory measures to help new entrants into the market such as start-up financing and assistance with meeting health and safety requirements. For example, Jacobsen and Vollset report that grants have been used to stimulate the establishment of new childcare places in Norway, while Moss notes the start-up support in the UK for private providers in poor areas where markets might struggle to get established.

Employer-supported childcare

If the use of childcare has social benefits which accrue to employers in terms of maternal employment enhancing the productivity of the workforce, it may be justifiable for employers to bear some of the costs of the childcare that they benefit from. Government financial incentives or regulation could be used to encourage firms to provide financial support to employees to cover childcare costs or to directly provide childcare on a subsidised or non-profit basis. The former of these is a variant of a childcare subsidy based on a work requirement and has the same advantages and drawbacks as other subsidies discussed above. As described by Plantenga, the substantial employer involvement in the financing of childcare has been unique for the Netherlands and made it possible to realise a large increase in childcare, while Moss reports that corporate spending on childcare through vouchers has increased dramatically in the UK.

The direct provision of care at subsidised or cost prices has the advantages that larger employers are likely to have the financial resources to set up facilities with an immediate customer base to ensure financial viability and, being both the producer and consumer, can directly monitor and control cost and quality. Penn also notes that much of childcare in the post-socialist countries used to be subsidised workplace-based provision.

However, there are a large number of drawbacks to employer provision of childcare (Paull and Brewer, 2003). First, the monitoring of cost and price is dependent upon the firm having incentives to do this and to make choices, particularly in quality, which match parental preferences. In addition, parents would be in a weak position to voice concerns as they would have few comparable alternative childcare arrangements available. However, the coordination of parental interests may be facilitated by the common workplace and firms may have a vested interest to respond to parental concerns by a desire to keep employees. Second, childcare would be located near the place of work (rather than near home) and would be centre-type care. Third, it is likely to reduce the employment mobility of parents if they are reluctant to change their childcare provider. Fourth, the costs of the care may actually be borne by the worker if the benefits are part of a package which offers a lower wage. Fifth, the subsidised care would only be available at larger establishments and firms. Finally, employers may prefer to hire workers without children to avoid the costs of subsidising or providing childcare.

Given these drawbacks, particularly that employer-provided care may have particularly weak incentives to meet parents' preferences; the case for government support for employer-based care is weak.

Direct government provision or commissioning of childcare

Direct government provision or commissioning of childcare lies at the other end of the spectrum from a freely functioning market in childcare, with the key elements of public funding and public choice in providers. In the UK, Moss notes that government provision is currently only the 'last resort' to plug gaps in the private market, but his discussion of non-market alternatives includes a type of commissioning system based around Children's Centres.

There is an extensive literature in the field of public economics on the theoretical and practical advantages of private versus public provision of goods and services (for example, see Le Grand, 2007 or Besley and Ghatak, 2003), but the key issues applicable to childcare have been highlighted in the discussion of social decisions above. Essentially, the social choices made by collective government bodies may overcome some of the disadvantages of parental decision making and lack of competitive elements through better information, longer-term interests and greater influence over providers.

But whether government involvement generates better outcomes than the market depends critically on the incentives and ability of those making childcare choices and the mechanisms shaping those choices. This point is most applicable in the case of direct provision or commissioning of childcare where the range of options available to parents wishing to use public support is completely determined by the group of individuals involved choosing those options. Indeed, Yuen reports that concerns for flexibility and diversity in childcare provision was a key reason why officials in Hong Kong decided that universal provision was not suitable in the local context. In addition, the public cost of commissioning or directly providing childcare would be substantial and would require broad support from taxpayers and society more widely to pay these costs.

The system closest to childcare commissioning is the Norwegian kindergarten system of publicly financed childcare with block grants to public and private providers and municipality responsibility for ensuring that childcare demands are met. However, this system also includes strong regulation and caps on fees but, at present, no regulation of profit. In addition, there is no mention of the cost of the system, but the long tradition and development of the childcare system in Norway suggests that social support for public provision and the willingness to pay for it is considerably higher than in other countries.

Conclusions

Childcare is unusual in its multiple objectives and social impacts, the complexities involved in making choices and the barriers to effective competition among providers. Many of the consequent market failures are similar to those in markets for other goods and services, but the inherent characteristics of childcare raise a unique set of problems which need to be addressed whether provided in a market or non-market framework.

There is wide variation around the world in the issues seen as key problems and how governments have intervened in the provision of childcare. A critical divide in government intervention has been whether the objective has been to promote better and more equal educational development (requiring support for universal part-time provision) or to promote maternal employment among poorer families (requiring support for means-tested full-time provision). Yet the response in most countries has been to seek to address specific problems within the market rather than replace the market with alternative methods of delivery. This may be due to sociopolitical reasons that childcare provision has mainly developed as a private market and policy inertia constrains governments to incremental intervention. Or it may be because of an explicit social choice to limit the degree of redistribution towards families with children. Or it may be the case that parents, for better or worse, are reluctant to risk having their childcare choices restricted by public decision making bodies. On the other hand, it may indicate that the advantages of market provision are not easily replicated in other modes of delivery, while policies operating within the market can mitigate the more major market failures and promote social objectives. Importantly, the evidence presented here suggests that these policies need to be multidimensional and critically need to command sufficient support from the wider population to pay their cost.

There is considerable scope for countries to learn from the experiences of others on the best mechanisms for childcare provision. However, given the variation in social objectives for childcare and in cultural conditions, it is likely that a considerable degree of international diversity in the role of the market and government in childcare provision will remain.

References

Besley, T. and Ghatak, M. (2003) 'Incentives, choice and accountability in the provision of public services', *Oxford Review of Economic Policy*, vol 19, no 2, pp 235–249.

Le Grand, J. (2007) *The other invisible hand: Delivering public services through choice and competition*, Princeton: Princeton University Press.

Paull, G. (2003) 'Childcare subsidies', The IFS Green Budget: January 2003, *The Institute for Fiscal Studies Commentary 92*, January, London: Institute for Fiscal Studies, pp 85–104.

Paull, G. and Brewer, M. (2003) *How can suitable, affordable childcare be provided for all parents who need it to enable them to work?* Submission to House of Commons Work and Pensions Committee Inquiry, The Institute for Fiscal Studies Briefing Note no 34, March, London: Institute for Fiscal Studies.

Vincent, C., Braun, A. and Ball, S.J. (2008) 'Childcare choice and social class: caring for young children in the UK', *Critical Social Policy*, vol 28, no 1, pp 5–26.

Index

Please note: ECEC refers to 'early childhood education and care'